LOOKING FOR GEORGE

Helena Drysdale is a journalist and author of two highly acclaimed travel books: *Alone Through China and Tibet* and *Dancing with the Dead*.

Helena Drysdale

Looking for George

Love and Death in Romania

Foreword by Tobias Wolff

PICADOR

First published 1995 by Sinclair-Stevenson as *Looking for Gheorghe*

This corrected edition published with a foreword by Tobias Wolff 1996 by Picador
an imprint of Macmillan Publishers Ltd
25 Eccleston Place, London SW1W 9NF
and Basingstoke

Associated companies throughout the world

ISBN 0 330 34792 6

1 3 5 7 9 8 6 4 2

A CIP catalogue record for this book is available from
the British Library.

Phototypeset by Intype London Ltd
Printed and bound in Great Britain by
Mackays of Chatham plc, Chatham, Kent

Much madness is divinest sense –
To the discerning eye –
Much sense – the starkest madness –
Tis the majority
In this, as all, prevail –
Assent – and you are sane –
Demur – you're straightway dangerous –
And handled with a chain.

Emily Dickinson (1830–1886)

Posterity will remember
And will burn with shame
Remembering these strange times
When common integrity was called courage.

Yevgheny Yevtushenko

Foreword by Tobias Wolff

I first came across *Looking for George* while serving as a judge for the Esquire-Waterstone's-Apple Award for Nonfiction. I'd read some thirty books by the time I picked this one up, with an equal number still to go, and a certain detachment, not to say dread, had begun to dull my responses and my zeal for the task at hand. But within a few pages of beginning this book I was completely captive, and forgetful of any motive for reading save the apprehension and wonder generated by Helena Drysdale's account of a youthful holiday romance that led her down darker roads than she ever meant to travel.

What kind of book is this, exactly? Hard to say. One of the intriguing qualities of *Looking for George* is its resistance to classification. It falls into no single category of literature, yet at different times takes on the method and tone of the personal memoir, the psychological thriller, the love story, the travel book, the detective novel, and the cultural portrait, in this case of Romanian society in the twilight of Ceauşescu's rule and the years just after his overthrow.

The events that form the basis of Helena Drysdale's narrative began in 1979, when she was a nineteen-year-old undergraduate travelling around Romania with two friends. While visiting the monastery at Putna they encountered a tour guide and former monk, the George of the title, a moody, idealistic, literary young man who, after some hours of drink and talk, invited them to spend the night at the home of his friend and neighbour Vasile. On impulse, George decided to accompany them when they resumed their travels the next day, and by the end of the week he had formed an attachment to Helena Drysdale, who responded to his exotic intensity and refusal to be ironic or 'nice' in the conventional English way. She left George in tears at the Yugoslavian border, and resumed her former life of 'swanning about Cambridge' and travelling between terms.

He wrote to her for several years, high-flown, romantic, often inscrutable letters – one of them ninety-two pages long – in which he described his growing troubles with the Romanian authorities and his incarcerations in a series of hospitals. The letters grew more runic and desperate, then stopped. This was in 1986. In 1991, Helena Drysdale went back to Romania to look for him. Her search for George is the substance and contagious obsession of this book.

It sounds like a romance of the oldest kind – Orpheus descending into Hades to redeem his Eurydice. It isn't. There had been flickers of ardour between George and the young Helena, but their flirtation never came to anything: she was made skittish by his urgency and awkwardness. At the time of her return to Romania twelve years later, she was married and, during the last leg of her search, pregnant. One of the things I admire most in Helena Drysdale's story is her refusal to dress her experience with George in operatic costume. She is modest and exact in her rendering of what they shared, which was not grand passion but a raw, undisguised humanity and love of freedom. It was this that brought them together, and finally drew her back to look for him – a chance, somehow abiding connection between two people of good will.

And she had another reason for undertaking the search. As she later discovered, George's week of grace with her and her friends was a violation of Romanian law, and put him at the mercy of the Securitate, the secret police, who did not deal gently with him. A blithe, privileged young woman unaccustomed to governmental terrorism, she had given no thought to the price George might have to pay for his brief vacation. As she herself says, 'I meant well, but there are few forms of innocence more dangerous than the innocence of the well-meaning traveller.'

Helena Drysdale's guest leads her inevitably into Romania's totalitarian past, its institutions and psychology and the enduring pathologies which are its legacy. Even after the 'so-called Revolution', as her Romanian acquaintances refer to Ceauşescu's downfall, it is hard to break through evasion and paranoia long enough to get a straight story out of anyone. To Romanians, every question is suspect, every questioner; and they have good reason for circumspection. The Securitate invaded the whole of Romanian life, holding nothing sacred, neither friendship nor family nor one's own home. 'Even if you weren't bugged,' says one of Helena Drysdale's sources, 'you thought you were, and the effect was the same.' This same woman, a stylish Ceauşescu-hating intellectual, reveals that she herself had served as a police informant, and that this caused problems in her marriage, because her husband was fond of making political jokes. 'Now people suspect me. That's why I don't have many friends.'

While looking for a man, Helena Drysdale finds a country. Suspicious as Romanians have learned to be, she clearly has the gift, which must sometimes seem a curse, of inviting trust and the confidences that follow. After a ritual show of doubt, people open their lives to her as if they've been waiting for the chance for years. Peasants, priests and monks, doctors, factory workers, intellectuals (that is how they describe themselves), missionaries, teachers and students, all tell their stories, and the resulting mosaic shows a people traumatized and corrupted by nearly half a century of state terror, but still proud of what their country once was, and hopeful of what it might yet become.

The situation of the people is figured in the land itself. Vast expanses have been defiled by collectivization and industry, but Helena Drysdale also notes with a lingering eye the beauty that remains in Romania's ancient forests and small farms. Her pictures of rural life are vivid and precise, and infused with affection. The truth is that for all its scars, she loves this country, and loves it more as it shows more of itself to her.

In coming to know Romania, she also comes to know George. With exquisite care and patience, like one reconstructing a canvas slashed to ribbons, Helena Drysdale assembles a complex and detailed portrait of George, unravels the history of his treatment at the hands of the Securitate, and finally plumbs the mystery of his disappearance. To accomplish all this requires great persistence and courage – she is, don't forget, a nosey women alone in a country still run by secretive thugs. It would be an act of treason to say how her search ends, but she does after all descend into Hades to find George and in so doing complete a story that has haunted this reader for over a year now, and will no doubt continue to haunt him in the years to come.

One

Each of us was looking for romance of a sort. Maybe we mistook the idea of each other for the reality, which was inevitable since we were together for only a week, but it was a week that changed things – my life for the better, and his, as it turned out, for the worse. People say I shouldn't reproach myself, that it's arrogance to do so, but it's hard not to; after all, it was I who encouraged him to dream of escape, when I could leave while he was forced to stay behind. So when I returned to Romania twelve years later, just over a year after the 1989 revolution, it was with a certain amount of dread as to what I would – or would not – find.

I reached Putna late one afternoon in April 1991. Tired and hungry after a ten-mile walk, I was thankful to arrive at the avenue that led straight to the monastery gate. Here Viorica, George's sister, left me. Her support would have been helpful but she was determined not to come on, seemed afraid even, and she gestured towards a hovel near the river, muttering about friends. She would wait there until her train home. She kissed my hand, then protested and twisted away – shocked – when I attempted to return the politeness and kiss hers.

Pausing in front of the arched gateway, I remembered, now that I was back, how the steep black fir trees bank around Putna's white

1

stone, and how the walls, like arms, embrace and protect their church. Centuries ago Putna's towers were lavishly decorated with gold; now the only gold was a gilded memory of an afternoon here twelve years earlier when the sun had hinged the church to its long shadow.

But memory works in mysterious ways, and nothing was quite as I recalled. The turrets, the forests stalked by bears and wolves, the mountains pressing in – they all resembled my memories, but were not identical; present and past jarred like a double-exposed photograph, each slightly out of synch. Disorientation added to hunger (and to anxiety about the outcome of my enquiries) to exaggerate my feeling of unease.

No time to explore: I wanted information, and now. I crossed the quadrangle, leaving the church on my left. A flight of steps ascended to a pair of glass swing doors and to the lobby of the museum, which was furnished with green leather chairs. I dropped my rucksack on to one of them and sat beside it. I was exhausted. A novice robed in black, who stroked his wispy beard as though teasing it into the luxuriant length of his superiors', hovered over me, waiting to sell me an entrance ticket. He had the ghost of a moustache and he tapped two coins together.

'Excuse me,' I began, gathering myself up, 'does anyone speak English or French here?'

'No.' He snickered at the absurdity, tucked as we were up this remote Carpathian valley in Bucovina, Upper Moldavia, hard against the Ukrainian border. 'No English and no French.' That then had changed; twelve years ago there had been just a handful of monks left at Putna but amongst them were some who spoke not only English and French, but Italian, Spanish, German, Russian, Old Slavonic, Hungarian, Greek, even Latin. Isolated and introverted, hidden from the outside world, their minds had ranged across all of Europe, both ancient and modern. It was one of them I had come to find.

'Did you ever know Cupar George?' As I would have to struggle in my month-old Romanian I said it surname first, Romanian way.

He shook his head, and called to a colleague behind the postcard counter.

'Cupar George? Mean anything to you?' The colleague, another novice, giggled. George kept expanding and contracting; when I knew him he seemed huge and filled up all of my mind; now he shrank to a nobody, forgotten and belittled by their laughter. 'Sorry. We've never heard of him.'

'Surely people have mentioned him? He was here in the 1970s. I met him in 1979, just after he left Putna. He was brilliantly clever. Everyone knew him. He worked as a guide and he ran this museum, but he had some trouble with the Securitate. I want to talk to someone about him. Anyone.'

The monks exchanged uneasy glances. I saw at once that I had said too much. Again and again I blundered against Romanian subtlety. Hoping that sixteen months after the revolution I would be able to talk freely about George, I realised, often too late, that almost everyone had something to hide. Intrigue, bluff and double bluff: it was not just the recent stifling years of Communism, but centuries of artful survival under Turks, Phanariots, Habsburgs and feudal Boyars. This was an old people, old and sophisticated.

'We can't help. We've both only been here a few years. Almost all the personnel have changed since 1979.'

'What about the Father Superior? Can I talk to him?'

Neither of them moved.

'Please. I've walked all the way from Bucov de Sus. In fact I've come all the way from England.'

The novice hesitated. 'All right. I'll go and see if he's free.'

'Thank you.'

The Father Superior, Viorica and her mother had assured me, could tell me all I wanted to know about George. Everything would be fine: I still persisted in believing in the integrity of these men of God. The postcard monk whistled and strolled around his stall; there were no other visitors.

'I'm sorry. The Father Superior is busy. He can't talk to you.'

'What do you mean? Did you ask him about George?'

'He said that George had already left when he joined Putna in 1985, and he never knew him.'

'I see. Thank you.' I had been a fool, barging in here without observing the Romanian protocol, no letter of introduction from a church official, no preliminary phone call. I was alone, without influence, struggling with my unimpressive rucksack. 'Aren't there some older monks who remember him?'

'I don't think so.'

'There must be!' I was on the verge of tears; I began to plead, cajole, threaten. Would these men of God refuse to help me? How would it look? After I had come all this way, couldn't he try? Eventually I bullied him into braving the older monks, but he returned to say that although they did remember my friend, when George was at Putna he was crazy and, he added, they did not wish to discuss the matter. *Crazy*. I hated the way they dismissed him.

'Then I will go and see the monks myself.' I stood up.

'No, no!' The novice flung his arms across the glass doors.

'Why won't they speak to me?'

'I don't know.'

'They must!'

'I'm sorry. I can't do anything.'

I sat and put my head in my hands. It was not just the walk, nor the weeks of travelling, travelling, searching, searching; it was the betrayal. I saw now that the monks were guilty and afraid: they could not have treated George well. The novice dropped his arms, embarrassed by my distress.

'What's so special about him anyway? Was he someone important?'

Perhaps I was tedious writing so much to you. I don't pretend anything, but I want you to know who was that Romanian young man you met during your summer holidays from 1979. Yes, who am I? Nobody. Just a guy!

'Well.' The novice shrugged. If I was not going to buy a ticket he would close the museum.

I wandered forlornly about the monastery. There seemed no point

4

in going on; my journey had reached a full stop. I sat on the steps and punched the stone. What a waste, waste, waste. Across the courtyard the monks, their black skirts flapping pompously, paused with undisguised impatience to allow the visiting faithful to kiss their hands. Putna's founder, the medieval Voivode Stephen the Great – Moldavia's greatest (and only) hero – had intended his monastery to be a refuge, and to the local villagers it retained something of that. It formed a refuge not from Seljuk Turks or Cossacks, but from the death of their souls and, in its order and traditions, from the growing chaos of their post-revolution lives.

I remembered Putna, but in fact twelve years had wrought many changes. The church, silent and safe, still rose out of its courtyard like a white ship in dock, mast-like turrets clustered to the bows, unsure whether to sail east to Byzantium or west to the Gothic world. But like the entire monastery it had been restored since my last visit. I ought not to have minded since throughout its 500-year history Putna had been burned, pillaged by Cossacks, demolished by earthquakes and repeatedly vandalised by restorers, but the last attempt had given it a municipal look. It was too white, too smooth, and the crumbly red-tiled roofs had been replaced with tin. The car park, which had previously been hidden discreetly behind the fir avenue, had now been moved up against the entrance tower, a crude juxtaposition allowing tourists to spill from their buses almost into the courtyard itself. It was another betrayal: as well as George himself, my fragile memories – my own youth – had been wiped out by the new reality. Plastered over like the church walls.

But I had to risk that; I had to come back; I needed to know. And perhaps I exaggerated the changes; after all, memories tend to have a life of their own; and although twelve years is not so long, in that time many things had happened both to me and to Romania to overlay what had gone before.

Near the gate stood a statue of the nineteenth-century romantic poet Mihai Eminescu, admired by every educated Romanian, 'like your William Shakespeare' – not a good comparison, although I was too polite to say so (perhaps 'like your Byron' was closer). George had said, 'You know why we don't have too many famous writers and artists in Romania? Because for hundreds of years we were busy defending you from the Turks.' Some students clambered over the poet, photographing each other perched on his head and shrieking, like birds; they annoyed me until I remembered that I had been equally irreverent on my last visit here, when I was their age: the beauty of the place had made me want to run around and shout for joy.

The church interior was mysterious, womb-like, with its play of void and solid. A monk sold candles in the pronaos; he was old, but had never known George. Too weary to take in the tomb of Stephen the Great, I settled into a seat beside his wife, Maria of Mangop, and dozed off.

The museum reopened for a party of Romanian tourists; I followed them back in and again pinioned the poor novice. Looking wildly about him for some means of escape, he suddenly brightened. 'There's Brother Gregoriu! He will talk. He will be much more open.' Alive with relief the novice ran after the monk and grasped his arm; they returned together.

'*Hristos a înviat!*'

It was soon after Easter and he greeted me with the traditional Easter invocation, Christ is risen!

'*Adevărat a înviat!*' I replied. He is risen indeed. 'I wanted to ask if you ever knew Cupar George?'

Milky blue eyes with pale rims, sympathetic eyes.

'Please. If you did, I must talk to you about him. I have come all this way. Please help me.'

Beneath his black cap, his long red hair was tied in a ponytail, his mouth muffled by a red moustache and beard. He nodded. Yes, he would talk. He would be back in a minute. I watched him lift an oar from the church wall and, where there was a notch cut out of it, fit it on to his shoulder. Taking a wooden hammer in his hand, he circled the church, beating this hammer languidly against the oar, its flat rhythm summoning the monks to vespers. Having completed his circumnavigation Brother Gregoriu replaced the oar and another

6

more energetic monk lifted down a second hammer which he carried into the bell tower. There followed a virtuoso performance. Now faster, now slower, the hammers were drummed against a plank, the great brass bell tolled, the plank drummed again; I had never imagined that a plank of wood hid so many tunes inside itself.

'You liked the *toacă*,' Brother Gregoriu observed, smiling faintly. He sat down beside me on one of the green leather chairs. His veil of a moustache and his soft voice made him difficult to understand, so the young novice, curious now, repeated his words, still in Romanian but louder and clearer.

'About George,' Gregoriu murmured. 'He had an extraordinary understanding of languages, but he was unable to understand certain other things.'

'Do you mean he was mad?'

'No, it was much more complex than that. Much more delicate.' He closed his eyes, seeming to meditate. 'I don't want to get it wrong. How can I put it? When I knew George he was a highly cultivated person. He ran this superb museum. You've seen the medieval icons? The embroideries and vestments? Priceless things. He also interpreted for foreign radio and television companies, guided parties of foreigners around the monastery.' Brother Gregoriu stood up and almost imperceptibly steered us into the courtyard, his black robes eddying around his ankles. He spoke slowly and softly, as if he did not want us overheard. 'But George's problem was that he could not bring himself to join in the cult of a certain personality. You know who I mean.'

'Of course.' I lowered my voice to match his.

'As a result he had many problems.'

'What sort of problems?'

'The usual sort. Listen. A monastery is like a family, we take care of each other. But when someone doesn't fit, he is pushed out. It is as simple as that.' He glanced around him. 'There's an old monk here now, he's seventy-two years old. He also has Costina hanging over his head. Nothing's changed.' We paused beside the neat green lawns and I found my mind split in two, one half absorbed by George and the old monk, the other – absurdly – transfixed by flecks of dandruff on Gregoriu's shoulders. His black collar was shiny with grease. The novice looked expectantly from me to Brother Gregoriu and back again.

'I need as many details as I can get about George. Dates. When he was here, when he left, where he went.'

We strolled on. I became aware that Brother Gregoriu was steering me towards the gate. 'I can't help you with much, I'm afraid. I barely knew him. I'm not even sure what years he was here. On and off throughout the 1970s and '80s, I think. In those days it was difficult to . . . communicate. I think you understand. But there is one person who could help you. His name is Iacov.'

'Oh yes!' The novice clasped his hands together. 'He will know everything.'

I was sceptical; I had heard this so often: the Father Superior will help you, the monks will help you. Passing the buck. 'Who is this Iacov?'

'He is a priest,' the novice explained, excitedly. 'He will help you. He was the guide here, and in charge of the museum.'

'He is a highly cultivated man,' Brother Gregoriu murmured. 'He also speaks many different languages and will be able to be much more open with you. He knows about George. They were friends. He also had problems with the Securitate, but he was lucky. He had studied in Bucharest and had contacts in the church, friends in high places. George had none of those things. He was much younger, and on his own.'

'Where can I find this Iacov?'

'In the Moldavian Metropolitan Bishopric in Iaşi.'

Iaşi was over 170 miles away, a good six hours by train. 'Is it worth my while going all that way? How do I know he'll be there?'

'He'll be there.'

The novice wrote down the address. At least I had another place to try, a straw to grasp.

'And what about the Father Superior, Gherasim, the one who went to Arad? Should I speak to him?'

'Oh yes. Of course he was part of the trouble.'

'But he was George's friend.'

'Challenge him. He'll tell you nothing, but you could challenge him with what you learn in Iaşi.'

We reached the gate. Fir shadows had stretched and striped the road. I was not sure how to say goodbye – did I kiss their hands? Brother Gregoriu pre-empted me by taking mine and shaking it.

'Good luck,' he said. 'I think you'll find what you need.'

'Where will you stay tonight?' the novice asked as we stood in the porch, comradely now that he had been able to help me and would at any moment have me off his hands.

'I don't know.' I had been assured of a guest room at the monastery, but he made no offer. 'Somewhere in the village, I suppose.'

'Yes, there is a hotel.'

The man I knew as George Cooper I met on the terrace of the Putna Hotel bar. I had seen the face a thousand times: white skin, black hair, thin features, long narrow chin; but his was given an elfin, almost naughty, look by the typical brown felt hat – apparently *de rigueur* for every Romanian male in 1979 – which he wore at an untypically rakish angle. He sat with a larger, thick-set man in the evening sun over two enormous bottles. Conscious of us, he pretended not to be. I watched him: a sensitive, intelligent face, and humorous, but with eyes so dark and sunken that, shadowed by his hat brim, they became not eyes but two black discs. I was nineteen. He turned my way and this time he bowed slightly, then stood and edged between the tables.

'Have you got a cigarette?' A conventional opening. 'And one for my friend also?' One of us – I forget who – held up a flame. He summoned his friend, whom he introduced as Vasile. Vasile carried over George's two-litre bottle of wine and his own *rachiu*, raw alcohol. I wondered what these two had in common, one so refined, the other a red-faced peasant.

'How did you know we spoke English?' I asked George.

'I saw you running around at the monastery.' He was referring to our rather shaming display of high spirits, and he added disconcertingly, tossing his chin at Alex, 'I wondered what a powerful man he must be to have two wives.'

'Wives!' Alex expostulated. 'I should be so lucky.' He was embarrassed and flattered.

I explained, 'We are just good friends.'

George raised a quizzical eyebrow.

In fact we were three Cambridge undergraduates spending a summer in the Eastern Bloc, travelling around, sleeping in the car on the roadside or staying three to a room in cavernous hotels where the sheets were starched and the loos were blocked. My photographs – yellowing now – show me smiling out of a blue nylon dress from Help the Aged (caught at the waist with a pink nurse's belt) worn with yellow lurex ankle socks and black plimsolls. This costume alternates with red and black stripy jeans from Boy, worn with white plastic sling-back open-toed ankle-boots; I still have them and sometimes wonder where I could have come by such hideous footwear. Ali wears a green T-shirt dress without a bra, and espadrilles with ribbons which she tied up her legs, while Alex sports empire-builder shorts, knee-socks and a T-shirt bearing the slogan 'Accidents will Happen'. They never did, at least not then.

I had brought my grandfather's picnic box of false leather 'Rexine', which was designed to strap on to the running board of his pre-war Mercedes. It was equipped with a kettle and gas burner, and, in a spirit of defiance, as soon as we crossed the Iron Curtain into Czechoslovakia we parked beside a Soviet tank on a pedestal to brew Earl Grey tea and eat digestive biscuits. Ali, in case of emotional upset, had brought her own private tin of Ambrosia creamed rice.

Ali was the energy behind the trip. It was her idea, and she who persuaded Alex to drive us. We nearly didn't go. Just before leaving she went parachuting and damaged her hip. Then Alex was caught driving drunkenly up Trinity Street after a May Ball, and lost his licence. But Ali recovered and Alex had a few months' grace before his court case came up.

Of all Eastern Europe, the prospect of Romania was the most

romantic. It was the legends we were after, the forested crags of Transylvania haunted by vampires and Count Dracula. Every castle or sinister, deserted street that might (fictionally) have been visited by Bram Stoker had to be visited by us. There was also the charm of Romania's remoteness, buried as it was in the back regions of Europe, deep down in the ice-box of the Cold War. I knew no-one else who had been there.

However, our goal – if anything so haphazardly aimed at could be called a goal – were the Orthodox churches with tattooed walls that ringed Bucovina in the north-west corner of Moldavia.

We entered Moldavia over the Prislop Pass. The road through the forested pass was still only half built: conscripts leaned on their shovels as we struggled up and over, and tapped fingers on their lips to solicit foreign cigarettes. Now another mountain range, the Eastern Carpathians, divided us from home. This was the outback.

We were delighted to find that, unlike the locked and smashed-up churches of Czechoslovakia, these were open not only to the few tourists who passed by but to worshippers too, albeit in a subdued form, and a handful of monks and nuns were still permitted to live in the stone-walled monasteries. We spent sun-filled days at Moldoviţa, Dragomirna, Humor, Voroneţ, Abore and Suceviţa, each more fantastically decorated than the last. There were hierarchies of saints, bearded patriarchs with dish-like haloes, devils with second faces in their stomachs who dragged their victims down flaming ladders into hell, and votive portraits of the donors who offered these churches to their Byzantine God. He sat on high, stern and forbidding. In brilliantly coloured Last Judgements couples peered over the edges of their coffins, astonished to find themselves resurrected, and beasts spewed forth bits of swallowed human limbs, while turbaned Ottomans remained firmly in limbo. What was most extraordinary about these murals was that they smothered not only internal walls, but external ones too, protected from harsh weather by the over-hanging eaves of the shingle roofs that perched like mushroom caps on the stone walls.

During the later fourteenth century an outstanding generation of rulers had taken control of Eastern Europe. They had founded cities and monasteries, summoned scholars to their courts, and built universities – Prague in 1348, Cracow in 1364, Vienna in 1365. All this had spread eastwards to the principality of Moldavia and flowered a century later under the leadership of Stephen the Great.

Ironically, what prompted this flowering was an event potentially disastrous for the whole of Europe: the fall of Constantinople. Four years before Stephen's accession in 1457 the Turks conquered the capital of the Byzantine Empire. For Stephen, this was a disaster. It not only cut Moldavia's trade route through the Bosphorus, but the desecration of Santa Sophia was also a blow to his Christian – Orthodox – feeling. After eleven centuries, the Christian empire had lost its capital to Islam. Stephen campaigned for both East and West to unite with him against the Turkish threat, but although Pope Sixtus IV named him 'Athlete of Christ', Stephen was left to defend Christendom virtually alone. When in 1475 he refused to pay the huge tribute demanded by the Sublime Porte, an Ottoman army under the splendidly named Soloman Hadamb, Beglerbeg of Rumelia, marched on Moldavia.

However, Stephen kept the Turks at bay, and managed to win thirty-four of his thirty-six battles. To thank God for his successes he founded churches and monasteries. Tucked in valleys between the claws of mountain ridges, nudged up against the Carpathian passes which were the trading links with the outside world, and also the main access for marauding tribes, these were to be strongholds as well as spiritual retreats. They also became centres for scholars and craftsmen, attracting icon painters, calligraphers, embroiderers, gilders, carvers, jewellers, carpenters and muralists. This flourish of Moldavian creativity found its greatest expression on the church walls.

An embroidered votive portrait of Stephen in the Putna museum shows him as a Christ-like figure, with a gentle expression and flowing fair hair. He is dressed in the elaborate princely attire of Byzantium, large funnel-shaped crowns with oak-leaf fleurons pendulous with gold chains.

The most glittering jewel in the necklace of monasteries was Putna,

Stephen the Great's first foundation – consecrated in 1470 – and final resting place. Legend has it that he stood on a mountain top and shot his bow, and where his arrow landed he built the altar. Three young boyars, the children of the chieftain, and two of his pages were also asked to shoot, and where their arrows landed he made the gate and the belfry. The candlesticks and candelabra were beaten out of the finest silver, and the walls both inside and out were painted with pure gold, more gold than paint. We reached Putna late one afternoon and had it to ourselves, a haven beautiful and remote. I remember the exquisite loveliness of the evening after weeks of rain, and the high white monastic walls which expressed purity and seclusion.

A notice pinned to the church wall, however, described the monastery as an historical rather than a spiritual monument, and spoke of the masses who were building their Socialist Future under the direction of the patriotic Comrade Ceauşescu with the same 'dignified modesty' as those masses who had been instructed by Stephen the Great to build Putna itself.

By then we were tired of all that wordy twaddle. Our studenty liberal seeing-both-sides, our flirting with socialism, had been battered by what we had seen of the obviously disastrous economy, the empty shops and oppressive state control. Romania was a frozen country, frozen in time; the remoter villages were medieval, but the drabness of the cities was pre-war. The streets were strangely muffled, as if covered in snow, the nights unlit, the people subdued. The faces of the women with stiffly controlled hair who stood painting their nails behind desks in hotels and banks or waited tables were blank and cold. Were they happy? Did they approve of what appeared to be the destruction of their country? Did they despise our bourgeois decadence? I wished I had heat-seeking perceptions to home in on their warmth.

But that evening in Putna we had had enough. We had been on the road for weeks. Normally Ali had the energy for yet another encounter, yet another struggle with an unknown language, yet another cultural exchange, but even she was exhausted. So we turned our backs on Upper Moldavia's Great Socialist Future and rediscovered each other. Exhilarated by the golden light and by the solitude, we ran about Putna's quadrangle and bumped into each other as if by accident, calling 'Darling!' in mock surprise, as if to say 'to hell with the lot of you, we'll be happy if we want to'. If someone was watching we never suspected it, and would not have cared. We would have a drink in the hotel bar, then look for a campsite – somewhere on our own. Time for the Ambrosia creamed rice.

But here was George with his black eyes, speaking fluent English and enthusing about (of all things) Cambridge. I was studying History, Ali Medicine and Alex Theology. George enviously imagined the free intellectual explorations that must have prompted our physical ones, both forbidden to him, and he put our frivolous tourism to shame. He was serious, intense, different from the rest. He had none of the aggressive/defensive hostility/charm of those who wanted something from us, yet despised us for having it. He asked for nothing – apart from two cigarettes, and they were just an excuse. Instead he welcomed our foreignness, and in his grandiose way saw our meeting as a bridge over the political breach. He also fancied both Ali and me.

He said he had been a member of the community at Putna but had been expelled for 'knowing a woman'. He was surprisingly candid. He had broken his vow of celibacy; his punishment was to genuflect one thousand times before the icon. Then he was asked to leave.

His friend Vasile understood not a word but found he had invited us to stay. We set off for the neighbouring village of Bucov de Sus, children scattering into the ditch as I wielded our Citroën between their wooden houses, Vasile and George on bicycles wobbling rather drunkenly alongside. A hundred yards ahead rose a cantilevered watchtower and, beyond a line of trees, the brooding mass of the Soviet Union. We had penetrated as deep into the wildest corner of Europe as we could. Tiny fields without fences rose to terraced orchards and then to pine and oak woods, and in those fields, pocked with stooks like Burmese stupas, men, women and children made use of the last of the sun to bring the hay harvest to a close. They clustered round wagons and forked hay up on to the teetering stack, dead grasses flying from their prongs and turning into an arc of gold. Horses, snorting, made their way to the track, wooden wheels creaking over ruts. From far away drifted the sound of bells, not church bells but sheep bells, and above them a boy's voice singing. It was a vision of pastoral Europe from long before my time, from long before it was killed off by motorways and out-of-town superstores, show homes and industrial units to let.

To the left: a narrow path. We parked at the top and followed George and Vasile down between fields. The women paused, hands on hips, expressions blank, to watch the strangers pass.

We knew it could be dangerous to have foreigners in the house. We had spent one night camping in the garden of a Romanian lorry driver, and while under cover of darkness he had been friendliness itself, come dawn he couldn't wait to be rid of us. Vasile's mother, however, welcomed us with unruffled hospitality. She was tiny, red-faced and round as a berry.

Vasile's family had two houses, one for winter, and another – which we mistook for a garden shed – for summer. It was August and they were in the summer house, so we were shown to the winter house. This was basically one room, half of which was occupied by an elaborate tiled stove. Stacks of brightly coloured blankets filled the spaces between the cupboards and the ceiling, and weavings covered the walls. Head to toe around the room were the beds. The mattresses had been removed and we sat on the wooden slats while Vasile's mother bustled about serving us fried eggs, *mămăligă*, a maize porridge resembling polenta, and mint tea.

Away from the neutrality of the bar the atmosphere grew awkward. George kept saying, 'Feel yourselves like home' (although this was not his), but he was an anxious host, and we were grateful but self-conscious: eating in front of an audience is never easy. Vasile and his family sat in a row at one end of the room, and we sat at the other end, with George between us leaning against the stove. He had a critical expression, as if he fitted neither with Vasile nor with us, but he did his best to act as a current between us all.

'They want to show you that the government of Romania is not the same as the people of Romania,' he said. He meant the generosity, the friendliness.

Our second week in Romania, but the first time anyone had even hinted at criticism of the regime.

Searching for some way of communicating with us, Vasile unpacked his treasures one by one (I remember an ugly glass fish) and carried them to us to be touched and admired. He was a coarse-looking fellow but he loved his precious things. Later he and George brought in three mattresses stuffed with straw; all night I could smell the straw through the bag, and feel it crackling beneath me. In a few months the family would be huddled in here around their stove, hiding from the *crivăţ*, which whips mercilessly south-west off the Russian steppes.

Lying by the stove listening to the animals rootling in the barn and, later, to the cocks crowing, I felt like a character in a children's book set in the exotic, mist-swathed East, full of warring counts and heroic but displaced monarchs. Frances Hodgson Burnett's Lost Prince, the poor yet noble Marco Loristan who is recognised as heir to Samavia, a mysterious East European kingdom from which he has been exiled by hostile factions, might just as well have been Romania's ex-King Michael, currently exiled in Switzerland. Valiant 'Samavia' might just as well have been Moldavia, a principality torn apart by internal feuds while struggling to maintain its independence from encroaching empires. After all, this was the land once ruled by feudal Hospodars with such stirring names as Alexander the Good, Basil the Wolf, Bogdan the One-Eyed, and John the Terrible.

We explored the farm in the morning. The barn was hung with wooden ploughs and sickles, ancient tools but still in use. The cow shuffled in dung as Vasile's mother milked it for breakfast. Like a nursery-rhyme milkmaid she squatted on her three-legged stool, squirting jets into a bucket. Chickens scratched freely about the yard and the swollen fields were ripe and golden. Someone was chopping wood. The few fences were woven from cut and laid willows – such trouble taken and such neatness.

George led us down the hill through a garden of chrysanthemums to his own family home. His mother, in headscarf and thick peasant skirt, smiled metal. She left the loom at which she worked to feed us apples and hot doughnuts. When we posed together for a photo she tucked her arm through mine, held it close.

'We were quite rich once,' George said, 'before the war.' Then the Russians had taken everything. They came one night, and suddenly most of the family land was on the other side of the barbed wire. He had relatives a few yards away whom he had never seen. In 1774 the end of the Russo-Turkish war had been marked by Russia losing the northern tip of Moldavia to the Habsburgs, who named it 'Beech-covered Land' – Bucovina. The result was an Austro-Hungarian-Ukrainian-Romanian-Jewish-Russian-Ruthenian melting pot. George himself was of Ukrainian descent. After 1918 Bucovina was returned to Romania, but its northern tip was reoccupied by the Soviet Union in 1940, and the desire to retrieve it was one of the reasons Romania entered the war on the side of the Nazis. Now Southern Bucovina was cut off from its heart, since its capital, Czernowitz/Cernăuţi/Černovcy, was buried in the Ukraine. George's family was left with only a smallholding.

Theirs was a simple peasant house, single-storey with three rooms in a row, one leading into the next. Although George had six younger siblings, some of whom still lived at home, the last of the rooms had been set aside as his study.

'Would you like to see my library?' he asked diffidently, pushing open the door. It was bare but for a table under the window on which lay *Das Kapital*, the Bible and an atlas. 'I read Marx because this government has forced us all to become political. But most days I read the Bible.' His fingers brushed the cheap covers. George had studied French at the local *lycée*, but he had become fluent by sitting at this table and memorising miniature foreign-language dictionaries from A to Z. In this way he had also taught himself English, German, Italian and Spanish. Languages were a passion, and his knowledge of European literature was shaming. He also wrote poetry and, he said, he had completed a novel. All this, yet he had spent his childhood as a shepherd, high in the mountains. Now he had grown away from the peasants among whom he lived.

'People say I'm crazy. I'm not considered a man because I study at home. And they say, "He's twenty-four, why isn't he married?" '

'Why aren't you married?' I asked. Twenty-four seemed glamorously old.

He looked at me. 'Because girls just break your heart.'

When we left George presented Ali and me with a bunch of chrysanthemums and roses, and pressed on us his Romanian–English phrasebook; his mother gave us a melon, apples, pears, tomatoes, all the doughnuts; Vasile was eager to sacrifice even his beloved glass fish. We managed to resist the fish, and George seemed pleased. I was surprised by how much I wanted his approval.

'I could come with you to Neamţ,' he suggested suddenly. 'I spent some time at the seminary there. I still have friends.'

'Yes! Why not?'

'You ask my mother. Then she can't refuse.'

She smiled indulgently on her eldest son.

Neamţ was beautiful, all pinky-red stone and brick and one of the oldest monastic foundations in Moldavia. A two-tier colonnade squared the eighteenth-century courtyard, stone below, wood above, always a centre of learning; I was reminded of my own Cambridge college. The church was a burial place of princes and another of Stephen the Great's foundations – laid, according to a votive inscription, for the redemption of his soul, and that of his wife and sons.

But the beauty was undermined by George's mood, so taciturn and uneasy. At the time I blamed it on us, feeling that we had disappointed him in some way. Our clothes were brash, and perhaps we had seemed irreverent during mass, when Ali had fallen asleep; it must have been disillusioning for George to discover that the England we came from was far more secular than Communist Romania.

Like the three bears, we found three bowls of soup steaming beside three hunks of fresh white bread in the refectory. But there was nothing for George, and he would accept none of ours. He looked morose and we could think of nothing to say to him except that everything was lovely. It wasn't, but we tried to make it so. This was our first full day together.

We were surprised then that when we offered to drive him to a station, he said he didn't want to go.

In the car he was silenced by our singing (sweet transvestites from transsexual Transylvania left him cold) and overawed by our daring in camping not in official campsites but by streams in the forest. What of wolves? Vagabonds? *The authorities*? Throughout our first night he kept guard, feeding the fire with 'ood' (he had trouble with his 'w's') which he never tired of gathering in the dark. He was a constraining presence on our happy threesome; Ali and Alex found him a drag, but I felt that with him our journey had taken on a new specialness. And he must have liked being with us or he would not have stayed.

After two bottles of red wine he began to relax. We were wrapped in rugs around the fire; it was August but we were high in the mountains and the night air was damp.

'I hate this government,' he said suddenly. 'Ceauşescu is a peasant, and so are the rest of them.'

We glanced at each other but said nothing. Romania's reputation was that of a brave little country standing up to the mighty Soviet Union. In 1968 Nicolae Ceauşescu had announced to an ecstatic Romanian crowd that he condemned the Soviet invasion of Czechoslovakia; later he condemned the invasion of Afghanistan, and called for nuclear disarmament. In 1978, a year before we crossed the border, the Ceauşescus were rewarded for their anti-Soviet stance with an invitation to Buckingham Palace, where Nicolae was presented with the Order of the Bath. Until as late as 1983 he would be hailed by the West as the maverick East European leader, in Vice President George Bush's words 'the good Communist'. But at home, where the quality of life was deteriorating, there was talk of nepotism and megalomania, and of an increasingly pervasive security service.

I felt a sort of exultation at George's bravery in speaking out.

'Do you have friends who feel the same way?'

'I don't know. We don't discuss these things. I feel safer without friends. They're only people to mistrust.'

'What about Vasile?'

'Vasile! He doesn't think about anything. We don't talk about anything. He just lives near, that's all.'

'What about your family?'

'I can't talk to them about many things. They do not understand.'

'You must feel lonely.'

'I have books.' He added, 'The authorities threatened me with asylum.' The fire crackled between us, its hypnotic flames thickening the night around into a denser blackness.

'What for?'

'They told me I was crazy. I was working at a factory in Constanţa, on Black sea, and I spoke up for a woman who had been sacked for refusing to know with the superiors.'

'To know?'

'To know as a man and a womans.' He said it 'oomans'. 'They sent me away. It was a terrible shame. They said I was crazy and a troublemaker. That was when I came home.' Once home, he had been approached by the 'chiefs', he said, but he had refused to work for them. There were several such 'chiefs' in Bucov de Sus, all hated for their corruption. I did not know it then, but he was referring to the Securitate. 'There are more of them this year. I think that now the economy is going down they worry we will start complaining.'

If George was a dissident, it was as much because of his personality as his politics. His disdain for the Communist Party was above all aesthetic; he despised the members for their ignorance and lack of taste, for what they *were* as much as for what they *did*.

There were others who felt as he did, but we had not met them, and outwardly there was no sign that the nation was not united in

20

veneration of its *Conducător*. In Suceava, a few days earlier, we had watched parades for 'Liberation Day' celebrating the end of the pro-Nazi Antonescu regime which was toppled by the Romanian Communist Party (or so they claimed) just as Soviet troops crossed the border in 1944. In bright sun workers and peasants in folkloric costumes had processed through Suceava brandishing red-tasselled portraits of Ceauşescu and the local Party leaders, along with banners proclaiming the massively increased industrial output of the previous five years and wildly optimistic plans for the next. On a dais in front of the Palace of Culture the suited *nomenclatura* had watched a display by gymnasts waving coloured pompoms, the usual Communist kitsch. *Extraordinary collection of ugly girls*, I noted in my diary.

Alex went to sleep in the car, and eventually Ali dragged her blanket off to the tent. I sat up with George beside the fire. He broke the silence. 'I'm sorry for what I said about marriage.'

'What did you mean?'

He stroked my cheek. 'I cannot tell exactly. At least not yet.'

I joined Ali, and when at 5 a.m. I levered myself off the ground to unzip the tent door, there was George in the bleak dawn, cross-legged beside his fire which burned still, though pallidly now. It was not just fear of wolves and authorities that kept him up; he was a poet, needed to be awake and watching the stars while the world slept. But after his night on guard he looked grey when presented with a plastic mug of tea, muesli with reconstituted powdered milk, and baked beans. 'I eat only natural things,' he said.

We crossed the mountains back into Transylvania in search of one of Dracula's castles that Ali's father had stayed in before the war. George did not share our enthusiasm; he had never heard of Dracula, and resented having to ask for him in a convent since *Dracul* in Romanian means 'the devil'. 'Where is the devil?' he found himself asking some mystified nuns. We embarrassed him. We climbed a ridge on the edge of town to look down on a yellow stucco mansion that had supposedly been lived in by a cruel nobleman, but George made it seem trivial. We abandoned Dracula.

Instead we took to the forest for a picnic. Inspired by George we discarded our practical sardines and baked beans for fresh bread, sheep's cheese and local wine, natural things. We lay by a stream enveloped in fir trees that crawled over the hillsides at random, wild and ancient, the stuff of Gothic tales; the only fir forests I knew were planted in rows. Leaving Alex lying on his back reading *Man without Qualities* (his bookmark was a photo of his girlfriend), Ali, George and I played about. Felled trees were strewn over the lower slopes and we balanced one mossy trunk on others to make a see-saw; as a forfeit for sliding off George was made to catch a cow and milk it. He taught us how, with one of us holding her horns and tickling her forehead, the other squeezing her teats. At first George's games seemed a bit forced, as if his playfulness had been buried under the stress of Communist life, of having to conform and watch his back, never letting go. He had tried to escape from all that into books and languages and monastic studies, but even as a boy he had worked hard, shepherding sheep, digging potatoes, feeding pigs: not much room for fun. Now, slowly, slowly, he creaked back into life. He remembered the names and properties of the toadstools we found sprouting from rotted stumps; he whittled himself a pipe, and smoked it in a den which he built for himself from fir branches.

How happy was I those days with you. I don't regret them, but I'm afraid that it will be for me only the first and last time. How happy was I. Perhaps I am ridiculous, repeating the same words, but those events meant so much for me. Do you remember that day when we made a see-saw in the forest, don't you: Well, Ali wore a red maxi-skirt! It was for this reason that a bull was following us. Bulls are so attracted by red colour, you know. She asked me suddenly, 'Why is this bull following us?'

'Because he's in love with you,' I replied. Perhaps she thought that I meant that I was following her for I was in love with her. I'm sorry I failed her. She was singing all the time. I think she was in love too with somebody.

George was as intrigued by us as we were by him. It was above all because we were English. He was fascinated by the language and the literature, so much so that an old man in Bucov de Sus had named him 'The English'. He was proud of this. He admired the British not only for their literature but also, he said, for their sense of duty and purity of soul. *First time I was proud to have foreign friends. Second time I could practise my English. Your car was for me an English island in a Romanian ocean. And then your infinite kindness!* Occasionally he had heard on the radio of political and cultural events in Western Europe, yet he was kept from them, trapped in years of lies and silence; now for the first time in his life he could pour out his frustrations. We were his escape from isolation and provincialism and we could share with him the intimacy of strangers. *All those days we were together, my feelings were boiling in my soul and in my heart, but I was so tired, I felt so sick that I couldn't express them. Yes, I couldn't express enough the joy of being together with actual friends who were so kind with me. They were more than friends for me: Alex was a brother (a blood brother), Helena and Ali were my sisters . . .*

Physically George and Alex could not have been more different, George dark as a pencil, Alex all fair and square. But because they had both studied theology, George felt a bond with Alex. He was unaware that Alex's real love was not iconoclasm or the Nicean creed, but horse racing. For his part, Alex grew fond of George, but found him irritating, not an easy companion. Alex was a practical man, good-humoured, good with money and the car, an open-faced, honest Englishman; he was impatient of George's mysteries and moods.

But it was those mysteries and moods that so appealed to me. He was never 'nice', never dull.

One night a summer storm closed in. The four of us squeezed into the two-man tent. There was no chance of sleep. We couldn't stretch and when we brushed the tent walls the rain dripped down our necks; wind bucked the guy ropes and thunder ricocheted off the trees. We crouched around a lantern drinking whisky and talked all night. Next morning I noted down some of the odd facts that George had let fall; for example, marriages were still arranged in his village and brides were expected to be virgins. As proof the blooded bridal sheet was hung from the bedroom window, a relic of Turkish influence which seemed brutal and primitive but which George found unsurprising. No contraceptives were permitted, nor abortions (unless the mother had already had five children), although they were performed illegally and under dangerous circumstances for large bribes. Unmarried mothers were a phenomenon unknown – and a sign of the decadence of the West, George had been told. One night his uncle and other friends had raped a girl, and the police, for fear of an unmarried pregnancy, insisted that she married one of the rapists; she chose George's uncle. He related this story without criticism of the uncle and his act of rape, or of the cruelty of the choice the girl was forced to make; he was simply stating the current situation.

George was learned about literature, but astonishingly ignorant about the world. How could he have known more? He was unable to travel, and had no access to non-Communist media. What he did know of the 'free' West – shops glutted with inessentials, striking workers, violent crime – he criticised. Although George had so little freedom, he was at least free from pressures to buy/want/aspire to/wear/own, not a freedom most East Europeans desired but one that George did value. So when he mentioned defecting from Romania, it was lightly, and I didn't believe he meant it. He loved his country and was proud of its past.

At dawn George said, 'I will remember this night for all of my life.'

He planned to leave us that morning; apart from his two-week annual holiday, he was allowed only four days off work before 'the authorities' clamped down. We promised to return next year; his father would build a caravan and George would find us a horse. We'd be like 'real' gypsies, he said. He carved on a trunk: 'Goodby [sic] till 1980 – Alex, Ali, Helena, George.' I suppose that tree still stands there in the Romanian forest. We exchanged addresses, books, photographs of ourselves. He said, 'When I go from you I die a little death.' But when the bus came he couldn't steel himself to go. The bus waited and Alex tapped his fingers on the steering wheel.

'George, you must make up your mind. We've got to get on. We've got a long drive ahead of us.'

George appealed to Ali and me. 'What shall I do?'

'Come with us.'

He put his bag back in the car.

With George abandoning himself to us, the journey took on a wild exhilaration. We crossed Romania, swooping up and down mountains, bumping across plains, windows down, George shouting into the wind. Villagers waved frantically as we sped past and we took turns to wave back. Why do they wave? They see a foreign car and hope you'll give them money. I don't believe you, George. Once, as we descended a mountain, a boy hailed us and ran straight down the mountainside, greeting us at each bend. When we stopped at the bottom he wanted nothing, just to look.

I remember little else. Whole days have disappeared, and no words in my diary bring them to life. I grope for images or sounds that lie beyond what I read, but nothing surfaces. Conversely other days are rich and full in my memory, but those were the days when I was too busy to write.

Once or twice the car became a battle ground between Communism and Capitalism. None of us knew what we were on about. Ali tended to make disjointed remarks that were several leaps removed and took some working out. George was confused, starting by praising his own system, but ending by condemning it. He despised our decadent ways, but equally he hated the ugliness and toil of Romania where beauty was resented, he said, for creating inequality. Life was work, work, work. Yet the only way to improve that life was through corruption – or 'stealing', as George put it. The government were corrupt, the doctors corrupt, the police corrupt. It was the norm.

During those drives George and I developed an unspoken understanding; I wasn't sure whether the others noticed this. Ali was distracted (as George suspected, she had another man on her mind); Alex distanced himself because George made him feel left out, but I was fascinated by George. I was intrigued by his Romanian-ness, curious about his language, his beliefs, his habits, his attitudes. He knew so much! Then there were those eyes, which when you got close suggested such sadness, such yearning. I found myself increasingly aware of his every mood. He was highly charged, his emotions threatening to burst out of him, and his silences I interpreted as profundity, as spiritual elevation. All that plus his love of poetry and music set him apart from any man I knew. Cambridge was a place of facts, of proof, of decoded mysteries and adolescent cynics. George went beyond all that; he was a dreamer. I loved the way he sat up all night. He made Alex, forced in his empire-builder shorts to represent all of British manhood, seem unbearably philistine. Later I realised I had never known George at all.

If George had anxieties about coming with us he hid them, and only as we travelled did I begin to understand what he risked. In Sighişoara I wept in front of a noticeboard headed 'Public Opinion'. It displayed life-sized mugshots of 'criminals' with shaved skulls who 'refused to work'. Their punishment was gaol and this public disgrace. A woman of twenty had been imprisoned for three months for not working; a man had been imprisoned for eighteen months for being an alcoholic. Another board displayed close-up photographs of car crashes and burnt children, warnings against dangerous driving and fires. I subsequently saw these noticeboards in China, and guessed that Ceauşescu had been inspired by his visit there in 1971: the stern morality, the sacrifice of individual privacy to the good of the masses. Passers-by studied the mugshots with a mixture of smugness and venom. Had not George left his tedious factory job to come with us? Would he too be judged as 'refusing to work'? He laughed it off, reckless in his new-found freedom.

What I didn't discover until later was that there was a law requiring every conversation with a foreigner to be reported to the authorities. George – so far as I knew – did not go near them.

Leaving it too late one night to find a campsite, we resorted to the squalid cabanǎs, wooden tents provided by the tourist board in which we should officially have been staying all along. The manager refused us two twin-bedded cabanǎs, insisting that we hire a third for George since a Romanian was not permitted to share a cabanǎ with a foreigner; we would infect George by our very proximity and spread foul-smelling ideas. The third cabanǎ was dirty, so after some toing and froing George was allowed to share Alex's, provided we paid for all three. When we argued, the manager threatened to call the police, which he suspected – rightly – was the last thing we wanted. There were no loos, but a field beyond a hedge was a field of human excrement. I wrote in my diary, *Suddenly I hate everything about Romania and the people and I want George to come away with us if he is to survive.*

That was my first mistake: I encouraged him without meaning to. I meant well, but there are few forms of innocence more dangerous than the innocence of the well-meaning traveller.

One day we ran out of petrol. George and Alex took the petrol can and hitch-hiked to the nearest town, where George was stopped by the police and asked why he was not at work. George, who had retained his monastic papers, claimed that he had been sent by Putna to visit the monastery's ex-abbot who was now Bishop of Arad, in the Banat. Not convinced, the policeman asked him to turn out his pockets. Alex had given George a hundred lei to buy the petrol, and this note the policeman held gingerly between his fingers. It was crisp, fresh from a bank: a tourist's hundred lei, not a Romanian's. From across the road Alex saw the two together, but wisely stayed away. The policeman took George's name and address; he would be contacting Putna monastery and the Bucov de Sus police to verify his story.

Ali and I waited in the car. One hour passed. Then two. We were bothered by gypsies who drummed on the bonnet demanding money and 'bic' biros. Eventually, to our relief, Alex ran towards us.

'He's alone,' Ali said.

'Let's get out of here!' he shouted.

'What's the matter? Where's George?'

'He's been arrested. They're taking him to Sibiu!'

Ali and I stared at each other. 'Oh my God.'

George rounded the corner behind him. He and Alex burst out laughing.

'Don't do that again,' I shouted. 'It's not funny.'

From then on George wore our clothes. Off went the felt hat and the cheap brown pinstripe suit, on went Ali's baggy cotton trousers and my red jumper. He was transformed into that rare and magical being: a foreigner. It began as a game. In the market in Rîmnicu Vîlcea, in the Olt Valley, he acquired a nonchalant swagger, an arrogance, as he addressed stall-holders in beginner's Romanian. *Do you remember friends when I asked at the shops in Romanian with English accent how much is a kilo of apricots? Naive and fun in the same time.* He eavesdropped on the stall-holders, peasants in from the villages, and reported that they were speculating on our origins and our wealth. He was delighted by the success of his performance. Only his shoes, brown lace-ups, stayed resolutely Romanian.

But what began as a game turned into a dream. He imagined that he too was heading for the border which he would cross with us, leaving the country for ever. Of course it was impossible; he had no passport, and as for the border, he dared not even go near it. But later I was to speculate if it was then, in Rîmnicu Vîlcea, that what had turned into a dream became, in his mind, a possibility.

We had accumulated a mass of surplus lei. We were each required to change ten dollars a day, but there was nothing to buy. I don't remember meals in restaurants. Our timing was wrong: we kept missing lunch, and by dinner time what food there was had gone. So that evening in Rîmnicu Vîlcea we agreed to spend our lei on a night of relative comfort in the Hotel Alutus. We all needed a wash. At first George, protected by his disguise and half-fooled by it himself, was untroubled. While he hovered in the lobby leafing through tourist brochures, we three checked in, completed numerous forms in triplicate and surrendered our passports. Then we joined George and strolled together into the restaurant. A gypsy band was playing a fruity, melancholy music. We listened and drank *ţuica* and the restaurant manager pulled a chair up to our table. We didn't want him there. George kept quiet. The manager said he wanted to learn English, so we gave him an impromptu language lesson, teaching him that sausages were 'turds' and salt was 'farting' until we were too suffocated with laughter to speak.

We four got up to dance. The manager watched but we ignored

him: we were a team, united against the world. Nothing could touch us. George was a gawky dancer but we didn't mind: we danced on and on, intoxicated by the violins and by the *ţuica* and our journey. That was our second mistake: we forgot where we were. In fact we never really knew. The manager abruptly left the room.

The music ended, the musicians packed up. Time for bed. Together, we would walk nonchalantly past the receptionist and up the stairs. If we reached the second floor unchallenged, we would secrete George into one of our rooms for the night. This was the plan. But when we opened the restaurant door George was intimidated by the red-carpeted lobby and sweep of staircase.

'Come on, George,' Alex said. 'Now's the time. Just don't look at anyone.'

We walked towards the stairs, but a group of soldiers had gathered around the reception desk. Amongst them was our 'friend', the manager. The soldiers were officers, large men in peaked caps with green and gold braid, and they turned to watch us.

'It's OK, they don't know you're not a foreigner. You're wearing our gear. Just keep walking.'

We reached the middle of the lobby, between the staircase and the entrance, when George glanced once more at the soldiers, broke away and fled from the hotel.

We carried on upstairs as if nothing had happened, and much later, long after midnight, when Ali was asleep, Alex and I followed George outside. He had become our responsibility; after all, by that bus stop we had made the decision for him to come with us. It was our fault. And there was so much still undiscovered, still unsaid, I couldn't bear to lose him already, so abruptly. We hoped to find him hovering near the hotel, waiting to be rescued, but there was just the still night. We went further, calling softly behind moonlit buildings: 'George! George!' Back in the market the peasants were bedding down on their stalls to guard their watermelons, piled high like an arsenal of cannonballs. Having pretended to be British a few hours earlier, it was unlikely that George would have sought refuge here. We came to a park and here we found him crouched beneath a tree.

'George!' I was almost crying with relief. 'You can come back now. It's safe.' But he stared past us blindly, paralysed. I tried to take him in my arms, but he was rigid with fear.

'Come on, George,' Alex coaxed. 'You're with us, there's nothing to be afraid of.'

'Please. You can't stay out here all night.'

'All the soldiers have gone to bed.'

'Nobody will know you're not a foreigner.'

But he shook his head, unable to speak. There was nothing we could do. We left him, but anxious about the cold we returned a few hours later. He had vanished. Now the market was silent, the streets hollow but for a lone policeman who shouted at us for being up so late.

In the morning the bedroom door opened, and there was George carrying breakfast on a tray. Wakey wakey. His hair was plastered down from the shower; Alex had woken to find him standing at the foot of his bed. We didn't mention the incident again.

By now George had become a tourist too, exploring places that were as new to him as they were to us. This made him less of a guide, more of a friend. We spent one day (a Sunday) at Hurez monastery, Wallachia's counterpart to Putna, later – seventeenth-century – but equally beautiful. Like Putna it nestled on the edge of forested hills and enclosed its church in a quadrangle, but the church itself was more square, less pointy, more horizontal, less vertical, more Italian Renaissance, less Gothic, as if we had travelled from northern Europe to southern Europe, just within Romania itself.

By unspoken agreement, George and I managed to lose the others in the Italian-Byzantine arcades, carved and twisted pillars gleaming in the sun, to escape into the chill halls of the museum. We glanced at the seventeenth- and eighteenth-century icons and embroideries, the chalices and candelabra, peering closer when one or another caught our fancy, but we were more interested in each other. For the first time he asked about me, my family, where I lived. I took it as a release from shyness, and was touched by his interest in me as a person rather than merely as an anonymous 'foreigner'

30

with whom he was having a special encounter. Back outside, a nun pushed a cart-load of plums up the drive and we helped her. Swallows swooped under the eaves and the silence was disturbed only by distant lowing of cattle. *Lovely day*, I noted in my diary, *Hurez amazing, all white and full of geraniums. Lovely nun said we could eat the plums. Fell in love with George.* Everything was 'lovely' and, looking back, that *was* the moment. It was not just the setting: many a man would have annoyed me here – too loud perhaps, too unappreciative, too jokey – but George somehow embodied the perfection; it was part of him, he was part of it, they were inseparable. He *was* Romania with all its exoticism and cultivation and refinement and intensity.

George was also childlike and this I found deeply appealing. Sitting on the grass beside the monastery's white walls he sang a song which went like this:

> It's Sunday morning
> I'm up with the lark
> I think I'll take a walk in the park
> Hey, hey, hey, it's a beautiful day.
>
> I've got someone waiting for me
> When I see her I know what she'll say
> Hey, hey, hey, it's a beautiful day
> Ha ha ha beautiful Sunday
> This is my, my, my beautiful day
> When you said, said, said that you loved me
> Oh! It was my, my, my beautiful day!
>
> Birds are singing
> You're by my side
> Let's take a car
> And go for a ride
> Hey, hey, hey, it's a beautiful day.
>
> We'll drive on
> And follow the sun
> Making Sunday go on and on
> Hey, hey, hey, it's a beautiful day.

It was our last night and our most perfect campsite, a clearing in an oak forest in the south-western Carpathians. We watched the silhouette of trees grow sharper as the sun slid behind the mountain, and until after midnight covered gypsy wagons trundled along the road below. We drank champagne and I ran through the woods down into the valley for the sheer joy of it. As we built our fire a tortoise snuffled out from the undergrowth and a great yellow moon swam low into an ultramarine sky. Alex sloped off to bed and then Ali. 'Don't go,' George whispered, as I sleepily stood to join her. 'You can sleep out here, under the moon.'

'I'm getting cold.'

'I'll find some more wood ("ood").'

Enjoying being taken care of, I lay by the fire in my blanket and he emerged from the dark bearing trophies of dead branches which crackled into life. My left side blazed while my right side stayed cool in the night breeze. It was good to be alone with him, just the two of us. While he kept watch I drifted in and out of dreams. I felt the top of his head against mine. 'I don't have a pillow,' he murmured, 'so I'll share yours.' I faded away again until I heard him say, 'If I kissed you I wouldn't be punished because I wouldn't be breaking my vows.' His head touched mine again, pressing harder, and suddenly he was beside me and kissing me. He had soft skin and a peasanty smell of mushrooms and close up his shoulders seemed massive. He was shaking and beginning to hurt me, and I got frightened and pushed him away. He gripped my wrist. 'Why are you so cold with me?'

'Please, I just don't want to.' I did want to, but I was afraid of him. He sat up. For one so ascetic, his body was surprisingly brown and strong. He put his head in his hands.

'What's the matter, George?'

He rounded on me, pushing my shoulders into the dead leaves. 'What a question! What's the matter, George? What do you think the matter is?'

'I'm sorry.'

'Sorry!' A sort of violence was bursting. He was trembling, trying to control himself. When the night began to spit with rain I went back to the tent. He joined Alex in the car.

Our visas had expired. We left George by the Danube on the Yugoslavian border, our farewells tearful. He planned to take a train north to visit his friend the Bishop of Arad.

'Come with me. Stay. Please. Come to Arad.' He held my hand.

'I can't, George. We have to leave now.'

'I am in love with you.' He said it in front of Alex and Ali, as if claiming me with this public declaration. They looked on sympathetically, and refrained from mentioning the love-bite on my neck. I gave him a flower and he handed me a folded sheet of paper which he said was something he had written for me at the *cabanǎs*. It was a love poem in red ink.

George's postcards and letters awaited my return home. The postcards, assuring me of his 'sincerity and constance', charted his journey from Arad to Oradea and then back across Transylvania, and his first letter came from Bucov de Sus. It went like this:

1 September 1979

My dear Princess,

I have to tell you that you left me broken hearted, my eyes full of tears. You pretty Gypsy! When shall I meet you again?

Now (when I am writing this letter) you must be in Venezia. Perhaps you are with your friends, laughing, dancing etc. I must recognise that I feel a little jealous. And when I remember your face so beautiful in the moonlight, so beautiful in the fire-light, so beautiful in the stars light, so beautiful in the day light! Then drops of tears fall down from my eyes. I hope you enjoyed my song (or poem or nothing). I promise you another one more successful.

Oh my God, give me patience because I shall not be any more my master, I'll run away to you to see you once more and then to die in peace. Oh my God, how wonderful and dangerous is the power of the love!

Your dried flowers feed my love. Your pictures are on my table,
Europe's map is every moment under my eyes.

O, darling, excuse me if I was wrong that wonderful night. What
about me? Well, I think I can't feel angry on you, anything you say.
It's dangerous to love a girl who is so far away from you, but 'Alea
iacta est'.

With love, George.
Please answer to me.

The prospect of a year apart was terrible. I wrote back with equal fervour and he replied, *What can I see in your letter? It's plain and simple to express: love's fire. Yes, love's fire which burns my heart.* On receiving my letter, he said, his longing for me grew worse. *O! I'm so glad you didn't forget me! Heaven bless you!*

Even that first letter of mine caught the attention of the 'authorities'. *I've got troubles with the police,* he warned. *They asked me to see your letter. . . How much I hate dictators! Damn them!* Tacked on to the letter was a playful but somewhat foolish PS: *To the Authorities: If you are obliged to open this letter, let it go to my English girl friend. If I am wrong, forgive me this time. I loved and I still love so much this pretty girl. That's why if you do not send this letter to England, I shall revenge myself. Take care, an awful revenge!*

I, and he too, disregarded the danger he was in. I could not believe that any 'authorities' would have the time or reason to notice letters between two such insignificant people. As I learnt later, I was naive and he was unwise.

In a prose poem he described his daily life, *For I want to write in a special language/To those who are far away, my friends.* In order to feel close to us he had established for himself an 'English programme', with early-morning tea and biscuits followed by a full English breakfast (*O, my God! How rich meal is an English breakfast!*). Lunch of roast beef and roast potatoes was followed by rice pudding, then afternoon tea and dinner.

> *'A tea again and go to bed, boy!'*
> *Says my father, but no, I can't*

I must take a look at the sky
To remember those lovely nights
We spent together.

He dreamed of *those wonderful days: friends, smiles,/Speed, dance, a nice company*, but woke to find himself alone, *the eyes in tears;/Where are my friends? Where are my friends?/O! I can't find an exact answer.*

He sent me more poems, both by himself and also, not wanting to be 'jealous,' by others – Yeats, Pierre de Ronsard, Coleridge, Longfellow.

His own literary style was unashamedly lyrical and romantic. He appealed to the Muses! O grievous night! Come, my grief: let's take a walk through the sky! Irony of fate! I loved all that, and the grand words he used, words like Death, Soul, Enemy, Spy, Destiny. Through it all loomed his loneliness and his longing. *Well, you left me a month ago. All this month of September I've got you on my mind. Yes, I shall call September the friendship month.*

Again and again he relived our last night together. *Perhaps I was wrong and a wicked man. But I must say, when you are twenty-four it's easy to make mistakes. Then excuse me, I am young.* Later: *Do you remember that last night, Helena? When you said, 'I don't want to.' Then I stopped flirting with you. In fact you broke my heart. I had no answer when you asked me, 'What's the matter, George?' O my God! That strange question: 'What's the matter, George?' Now I'm sorry I didn't go on with the flirting. Perhaps that moment I really hurt you. But I was hurt too.*

Flirting indeed! I was hurt that he should dismiss our relationship so lightly. To me it was more than flirting. Or was it?

In any case, when he first mentioned marriage I was both touched and relieved. He confessed that when he had tried to persuade me to remain in Romania, he had planned to take me to the Bishop of Arad and ask him to marry us, like Romeo and Juliet, he said, two lovers defying destiny to be together. It was a marvellously romantic idea. *Is it good to try to marry me? No answer. Nowhere. But still I wait. Yes, I decided to wait the answer.* I replied in some similarly poetic vein. But although I was moved by the uninhibited way in which he wrote, by a love so lyrical and unEnglish, and although I was intrigued by the idea of marriage to George, I treated it lightly. After all, we barely knew each other, and I was not sure that I totally believed in his love; he had a confusing tendency, for example, of following outbursts of feeling with such banalities as *You see, I have just used the past conditional!*

Twenty-one days after we left him at the border, George wrote from a tuberculosis hospital in Rădăuţi. This letter was in pencil on exercise-book paper and often difficult to decipher, the pencil faint and now faded along the creases, and it was ninety-two pages long. The first half was more journal than letter, written over a period of two weeks; the second half a Communist history of Romania from Roman times to the present day, of which half the pages are now missing. It was a rambling letter, a sequence of disjointed thoughts interrupted by hospital routines, and full of fragments and metaphors that added up to pieces of experience, but not to anything whole. Sifting out the facts, I gathered that during a medical examination for a job at a timber factory the doctors had discovered spots on George's lungs. These were thought to be early signs of TB or pleurisy. His parents had neither money nor space to keep him at home, so he had allowed himself to admitted to Rădăuţi hospital.

This was worrying. TB is a killer, and pleurisy not much better. But at first he seemed content. He described the daily life, the doctors' queries and the five-bed dormitories, bread and butter for breakfast, patients praying and reading, family visits. He was glad to have been given a place to eat and sleep, and hospital routines did not irk him since they were not so different from those of the monastery. But above all he had time to *read and live in my mind with my British friends*. He was allowed to walk in the fields around the hospital. *Oh my God, how I like to be in the middle of the nature. It seems to me that I receive a message from the trees, from the grass, from the winds, from the clouds, from the stars, from the moon, from the sun. It seems to me that they carry a message to me from you, my friends. A message of kindness, a message of friendship, a message of love. I feel nearly happy for I know that the same sun's rays comfort us, for you can look at the sky and see the same stars.*

However, during the course of the letter George grew tired and depressed. *Here what can I see?* he wrote on page forty-three. *Only white and white, and white, and white. Only pills and pills and pills. False smiles and false smiles and false smiles.* He was conscious of being different from his fellow patients who were workers, and that since he was an 'unuseful man' his cure was not as important as a worker's cure. He was also distressed by the number of pills he was prescribed, *sometimes unuseful pills but I must obey and take them. For instance they give me a kind of pills which make me feel like a half-drunk man. That's for I seem to be nervous. In fact I'm not allowed to be angry about anything.*

He was convinced that he suffered from neither TB nor pleurisy, and that the spots on his lungs were *from that accident and beating.* What beating? What accident? He had mentioned neither. He added – cryptically – that his ribs had been broken by 'that prior'. What prior? *If the monks pay the doctors they could destroy me. A lot of people say I am a dangerous man.* He mentioned a fellow patient, also from Bucov de Sus, who entered the hospital as a healthy young man and was now dying. *Yes, the reasons for what you come in a Romanian hospital are not only medical reasons, illness. No! There are political reasons too! That is why I don't trust doctors. Doctors help people sometimes to live and sometimes to die. What about the weather of yesterday?* Hold on! What political reasons? Why should anyone want George to die? I had no idea what to make of it all. Partly because of his theatricality, his fears for himself appeared melodramatic. I knew little of his activities before we met, or why the monks from Putna should wish to destroy him, but he seemed an unlikely target.

Certainly his letters were indiscreet. He spoke indirectly of escape, but only years later, when it was too late, did I realise the extent of the risk he was taking. *Perhaps my fate will force me to go abroad and have a political activity. Perhaps,'* he added, *I must marry Helena even against her will.* I understood this to mean not that he could force me into it, but that he could persuade me to help him flee the country even if I chose not to live with him. However, again I did not take him literally. He moved straight on to discuss the books he had read, to describe the doctor's last visit, and that small sentence was lost. I felt that he was simply toying with an idea and did not really mean it.

He did seem to be afraid. *Why do I write what's happened every day? Well, it's rather delicate. Perhaps you have the possibility and pleasure to come next year. Welcome every time! But I'm not sure if you will find me at home. I'm not sure if you will find me alive. What about my illness? Well, a man like me is never ill. I suffer only a social illness.* I didn't understand, and from the safety and stability of Cambridge again I dismissed this as melodrama. George, I thought, had read too many nineteenth-century novels.

It was impossible to pin him down and to extract facts from him without incriminating him further; besides, our letters took three weeks to traverse Europe, and always seemed to cross each other en route. Questions took six weeks to be answered, by which time the answers were no longer relevant.

George's criticisms of what he saw around him became increasingly overt. *There's such a great difference between papers and reality. They steal everywhere and I don't like it. What does it mean? It means I'm not the man of the time, and I'm not strong enough to change times. Again I cry and ask for pity, God, for my youth's mistakes.* He added his most profound insight into what was the tragedy of Romania: *Yes, now if you want a good life you are forced to have a dirty consciousness. But,* he added fatalistically, *the lie, the stealing, the soul murder, all that must have an end.*

Just as I convinced myself that I did love him enough to help him to escape the stealing and the soul murder, so he became disillusioned with the idea of marriage. *I'm not too much happy for I have not too much to offer her and I don't know if I could make her feel really happy. To be objective it would be difficult to marry an English girl.* I was disappointed, although to be objective myself I had to admit that I had not seriously contemplated anything permanent. Then he even went off my return visit. *Sure I'd like you to come again and visit me, but what's the use? To cry again at our separation. In any case your pictures will be icons for me in my mind and as long as I live, if I'm able to do it,*

I'll offer my support or help. Yes, Helena, there is no use to repeat a cruel separation. Now, instead of regrets, he expressed gratitude that I had forced him to keep his oath of celibacy, and he asked me to forget him. He said he was trying to turn my love into hatred for him. *Your love for me could compromise yourself and I should not like it. Just say that I wanted to practise my English and to try to be a writer or poet. Just say I am crazy.*

At the same time he admitted that his desires had alighted on Ali too. *She is a pretty girl after all and I would have like to feel her fresh flesh.* Fresh flesh indeed! I wondered if he really loved me or if he loved the words on the page.

He returned home briefly, then back to hospital. By now he had received several letters from me, and his mood had lifted. *I go walking every day round the hospital through the fields and sometimes in the forest. There I read your letters in a loud voice. I call your name and I imagine you walking with me.* He was happy. He had fun at the hospital, and described a fellow patient with a guitar who serenaded the girls in the agricultural *lycée* that was opposite their window.

Suddenly, in November, everything changed. He wrote in haste – apologising for his imperfect English – of 'troubles' with the other patients and the authorities. *Listen to me, Helena. My parents are poor. It will be difficult for me to find now a reasonable job, and I can't stay at home out of a job. I could go to study if I had money, but I haven't any. So, please ask your family and friends to call me, to ask your authorities to call me to go in your country. The reason might be to marry you or to study or never mind what. If you really love me, I want to give you a chance. Or perhaps it's better to tell you, 'Give me a chance to live my life by your side!'*

Help! Mentally, I ran a mile. Perhaps I had just been flirting. Mine was the luxury of being able to love and leave, flirting with the country, flirting with him, mobile and free. I suppose that had always been part of the charm. Now he was begging me to take responsibility for him coming to exile in England, for his living expenses, happiness, everything. He expected me to give up my freedom, my independence, my life. I was still only nineteen. Besides, while he was abandoned to a life he no longer fitted, I had slipped easily back into my student life which, I had to admit, he did not fit either. Did he love me enough to convince me that it was possible to make that commitment? His message was mixed. On one hand he wanted to marry me or study or never mind what – in other words to make marriage into some practical arrangement for getting him out – and on the other hand he wanted to live his life by my side. Perhaps if no feelings had been involved, if we could have made a straightforward business arrangement of marriage followed by immediate divorce, then it might have been easier. But the idea of us being tied together forever, him dependent on me? No way.

And again, I doubted the seriousness of his desire to leave. The letter was followed by a curious PS: *Even if our authorities don't allow me to leave Romania, your demand will mean an advertisement for me, an increase, a raising of my value, of my popularity.*

It was hard to know how to respond. If he simply wanted to raise his status, then marrying me was not going to achieve that. Quite the opposite. He would have additional problems before he managed to leave, if he ever did. And as for me going to live there, that was out of the question. I felt slightly betrayed, that he had used me, and that all the time we were together he was planning this, that his professions of love had been a trick. As for asking my 'authorities' to 'call' him to my country, did he imagine the Free West that we had praised so lavishly would step in and rescue him? No, the whole idea was absurd.

Choose, Helena. It's your turn to decide! I'm free and you are free. Before I had a chance to reply, another letter arrived, more urgent still. *In my last letter I asked you so much to call me in your country. Well, I dared to ask too much, but I was forced by the circumstances. Of course, your risk is considerable, but you can try.* He enclosed a letter for Alex ('*How are you, old boy?*') reminding him that on the Yugoslavian border he had promised to help him. *Call me in your country,* he repeated. *I want a legal call if it is possible. What do you say? During the winter holidays you've got plenty of time to decide my fate. Come on, Alex! A friend in need is a friend indeed! Risk for me!*

It was still unclear what that need was. He wanted to escape but could not say why. Ali and Alex and I got together to decide what to do. Marriage was out; as for enlisting the help of some international pressure group like Amnesty International, that was out too. So far as we knew, he was not suffering torture or abuse. We had no information that would interest them in his case. Finally we suggested that he wrote to the British Council and the British Ambassador in Bucharest to ask about scholarships.

Out of the blue came an abrupt change of heart. Suddenly he no longer wanted to leave Romania; instead he apologised for his previous letters. *They were written*, he said, *under the influence of my former teacher, and by Shakespeare's Timon of Athens*. I had no idea what to make of this. Lucky I had not set any marriage process into action.

He added that he had written to the Archbishop of Canterbury and had received a reply congratulating him on his English studies, by which he was touchingly thrilled. *How would you like to interpret the letter? What means Archbishop Designate of Canterbury? What must I understand by Christian Discipleship?* I did not tell him that it was a letter of platitudes which offered him no hope.

A Christmas card arrived. On the front was a classic folkloric scene of a Christmas tree streaked with glitter inside a traditional Bucovina house; the walls were hung with hand-woven fabrics, the table draped with a striped cloth. I opened the card and up popped a traditional carved wooden gateway charmingly thatched with snow, and beyond the house itself was a pretty young girl in traditional dress greeting three wise men. The stars were bright against the blue sky, the snow icing the haystack like some delicious cake. It was Bucovina as Bethlehem. Merry Christmas, George had written. A Happy New Year to you, to your family and friends! But he had lifted the pop-up part of the card and written words that were distinctly unseasonal: *Being very sad and indeed depressed, I know that I was guilty, but the world is more guilty! That's the reason for what I curse the world; pains and hurricanes, tears, blood and fire! So I express my deeply hatred against the mankind.* The card arrived in Cambridge on great flapping wings of anger. It was altogether perplexing.

A long letter followed. Half of it was the plot of a film he had seen, the other half five pages of a play (in French) by Françoise Sagan which I didn't bother to translate. I was fully absorbed back into my own life, and getting a bit tired of his long literary extracts; they had nothing to do with *us*. Now marriage was referred to, but only jokingly. *Here in Bucovina people used some years ago to steal their brides! So I shall steal you and force you to stay with me in Bucovina. I know that English people complain of their climate being damp and rainy, so England is no place for a person like me. What's the matter? I imagine you already shouting, 'Au Secours!'* He planned to leave the hospital as soon as possible – he had been there for four months – and take to the mountains as a shepherd. He yearned for fresh air, better food and time to '*think of you!*'

I asked him what he had meant in a previous letter about being *a man who refused to accept his fate and decided to restore his honour.* He replied, *I can't explain it exactly. Perhaps I was influenced by one of Boney M's hits.* Boney M indeed! It was all very well being influenced by nineteenth-century novels, but a pop group with the tritest little songs – that was positively embarrassing. He apologised for being tedious in writing so often, and I had to confess that a tiny part of me was beginning to find him tedious with all his toing and froing, and his obsession with himself and his own problems; he expressed no interest in my life. This was understandable, since I had the advantage of being able to picture his life, while he was unable to picture mine, but when he did make the attempt he was miles off the mark. Boney M! Every few days the man I shared a house with called up the stairs, 'Another letter from the mad monk', and I wrote back less often.

In January 1980 he returned home, having been diagnosed free of TB. Ten days later he was summoned by the village mayor, who suggested he should study in Suceava or Iaşi, and then sent him to the 'Sheriff', who offered him a job. *Perhaps my letter didn't reach the Ambassador*, he wrote, apparently hoping it had not, or resigned that it never would. *Anyhow they were very kind to me. My job is tiring and sometimes dangerous because the men of the law are sometimes hated by people. But risking my health and my life, I've got a chance now to prove my good intentions towards government.* Why were the authorities suddenly being kind to him? What did he mean by 'men of the law'? Why did he want to prove his 'good intentions towards government'? I had no idea what to make of this turn-around.

Instead of apologising for the number of letters, now he apologised for their lack. He was too busy being a man of the law. In March he wrote that *people say that Alex was a spy and that you (the ladies) were his bait.* He did not say whether or not he believed this himself, but he suggested that we should 'interrupt' our correspondence for a while. *In case I need you, well, I know your address by heart.*

An Easter card followed saying, *Christ is risen! Please, don't write to me any more. For my sake! And safety!*

I did as he asked and heard nothing more. The following summer I did not return to Romania. Instead I went to Turkey. But when I came home I found letters from George.

My dearest Helena,
Maybe my fearings are useless but I think I have to be prudent. Do not write to me!
 This summer in my previous letters I asked you as politely as I could that you would come again in Romania on August 15–20. Well, I shall be at home between August 15 and August 24. Our meeting place: Putna Hotel restaurant, every day at noon.
 'Have you got a match?' will be our pass word.
 When you reach Suceava or Rădăţi, send me a postcard on which you may wright 'Success!' and an indecipherable signature.
 This way we shall easily be meeting after one day at the most.
 My dearest Helena, I count on your arrival! Don't forget it!

There followed photographs of him *for my possible passport. I'm sure Alex will help you. He promised me so at the Yugoslavian border last year. PS Remember our date: Putna restaurant (where you and I met last year) August 15–20 every day at noon, between 12 and 15 o'clock.* A postcard had been sent separately, inscribed *Good luck!*

I was to smuggle him out of the country. I wondered if all the times he had begged me to return, this had been his plan.

But it was too late. I returned from Turkey at the end of September: the letters had been waiting for two months and our assignation had long past. Like Angel Clare, his letter for Tess slipping under the carpet, never to be found. When I wrote to explain – as discreetly as possible – I knew that while sitting at that hotel bar near Putna monastery, watching for me to come up the dusty track beneath the avenue, he would never have imagined that I was far away, with my thumb out on the road to Turkey. It would not have entered his head.

He replied: *Never write to me again. I have joined the police.*

Two

During the 1980s Romania vanished into its darkest times. As far as the outside world was concerned, it almost left the map. I made other journeys, met and married someone else, and hearing nothing from George thought about him less and less. I didn't forget him – stills from that summer often surfaced in my mind – and I wrote to him in 1985 asking him to let me know how he was. He didn't reply, and I didn't persist for fear of endangering him further. Alex I lost touch with almost as soon as we got back but Ali and I remained friends. We spoke of George now and then. We both felt guilty. We had helped to make him dissatisfied with his lot, but failed to help him change it.

Then in autumn 1989 Eastern Europe began to burst at the seams, and we watched while the Warsaw Pact started to crumble. By now it was clear that of all the East European dictatorships, Ceauşescu's had become the most repressive, the most Stalinist, the most paranoid, the most cunning. There were few signs, however, that Romania's *Conducător* would lose control. As late as the end of November 1989, at Bucharest's fourteenth Romanian Communist Party congress, more than 3000 delegates unanimously raised their hands to re-elect Ceauşescu as their leader for another five years. The future looked bleak.

But during December revolutionary fever spread eastwards across Europe. The unimaginable happened. In support of a Reform Church Hungarian priest in Timişoara who was threatened with eviction, the Romanian revolution began. Over eleven days between 15 and 25 December, riots fanned across the country. In Bucharest there was the last faltering speech from the balcony, the panicked helicopter escape, and on Christmas Day 1989 Nicolae Ceauşescu and his wife Elena were executed.

In my parents-in-law's house in Somerset we watched the rioting on TV. We were eating Christmas pudding at the time. We sat around the table while grenade-hurling Romanians pressed up against the screen as if trying to climb into the safety of the old nursery. As the revolution exploded in front of the cameras, the entire world found the immediacy gripping, horrifying; but I also had my own private memories of George. Was he among them, I both hoped and feared?

I wrote to him at once, but again heard nothing. It wasn't just that I was concerned for his safety, there were also so many mysteries, so many unanswered questions, and I hate to leave things unresolved. What had happened to him? Where did he live? What did he do? Did he join the police, and if so, why? Those cryptic letters had hinted at something – discreet references that were lost on me, messages I ignored – and with hindsight, once the horror of the Ceauşescu regime was revealed, I could recognise my own blindness. I wanted to discover what had gone wrong, even who George was, and in some way to make amends. Only now could I do that in the knowledge that George was safe from the evil that had shadowed Romania. In the so-called 'dawn of democracy' George had nothing more to fear. Or so I thought.

Since he failed to write – and of course he had no telephone – the only solution was to find him. I toyed with the idea of going back to Romania. I prevaricated, kept busy with other things; I admit I slightly dreaded leaving my comfortable life, my husband, our cat, for food queues, freezing trains and robberies. An exiled Romanian friend who had returned to Bucharest for the first time in ten years described the people as desperate, poor, frustrated, weary and ill-fed. Anarchy, she said. Nevertheless, I had to know. And besides, there was an air of excitement about the New Romania in the midst of change.

Richard, my husband, understood that this was one journey I would have to make alone.

Eventually, in March 1991, I crossed Europe by train. I wanted to take it slowly, to comprehend the vastness of the continent and Romania's isolation at its far end, something impossible to gauge during a three-hour flight. Red-brick Belgian houses evolved overnight into yellow-ochre churches with Baroque bell-towers, the first sign of the Austro-Hungarian Empire which spread its influence – architecturally at least – as far east as Bucharest. Then we were rocking across the great Hungarian Plain, its flatness pierced by the verticals of factory smoke-stacks, wintery trees, and stalagmites of high-rise blocks.

I changed stations in Budapest. My Hungarian taxi-driver was appalled to hear I was heading for Romania. 'When you shake hands with a Romanian you have to count your fingers when you get them back,' he warned. Anticipating food shortages, I stocked up on last-minute supplies of bread and packet soups.

Romania's approach had been heralded from Vienna by a steady deterioration of the trains. Now a single strip light illuminated frayed plastic seats and a lino floor littered with fag ends and a rolling bottle that no-one bothered to pick up. My rucksack rocked dangerously overhead, straps swaying. Teenage conscripts on military service squeezed into the corridor, their green backsides flattened and bleached against the carriage's glass doorway; I was lucky to get a seat. A middle-aged woman in a crocheted cardigan and tight hair couldn't stop knitting, knitting. We ignored each other until the entrance of a pock-marked gypsy provoked an exchange of fastidious glances. He clung to the door frame, apologising as he was flung about. When a seat became free he nipped in and was soon snoring; the knitter clack-clack-clacked with ever greater ferocity. As I was nodding off the gypsy blasted a sneeze and a shout of laughter, then snorted into a filthy towel. Everyone winced.

With me I had copies of George's letters, and his photograph; ironically, it was the photograph he had asked me to bring to Romania in his 'possible passport'. I also had a sheaf of addresses, friends of friends, but looking through them now, on the train, I discovered I had left the most important one behind. Never mind, I knew the name of his village; neighbours could direct me.

I was full of other misgivings about this journey,

1. I was alone.
2. I did not speak Romanian.
3. Romania was in a state of chaos.
4. If George's family had suffered because of his foreign correspondence, would they not resent my arrival and want me to leave?
5. If he had joined the police, would he and his family resent me for having forced him into this position?
6. If he was married and happily settled, would he prefer his life not to be disturbed again?
7. How would I reach his village?
8. What if I travelled all the way there to find he and his family had disappeared?

The conscripts metamorphosed into broad-beamed women in head-scarves, and men with long sideburns in cloth caps and earth-coloured jumpers who smoked a lot. Wide cheeks, squat necks, long noses, black hair, drab clothes, cheap bags. The past is another country, another country is the past: we had arrived in Romania and shunted back fifty years.

Waiting in the drizzling pre-dawn for a taxi (should I walk?), I felt abandoned in this dark strange country. Yes, I had been here before, but that trip was evasive as a dream. I wanted to resuscitate that dream, to turn it back into reality, but right now it was as if I was here for the first time – with no hotel and no lei. I arrived in Romania as if jumping from some great height, hoping someone would catch me. Fear and excitement. Free fall.

But Oradea – where we had also crossed the border twelve years ago – looked beautiful. My spirits lifted. Buildings are best seen by night, without the distraction of life down below or the cruelty of daylight. Neo-classical and baroque facades loomed each side of wide boulevards. One building more flamboyant than the rest – arbitrary windows, superfluous Jugendstil decoration that had no function except to be easy on the eye – housed the hotel Vulturul Negru, the cheapest in town. Here I changed money with the taxi-driver at nearly five times the official rate; he held a crisp twenty-dollar bill up to the light, then folded it lovingly away and didn't bother about being paid for the ride.

My room had a basin but no water, and a light but no bulb. There was, it transpired, a nationwide light-bulb shortage. The receptionist gave me a paraffin lamp which illuminated decayed formica furniture, grey net curtains dangling from string, walls stained with damp: it looked better in the dark. But it smelled good; if I closed my eyes I could have been in Liège, Munich or Madrid, but never in England. It was an indefinable smell, a sophisticated continental smell, a mixture of coffee, floor polish, sun on cobbles – I never worked it out.

Morning revealed a building opposite once topped with the words TRĂIASCĂ REPUBLICA SOCIALISTĂ ROMÂNIA, but SOCIALISTĂ had been ignominiously torn down. Just over a year after the revolution, the scars still looked raw. How quiet the place was – a few cold people in anoraks waited for trams, heads down – and how crumbly the buildings, how dowdy the women, how bleak the shops. A supermarket's shelves were stocked only with cigarettes and alcohol and rows of grey bottled apples, like specimens in formaldehyde. Even market stalls were bereft of any produce but withered carrots, pumpkin seeds, paprika in paper cones, and a heap of nettles. People queued for bread, and a restaurant tempted diners with a window display of a bag of potatoes on an enamel tray. I ate school-dinner meat with tinned peas and ersatz orangeade in a state-run 'Lacto-

49

Vegetarian' restaurant. The waitresses wore my hideous white plastic open-toed ankle-boots with their sling-back heels.

Slowly, I made my way east to Bucharest. Street corners in Cluj were dotted with memorials to the 'heroes of the revolution', makeshift wooden crosses that marked the spot where they fell, adorned with a photo of the dead and a poem in a plastic bag and fresh flowers and candles which dripped wax on to the pavement. The crosses were hasty and spontaneous, like the deaths. In Braşov the buildings on the main drag were pitted with gunfire.

But surprisingly, life went on. Flower-beds were tended, trams wobbled over cobbles, gypsies sold hyacinths, a boy pissed in the park while his mother waited.

Before finding George I planned to return to some of the places we had visited together. This was not foreplay; I did not want to titillate myself with other experiences first – far from it. But I did want to see what had changed, and also to make sense of what had happened. The difficulties of communication and the gulfs in our understanding of each other's lives – the social mores, the political undercurrents – meant that mistakes had been made, and now I had no wish to barge ignorantly back into George's life. Instead I wanted to put George in context and get to know him before we met again.

We had avoided Bucharest in 1979, but this time I began my journey from the capital. The city loomed frightening and dangerous, a mishmash of preconceptions: Olivia Manning's *Balkan Trilogy*, the earthquakes of 1977, recent news reports of violence and strikes, gypsies, baton-wielding miners, thieves. On cue as I left the Gara de Nord a black-market money-changer tried to rob me with a sleight of hand.

Where, according to my map, once stood a string of hotels, there remained only one, alone amidst a heap of ruins. Men wearing black leather jackets clustered like stag beetles in a cigarette-smoke fug at the counter, one of them yelling down the phone. The room was too expensive.

'Is it a good room?' I asked.

The receptionist shook his head. 'No, it isn't. But you won't find anywhere cheaper.' Dim light illuminated a flattened Fifties carpet and posters of large women in large bikinis cavorting in front of tower blocks beside the Black Sea. I could not stay here. My only hope was Nicu, a friend of a friend in London, so I forced myself to call this stranger.

'Wait there,' he said at once. 'Give me forty minutes.' This was one of many such spontaneous acts of kindness.

Nicu was tall, bearded, handsome in a soft-centred way. He spoke English with an American accent. He had a friend, Roxana, with a spare room: I could stay there. He led me through tumbledown streets, tripping over potholes as I tried to spot the remains of neo-classical ochre villas and nineteenth-century *belle epoque* apartments behind the tower blocks. At first glance, Bucharest lacked charm. Nicu, however, was proud of his city. He pointed out landmarks – the Calea Victoriei, the University, the School of Architecture – and said that unlike our mutual friend in London, he had never wished to escape. This was home, his roots. He talked all the time (carefully choosing his words, thinking of his grammar), about his family, his work in a state publishing company. He was planning a different style of publishing. During the *epoca Ceauşescu* they had had to take care; certain books were not published because a negative reaction from the Securitate could lose the editors their jobs. Aware of this, writers wrote other books, books that would be published.

'It was a question less of censorship than of self-censorship,' he said. 'This was the New Socialist Man that Ceauşescu managed to create, whose own thoughts were censored.' We were waiting for a bus. An editor himself, Nicu had toed the official line in order to survive. And now, he announced, he hoped to publish more courageous books, particularly memoirs of people who opposed Communism and suffered for it. Our mutual friend had proposed that he translate and publish Koestler's *Darkness at Noon*, and although not strictly memoirs, and not about Romania, Nicu thought this the perfect choice. It gave Romanians if not the actuality then the flavour of Romania's Stalinist history. 'We need to know the truth about what happened here, you know. And we need to know the truth not only about our past, but also about our present.' He was referring to the revolution, and to the unsolved mysteries that still, fifteen months on, shrouded it.

Roxana's was a large apartment in an art nouveau block much sought after by the élite. She met us on the stairs, her sleek black hair coiled in a ponytail, her eyes behind their big expensive glasses rimmed with green and blue. She wore a flamboyant skirt and long green beads; in her mid-thirties, she looked sophisticated, independent. She must have been disappointed by her train-stained foreign guest; she had prepared herself for someone more glamorous.

The walls were grey, and cracked since the earthquake. Roxana had neither the money, nor, because the flat was not hers, the inclination, to repair the cracks, but she had covered the worst with Japanese prints. She strove for a cosmopolitan look, though she had rarely left Romania. She produced teabags, a saucepan of boiled water, and tiny patisseries for me, neat gin and Kent cigarettes for herself and Nicu. The status symbols were important; most people used Kents as currency for bribing doctors and bureaucrats, but Roxana, who worked for a foreign oil company and was paid in dollars, could afford to smoke hers, and King Size too. She was full of company policy, contracts, gas and lubricants; like Nicu she displayed her excellent English, occasionally lapsing into French, a shiny person. Small talk was dispensed with; I longed to curl up on her sofa bed, but they were desperate to plunge into a comparison of neo-platonism and Zen. For years Eastern philosophies had been suppressed.

'You remember when the rest of the world got interested in transcendental meditation?' Nicu asked. 'It was banned in Romania because Ceauşescu was afraid people would escape. Metaphysically. At least, that's what we were told at the time.'

Now TM, Krishna, Buddhism were the vogue. Mircea Eliade, a Romanian-born historian of religions who spent a long time in the East and whose works had been banned, had just been published in Romania for the first time in many years and had inspired a generation. Roxana was practising yoga and astrology while Nicu had plumped for occultism.

We moved on to the inter-war history of Europe, and their knowledge of pan-European culture made me feel provincial. I was excited by the unEnglish way they wore their learning on their sleeves, unafraid of seeming to show off. No self-deprecating smirk, no modesty: it seemed daring and liberating. They were immensely cultivated, and they despised the shallowness of the 'developed' world. If we'd had the opportunities you've had, they said. . . .

'In a way it was a good thing we had no television to speak of,' Roxana observed, 'because instead we read books. We only had a few, but those we had we devoured night after night, then passed on to friends. You were distracted by pop music and discos and so your people are crass and ignorant. Not all, of course,' she added (kindly), 'but many. You only have to look at the American rubbish we get on TV now to see what I mean.' Nicu had studied classics and liked to quote from Cicero and Horace, while Roxana was keener on Lawrence Durrell. Bucharest society was small, so Nicu knew many of the eminent contacts I had been given by friends in London, and at the mention of one he kissed his fingers. *'Moah!* The Number One Intellectual!' Fifteen months after the revolution it seemed almost quaint to hear the old Marxist stratification of society into intellectuals, workers and peasants, but they were proud of being 'intellectuals', in other words degree-holders. Roxana expressed bitterness at having to leave her intellectual's job as a teacher to soil her hands with the oil company although she liked the money and status; at least she was not dabbling in *business*, that really was the lowest of the low, the work of gypsies and ex-Securitate.

I thought of George though did not mention him. He had yearned to study as they had done, but never had the chance. *Today my brother Constantin (the student) payed a visit to me. I must recognise that I was very proud to tell to the other patients that my brother is a student. He worked this summer and he was so kind to bring me some presents and a book to improve my English.* George was a world away from these urban sophisticates, but he shared their passion for learning, and their hothouse *lycée* education. He too loved to escape into books.

'How do you find Romania?' Roxana asked.

'Not as bad as I expected. I mean, life goes on.' I was wary of seeming patronising.

'Not as bad! How people respond to Romania depends on what you compare it with. If you compare it with the Third World it's not so bad. People have food. We have clothes, education, cinemas, transport, electricity.'

'Occasionally,' prompted Nicu.

'Yes. And running water.'

'Sometimes.'

'Sometimes. But if you compare Romania with anywhere in Western Europe, as we have every right to do, then it's awful. Did you know that during the inter-war period this was known as the Petit Paris? We had wonderful food, beautiful clothes, hot water, when you in England had nothing.'

It was true. Olivia Manning had described the almost obscene amounts of food spilling off tables in crowded restaurants, and the women, puffed up like pigeons, strutting the Calea Victoriei in furs while the British slid into rationing and war.

'We were part of Europe then,' Nicu said.

'Yes, and now, because Churchill betrayed us to Stalin at Yalta and threw us into the arms of the USSR, it is your duty to help us out of this mess.'

Nicu leaned forward. 'You know Ceauşescu succeeded in one thing? He put us in Africa.'

'Bah! We're Europeans, we have a Latin culture, and here we are with no water between ten at night and six in the morning. You'll see that the bath is full. I have to fill it before 10 p.m. or I have nothing to flush the toilet with. So if I don't get back in time, no flushing. It's humiliating.' Roxana dragged on a cigarette. I needed fresh air, but it was too cold to open the window. In winter, Nicu joked mordantly, they apologise to the radiator for touching it because their frozen fingers make it feel even colder. Then they light the oven, open the door, and crouch in front of it. As the kitchen is no more than a passage they have to take turns. Sometimes people would nod off, and while they slept the gas would go off and the pilot light go out. Then it came back on again, but the people never woke.

In Roxana's mind Romania was the nadir, and although criticism from me was unwelcome, I also insulted the stoicism of the Romanian people by belittling the awfulness of their situation. When I asked her about *The Dean's December*, in which Saul Bellow compared Bucharest with Chicago, two opposite extremes, with Chicago finally coming out worse, 'How dare he?' was her reaction. How could some outsider know what they had to tolerate, when he came from Chicago with its unlimited food, unlimited warmth and clothing and streets lit up by night and no-one looking over your shoulder? Roxana despised the liberal shilly-shallying of anyone who might try to imply that there was something good in the Communist system.

She was more pessimistic than Nicu. She saw nothing but evil in the present government: all the leaders were ex-Communists, the revolution was only a 'revolution' which returned the same old lot to power. As for the Romanian Intelligence Service (the SRI), it was simply the old Securitate with a new name; the front-runners had disappeared and their underlings had risen up to replace them.

'What were your lives like before the revolution?' I wanted to know for George's sake, but I was interested in them too.

'Please,' Nicu interrupted. 'We call it the "so-called revolution".'

'OK, before the so-called revolution.'

Roxana replied, 'We could hardly trust anyone, even our own families. You know one in three people were informing to the Securitate? That means that one of us here this evening would be an informer, and everyone would be aware of that. The phones were bugged. It's rumoured that the Securitate could listen to 10,000 lines – that is, to half the country who had telephones.'

'So who did you see, socially?'

'Just a small group of friends. We were students together at Bucharest University.'

For all the awfulness, I did envy this group's unity against the common enemy.

'It was a crazy time, you know,' Nicu said. 'I remember once we were together in a friend's apartment and there were two TV sets on, one with an illegal video of the film of *1984*, and one in the next room with Ceauşescu making one of his long speeches, which was all we ever saw on TV. He used to go on and on. I stood in the doorway between the two rooms and I realised that they were both the same. One was fiction, and the other reality. But it was Ceauşescu who was the fiction, and *1984* the reality.'

We laughed. 'But now things are better?'

'No,' said Roxana. 'Actually one thing has changed. Before the so-called revolution we were always afraid. Now we have lost our fear, but not our suspicions.'

Although allowed to travel, they were restricted by their lack of foreign currency and by their need for a formal invitation from someone in the host country, and they hated being stuck away in their provincial little backwater – Europe's poor relation.

'You'll notice we have a terrible inferiority complex,' Nicu smiled.

Roxana's husband had had trouble with the Security Service; he had sought refugee status in France, and she was thinking of joining him. Although he had been gone for months, she now reached into a basket for a packet of contraceptive pills, ostentatiously checked the date and swallowed one. She wanted me to see, I guessed, partly because until the revolution all contraceptives had been banned; now they were legal but elusive, so they were still high-status goods. Perhaps she was also indicating that she had lovers. Bucharest was always promiscuous, even during the prudish years of Communism; people were clustered together, unable to leave, with nothing much to do. Without any cause whatsoever, I wondered idly about her and Nicu, sprawled in her armchair obviously at home.

I needed sleep, but Roxana demanded to be listened to. Nicu returned to his wife and daughter, and while Roxana brewed Turkish coffee and lit another Kent ('Vitamin K') I explained a bit about George, why I was here.

'You say he didn't reply to your recent letter?'

'Nothing.'

'He could easily have moved house. Or perhaps he is still afraid of having a foreign correspondence. Or maybe he never got the letter.'

'Is that possible?'

'Of course! Many letters from my husband have never arrived. You realise we are not allowed to seal envelopes with scotch tape? It's illegal. Because it stops them reading the contents.'

'Maybe he's forgotten me.'

'I doubt that. Meeting a foreigner like you would have been a highlight of his life. You were his escape route. You do realise that he could have been a spy for the Securitate?' Roxana had a flat, hard voice.

'What are you saying?'

'Look, as I told you, it was a one in three chance.'

'You mean right from the beginning?'

'Why not?'

I remembered his terror in the park in Rîmnicu Vîlcea, his desperate letters. 'No, it simply isn't possible.'

'Then when he asked you to come back and bring a British passport, that could have been a trap. By then the Securitate would have got a hold on him and set the whole thing up. He could have been an *agent provocateur*. Think what a coup it would have been for them!' She laughed and tossed her gleaming hair. 'British tourist caught attempting to smuggle Romanian out of the country! It would have been great propaganda.'

I was silent. This had never occurred to me. It was the first of my doubts, but a betrayal of George even to contemplate it.

'After all,' Roxana continued, 'he did write to you that he was in the police. But then, he could have been forced to write that. Now he's probably lying low up in Suceava somewhere. One thing that I do advise is that when you meet him you should make your intentions clear.'

'That'll be easy. I am a married woman.'

'I don't mean that. I mean about whether or not you intend to help him leave the country. It would be very easy for him to get the wrong impression.'

'You're suggesting that he got the wrong impression last time.'

'It sounds like. It can be so easy to make those sorts of mistakes. My family also came from Suceava. In fact I want to tell you my story,' she said, 'because it might help you to understand why certain things happened here. Why your friend George might have joined the police. Why he might have lied. When I joined the Party, I also had to lie.' She watched me, green eyes narrowed behind big glasses. From what she had said, I had assumed that she and her friends had remained outside the system, bravely critical. I had presumed that to be true of any friends of friends of mine: there were the good guys and there were the bad guys, and I would be able to distinguish between them. This was what I had hoped, that there would be good and evil, black and white. But that was too easy: Romanian life was more convoluted than that, more grey.

'Why did you join the Party?'

'Yes. I thought you would ask. You must understand it was very difficult for us. It was impossible to get on without joining the Party. That's why your friend George might have joined the police or whatever.'

They [the authorities] said I would have real troubles if I wanted to become member of the Party ... But risking my health and my life I've got a chance now to prove my good intentions towards government.

'There was nothing unusual,' Roxana defended herself. 'Three million people did it. It didn't mean much. Nicu joined, most of my friends joined. But we weren't the ones who raised our hands at every proposal – we weren't the slaves.'

'Why then?'

'I knew I had to join the Party if I was going to escape from my parents' dead-end life. They were workers in Sibiu. So I was given this form to complete, ten pages long, all about my family's history. What my father did, what my aunts and uncles on both sides did, cousins, in-laws, grandparents. You wouldn't believe it. And of course

58

I had to lie because by then I knew the truth, and had I told the truth, I would never have been accepted.'

The truth was this: when Soviet troops crossed the frontier in 1944 her grandfather, a Moldavian landowner, had been sent to labour on the notorious Black Sea Canal, while her father, a lawyer, was transferred with thousands of Moldavian peasants to the factories of Sibiu in Transylvania. With that on her files she would never have got a decent job, so she lied, and then applied for a post in the oil company. She waited two years, an expensive time. Every month she took plastic bags filled with Kent cigarettes, brandy and soap for the ladies in the office. It was quite open. One time a woman even opened her bag in front of Roxana to check that nothing had been forgotten: it was that brazen.

Having succeeded in getting the job, she was immediately contacted by the Securitate. In an international company she would meet foreigners, and each of these encounters was to be reported. Because she was being watched, and her phone was tapped, she had to obey. To impress the Securitate with her diligence she did not even wait for them to call her, but called them first. After every gathering at, say, a foreign trade fair, she was required to write a report: who said what to whom, who formed a group with whom, who sat beside whom at dinner. Even if the delegates included Romanian government ministers, she was required to report on them. Particularly on them. She was unable to liaise with colleagues to agree on a story because she could not trust them.

'I couldn't protest about it too much either, because then it would look as if I was hiding something. My reports became quite an art; I couldn't write too little because they would be suspicious, yet at the same time I didn't want to write too much.' I wondered what kind of a conversation we would have had on my last visit, when she knew she would have to report it. How many people like her I must have met, with that impenetrable Communist blandness and superiority, without realising how much they were longing for contact. How brave – and foolish – George had been.

'By then my husband had become a liability, making endless political jokes. This put my job at risk. Many couples were having problems. Now people suspect me,' Roxana continued. 'That's why I don't have many friends.' The sophisticated girl-about-town . . .

Yes, now if you want a good life you are forced to have a dirty consciousness.

'I never reported anything that might incriminate people. If they would only show us the files I could prove that. But here nothing is clear. That's what's so awful now. Everything's still secret. And that's the one thing we ask for. After the so-called revolution we thought all the secrets would come out, but in fact we still have no idea what really happened.'

She and her friends were reeling from the revolution and lost in the rumours that surrounded it. Like the rumour that the crackpot Securitate troops were in fact Arab 'terrorists', or the rumour that Ceauşescu was not really dead at all, or the rumour that the entire revolution had been staged by the Securitate and was really nothing more than a *coup d'état*. Everyone had his or her own opinion about these rumours and argued it passionately.

I wondered why Roxana had confessed to me. I guessed it was not just to prepare me for George's possible collaboration, but because I was an outsider, uninvolved. There was a weight of guilt she needed to offload. We talked until after midnight.

Freezing rain drowned the city in a wave of grey. Grey concrete buildings, grey faces buffeted under grey umbrellas, grey trolley-buses wallowing over potholes and tramlines and spraying my legs with grey mud. Crossing roads meant wading through puddles which ebbed and flowed across the streets in the absence of drains. Tyres of tin-pot Dacias sloshed over drowned cobbles. Nicu was taking me across town. He was an informative guide, but the city had no style, no order. Later I was to become fond of Bucharest with its crumbly back-street villas and parks, but at that moment I loathed it. Petit Paris indeed! Where were Saul Bellow's Balkan-Haussmann boulevards? Destroyed by the earthquake or perhaps by Ceauşescu's attempts to rebuild Bucharest for modern Socialist man, for there was nothing so appealing now.

There was more recent destruction; of course there was, though I hadn't anticipated the extent of it. Nicu left me in what had recently been renamed Piaţa Revoluţiei, the heart of the 'so-called revolution'. I walked around the Piaţa at once fascinated and appalled by the violence. To one side, the Central Committee building with its notorious balcony. I could almost hear the crowds roaring their approval in 1968, Ceauşescu acknowledging their adoration with a small wave, then that same crowd baying for his blood twenty-one years later. I had seen it on TV, his confidence giving way first to confusion as his promises of wage increases had no effect and the chanting 'Ti-mi-şoa-ra Ti-mi-şoa-ra' just would not stop, and then to fear as he was hustled away under his small grey astrakhan. Below the balcony was a monument to the dead. On the other side of the Piaţa stood the remains of the University Library which had been gutted by fire and was now being rebuilt; opposite, the former royal palace, pitted with shrapnel and now under scaffolding; and beyond, the exquisite eighteenth-century Creţulescu church which was strafed with bullets. In the candlelit gloom an old caretaker noticed my interest and whispered, 'Terrorists.' She led me to the ancient silver-collaged icon to show me where the bullets had ripped through it: another icon had a bullet embedded in its side. Miming fear and guns she indicated the line of fire through the old door, which was destroyed. These 'terrorist' bullets had scarred the smoke-blackened ceiling. Now the white plaster gleamed through, like stars.

A café offered meagre respite from the weather, with cold people hunched in the draught surrounded by their streaming plastic bags and raincoats. The coffee was chicory mixed with acorns, and the cakes, which stubbornly refused to break down with saliva, tasted of chemical waste.

I had asked Nicu to show me Ceauşescu's final gift to the city, but he couldn't bear to go near it and had no curiosity to see inside. He said it made him feel ashamed. My first reaction was a sneaking sigh of relief. Light, symmetry of a sort, grandeur, style. The vast and empty Victory of Socialism Boulevard cut a two-mile swathe through the city and led to the vast and empty House of the Republic. Apartment blocks and broad pavements lined the boulevard, and between the lanes were a mass of trees, planted when already fully grown. But on second glance I saw that there was no unifying style. Every block was a mess of different styles – neo-classical here, Egyptian there, curved bits here, straight bits there – a post-modern nightmare, unfinished and impersonal and with no connection to Romania.

The House of the Republic itself was a monolith of exceptional ugliness, Stalinist and neo-classical, one style sitting on top of the other. Only when I walked around it, over building-site mud, did I realise that the enormous façade was repeated four times over in a square. It was less the ugliness than the megalomaniac scale that was so bizarre, competitive obsession made visible. The avenue was the *longest* – longer even than the Champs Elysées, the House of the Republic the *largest* – reputedly beaten by the Pentagon but only just. It was pharaonic, a monument to totalitarianism and folly. Like Vittorio Emanuele's Monument in Rome, it towered white above a mellow cityscape, but on an even more inhuman scale.

In order to build the House, the flat little green park that stranded it in a featureless void, and the boulevard, whole districts of the city had been razed. Ceauşescu and his fellow advocates of radical urban renewal had determined to transform the hotchpotch city of nineteenth- and early twentieth-century villas and apartments into a European Pyongyang. They were like British planners of the 1950s and '60s, only *more so*. The earthquake provided the pretext even though houses and streets declared to be in 'a state of imminent collapse' had in many cases withstood the shock. They were bulldozed nonetheless, and this Civic Centre begun. It involved demolishing not only people's beloved homes, inhabited for generations (for which compensation was derisory), but also parks, hospitals and churches. During the 1980s, the site was known as Hiroshima; lives, histories, memories, beauty, blasted away by a philistine. The few churches that remained were now imprisoned behind concrete apartment blocks and screened from the street, or had been moved, brick by brick, to another site where they remained, out of context, having lost bits and pieces – a cloister here or there – en route. Ceauşescu was like a child paying with duplo, putting up blocks and knocking them down again, by all accounts a hard taskmaster but an indecisive one who changed his mind on a whim often after a building had been built, or an avenue planted.

The residents were forcibly relocated in the outskirts. At Roxana's flat I had laughed over an English grammar book. One section had a conversation which went like this:

Adrian: *Did you also go through the new districts of houses for working people?*
Diana: *Yes, and everybody was very much impressed at seeing these thousands of blocks of modern flats forming little towns by themselves all around our capital.*

I met Roxana in town and we waited half an hour for the bus home. 'You see how much time we lose?' she muttered, staring down the empty street. 'It's like queuing for bread. I'm fed up with waiting for half an hour after work and finding that the bread's finished by the time I get there. I've given up. Most Romanians can't eat a meal without bread to go with it. We're like the French. But for me bread just isn't worth it.'

'I've seen queues for all sorts of things, not only bread. Loo paper, cabbages.'

'Oh, some people queue for anything. They're professional queuers. They see a queue and join it, just hoping something good will be at the end. Then on to the next one. It's a habit. Some people even enjoy it. They've got nothing better to do and they have a chat with other people in the queue. They turn it into a full-time job.'

I moved into a cheapish hotel off the Calea Victoriei. It was a squalid dive. Due to the light-bulb shortage I had to feel my way up four flights of stairs, patting the walls, teasing out each step with my shoes, sometimes forced to crawl on hands and knees, but the room itself was tolerable. I had a balcony overlooking the street. Leather-jacketed men slammed car doors; heels tapped on cobbles; young couples hand in hand in frumpy clothes sucked cartons of orange juice; a sparrow on the neighbouring balcony searched for crumbs amongst the fag ends.

Out on the main streets people milled around stalls selling meat-balls and stared with longing at expensive Syrian biscuits and shoes and Turkish cigarettes in the new 'boutiques'. These were little more than glorified market stalls, and the only sign so far of any private enterprise, apart from the black-marketeers.

It was a pleasure, after several years, to travel again in Europe: I was different, but not that different. Nobody stared or called me 'whitey'. Yet these people were alien to me, had had experiences I could barely comprehend. I attempted to envisage the eerie silence on the streets in the last days before the revolution, when everyone knew they were being watched and overheard by everyone else, when the shops were even emptier than now. I looked hard at the passers-by but they appeared satisfied with their lot, and I suspected that many hid secrets of their own little compromises. It was as if they shared in some multi-layered conspiracy which I could never penetrate, however hard I tried.

I spent one day with Adrian, Roxana's brother. He was a fifth-year medical student, dark and small. He had a nobility of bearing which bore out Roxana's confession about their aristocratic past, and a charming old-world courtesy. He held my coat, kissed my hand, walked on the road side of the pavement and guided me across the road. When I bought a Twix from a stall he was shocked by my extravagance (it cost nearly half a doctor's weekly salary) and he writhed with humiliation when I clumsily gave it to him in front of other Romanians. When a black-marketeer offered to change money he announced, 'My eyes and ears refuse to register such people.'

We walked and talked for ten hours.

He was proud of the University Medical School, a turn-of-the-century building with panelled lecture halls, a place of high learning, but debased, as Adrian described. Before the revolution it had been necessary to bribe the teachers in order to pass an exam. The gift would not guarantee a pass, but the students had to take that risk. Each term they made a collection, whilst observing the teacher's penchant for clocks, or drink, or cakes. One Easter a teacher made it too clear that he liked lamb, and he received seven hunks of lamb. Foreign students – mostly Africans and Arabs – were expected to be generous. One year the Romanian students were asked to leave a classroom; the remaining foreigners were informed that a consignment of imported televisions had arrived in the hard currency Comtourist shops. Enough said. Now some of those teachers had gone, but not all. We met one on the steps; Adrian kissed her hand with awful sycophancy while she raised her plucked eyebrows over her pink-and-black-rimmed eyes and stared into the distance, despising him.

Over the following days spring made its hesitant presence felt. I wandered amongst magnolias in the Cişmigiu gardens. Olivia Manning (or her *Balkan Trilogy* alter ego, Harriet Pringle) sought refuge here, the little café on the lake growing daily more desolate as war set in and food ran out. Now there was food, albeit basic and prohibitively expensive for everyone but the Securitate. Couples larked about in boats and I sat on a sunny bench wishing Richard was with me.

In my loneliness I rang Nicu and returned to the café with him as my escort – no substitute for my husband, but good-looking, tall. By night the café turned into an empty nightclub with outrageous prices; I had to borrow from Nicu to pay for our martinis, which he could not possibly afford himself. We talked of our mutual friend who had escaped to London before the revolution. 'We were together the evening before he left,' Nicu explained, 'but he never mentioned it. He just said goodbye and got in a taxi, and that was the last I heard for ten years. I didn't know if he was even alive.'

'Didn't he write and explain?'

'No, because he knew it would endanger me, you know? To have any contact with him? He had gone to another world in which I would never have a chance to see him, and he would never be able to come back. His name became unmentionable in public. Taboo. It wasn't even as if he was dead. It was as if he had never existed at all.' I thought of George, and wondered if, after his abortive attempt at escape with me, he had ever tried again.

'What was it like, the really bad years?'

Nicu smoothed his well-trimmed beard. I noticed that he was smoking Romanian cigarettes out of a Kent packet (one that I had bought from Duty Free) and I thought how odd it was, the tiny status symbols so important to one's image that meant nothing, *nothing*, to outsiders. 'It was like a nightmare for us, you know? Nothing seemed real and yet we were forced to live through it, like in a nightmare when you try to run and can't, you know? No-one believed in Ceauşescu or what he said, and yet no-one seemed able to do anything about it, like we were physically handicapped. Like when your legs don't work.'

'How does that affect you now?'

'Mentally now, more than physically. We're stunted. We've had no books, no television, no information, let alone the possibility of getting out and seeing and experiencing for ourselves, as you do. It's all very well, Roxana going on about reading so much and all the delinquents in the West; she just feels ashamed. She'd love to travel. I don't want to make you feel guilty, it's not your fault we could never do the same.' Besides, he added, it wasn't all bad. Even the worst of times had their humorous side. There were weeks, he recalled, when the only produce in the shops was alcohol and the only alcohol was champagne. At the same time there was a shortage of women's tights. So while families struggled to survive, the women were drinking champagne and wearing no tights. Such was the surrealism of Romania.

Tickets, taxis, changing money, extending my visa. I pounded pavements from office to office, only to find them closed for lunch. This is the labour of travel, aggravated by the old Communist bureaucracy and that self-important '*Nu*'. I queued in the drizzle at the Gara de Nord. Crowds propelled me and my cumbersome rucksack from window to window, but each time I began my prepared speech the ticket-seller rapped an impatient coin against her till and turned to someone else who lunged in front of me. Only when I shouted and my fellow passengers fell into gawping silence was I served, but to be berated for producing the wrong amount of lei. I was close to tears. Not a good start. Everyone seemed to be watching me, conspiring against me, angry with me. Branded by my clothes, my guilty secret was on display: I was a foreigner, a misfit. I had no fellow traveller to act as buffer. I felt as if I'd lost a layer of skin and every nerve ending was exposed; a sort of exfoliation by loneliness and hunger – hunger because I was too shy to sit alone in a restaurant. When I passed a bench my leg was grabbed; I turned to see a youth, leering.

Even my train compartment was no refuge; a man in a felt hat peered insistently over my shoulder to watch me write my diary. He kept calling me Domnişoară, 'Miss'.

'I'm not Domnişoară,' I almost yelled. 'I'm Doamna. I'm married. Look, here's my ring.'

'Well, where is he then? Why isn't he here?' His breath smelled of onions. Unusually for me, I did not feel like making friends. He wanted to know why I was going to Rîmnicu Vîlcea, but I was too peevish to explain. Besides, we could barely communicate in my fledgling Romanian. An elderly bourgeois lady tried, gently, to shut him up. She fussed about a wet patch on the brown plastic seat. She apologised for the state of the train. I was used to it: I had travelled in India and China and Africa, but that was the last thing she wanted to hear. In any case, I had grown fond of Romanian trains. They were punctual and incredibly cheap.

Our compartment had string bags for luggage and stank of piss. The windows were steamed up and striped with rain, but we were missing little: empty acres of mud, miles of pipes, fretworks of overhead cables. Oil derricks nodded in flat fields, twentieth-century mirrors of the nodding water wells with their buckets dangling from the ends of poles. Past smoking stacks of outdated industries into vast hedgeless communes – mile upon mile of black plough, ditches, newly planted wheat. Past a shepherd stretched out on a sheep-bitten bank, leaning on his elbow to watch us go by; he wore a black astrakhan and had hung his socks on two sticks which stuck out of the ground, like flags. At every halt the sudden quiet filled with rolled 'rrr's and thick 'pleasure' 's's: judging from the number of familiar names, they were talking politics in the next compartment. Sixteen months earlier, wary of informers or informers themselves, what would they have discussed? The weather, I suppose, so wet. A rare willow coming into leaf was the sole reminder that spring was on its way. Peasant women in mud-clogged wellingtons strode about the platforms, their men swathed in sheepskin and carrying staves.

Every back garden was a serious vegetable plot, no space wasted, with picket fences, crumbling sheds, cockerels perched on dung heaps; the odd baroque church with twin turrets and swollen cupolas rose from the flatness, the incongruity of long-lost grandeur. As if deliberately completing the East European scene, two gypsy violinists and an accordionist – travelling players – crossed the track.

A family got on. They were laughing and panting – had only just made it. The mother was neat and dark, like a Welsh woman, with sallow skin and huge, worried eyes. Her daughter had white cheeks with dimples and a mole on her chin, and an expressive curly mouth. We nodded polite greetings and when the man in the felt hat told them I spoke English the woman quivered with excitement. How wonderful! My daughter and I are studying English! Niculina, say something! We have a wonderful teacher, you will love her! Of course you will stay with us in Rîmnicu Vîlcea! Suddenly it was as if a light had been switched on; the irritant in the felt hat beamed and now I was sorry I'd been so hard on him. I had planned to return to the Hotel Alutus, to revisit the restaurant where we danced to gypsy music and the lobby from which George had fled, but the woman – Ana – appealed with her anxious dark eyes.

'Please. Niculina would be so disappointed. Wouldn't you?'

'Oh yes!' The little girl hugged my arm. No privacy, no independence, but then again, no loneliness.

'I'd love to.'

Mimicking my mood, the sun came out at Rîmnicu Vîlcea. It

softened the bleak vistas of flat blocks, many half-built, all identical, far more numerous than I remembered. As we walked to their block Ana and Niculina eagerly pointed out the few remaining older buildings, churches mostly, dwarfed now but intact. Their white towers were slit with diagonal windows that made their tops spin. The churches were the only reminders that this town was more than ten years old; modernisation had left it colourless and deserted, as if history couldn't stand it here any longer and had upped and left.

Ana took my left arm and Niculina my right, frightened that I might break free and make a run for the hotel. But I was happy to be their hostage. I liked them both. Ana exuded uncomplicated goodness; she was an ethnic Hungarian who had moved here when she married a local, and she had a firmness about her that Roxana and Nicu lacked. Transylvanians had assured me that they were . . . *different* . . . from Wallachians and Moldavians, largely because of their connections with honest, hard-working Austro-Hungarians and Saxons. They were less dreamy, less Oriental; they scrubbed their doorsteps. Ana fitted the pattern.

Ana was an outsider in Rîmnicu Vîlcea but both she and Niculina were determined that I should like it. Here was Niculina's high school, there her music school, here a bookshop, there the monstrous Palace of Culture, the cinema, the disco, the market. The market! My first flash of memory! I recognised the red metal poles supporting the canvas-covered stalls, the places where peasants had bedded down when we searched for George late that night. He had been so terrified of being seen with us that he hid in the park; now I was walking arm in arm with this Romanian family and would be openly staying with them.

When Niculina ran to the lift on the ground floor of their block, Ana said, 'Don't bother. You know it doesn't work.' We walked up the twelve flights of concrete steps, through smells of rotting food, and on each landing Niculina pressed the lift button.

'Maybe it will come tomorrow. I'm so sorry, Helena.'

'Don't apologise to me. It's you I feel sorry for, having to carry up all your shopping.' As usual, it was so dark that we had to feel our way, clutching the banisters; the solitary light bulb for the stairwell was protected from thieves by a jam jar, but it no longer worked.

Outside these blocks all vitality had been blasted away, but inside they were humming pockets of life, cells in a hive. The apartment was tiny but pleasant enough. The sitting room was crammed with heavy, dark furniture, including a veneer bookcase and display cabinet, shiny with varnish, that I would see in almost every home from then on. Beside the central table were two brown corduroy easy chairs which opened out to become Ana and her husband's beds. Every night they had to make up their beds, half under the table, and every morning put them away again. Niculina, their beloved only child, had a room to herself, large enough for a sofa bed and her privacy. The bathroom (windowless, paint grey and peeling) was often without water, while the kitchen sink had a tap that continuously streamed.

Niculina flopped down on the piano stool and trotted out a Chopin mazurka. Ana was a physics teacher, and when we guessed each other's ages I guessed older than her thirty-eight, she looked so tired. Hard times, she said. She hardly saw Camil, her husband. He was the new manager of a factory employing 6000 people; he worked all hours struggling to restructure the company in the switch from a planned to a market economy. It meant redundancies, and battling against public opinion, the public being of the opinion that he was destroying their local industry.

'It's very hard for Niculina and me. We never see him, and at weekends he goes fishing.' I tried to imagine a captain of industry in the West living in a two-roomed apartment with no lift and often no water, but failed.

'Niculina! Ring Ioana and tell her who we've got here.' I felt a bit like a trophy.

'Oh, yes. You'll love Ioana.' Niculina stood at the phone in the hall. 'She says she's coming at once.'

'Ioana's our English teacher, a wonderful person.'

Niculina whispered to Ana, who put her arm round my waist.

'Helena, please promise us something. When Ioana asks you to go and stay with her, say no, and stay here with us?'

I laughed. It was nice being in demand. 'I promise.'

They both spontaneously kissed me.

Ioana came panting in, long skirt flying, brimming with energy and strength.

'Ana, I am hungry,' she announced. 'Will you feed me, please?'

In our impatience to talk, our conversation ran ahead of Ana's English, so she busied herself with providing for us instead. We squeezed into the corridor kitchen; Ioana speared slices of salami with her fork.

Ioana's hennaed hair, greying at the roots, was cropped over a square face; I thought of Glenda Jackson. She was like a foreigner here, understanding the foibles of the people, yet detached, and it turned out that she, too, was Hungarian. She was brisk, excited.

'I live alone. Of course you must stay with me.' Appealing looks from Ana and Niculina. Ioana was hard to resist – she was used to being obeyed – but I had made my promise.

'In any case, you will stay at least five days because there is so much to see. Ana will show you the monasteries, won't you, Ana?'

Ana nodded, mute.

'You'll take her tomorrow to Hurez.'

'Oh yes!' I said. 'I'd love that.'

'The car . . . I'm not sure if I can drive it, if Camil will let me . . .'

'Come on, Ana! I'll handle Camil, don't you worry about him. But, Helena, you'll need to stay a week. And I want you to come and talk to my English class later this evening. Ana can be excused from her class because of you, but you must promise to correct her mistakes.'

I was flattered. These 'provincials' were very different from the Bucharestians. They had none of Roxana's inferiority complex, her chippiness or her pretensions.

Ioana was tense. She chain-smoked and had a facial twitch which bared her gold-lined teeth in a brief grimace.

71

'We all smoke because of the problems in our lives. No-one knows if they are coming or going. Ana, this salami's delicious.'

'Thank you. I made it myself.'

I had never thought of anyone actually making salami.

'Oh yes! It comes from a pig we were keeping at Camil's parents' in the country.'

'You see how townsfolk survive?' said Ioana. 'You can't imagine, but before – *before* – a year ago, there was nothing to eat.'

Ceauşescu, in his wisdom, had exported Romania's produce to pay off the country's foreign debt, leaving his own people hungry.

'How did you manage, bringing up a child, looking for milk and bread?' I asked Ana.

'We managed somehow. We could find things somehow. There were shops . . .' Ana was blushing; I couldn't bear to look at her in her embarrassment, but if I looked away it would seem as if I felt she was guilty in some way. 'There were always shops . . . for Party activists . . . you could find a way.'

Ioana went on briskly, 'Not only was there nothing to eat, there was nothing to do. Nothing. No books, no films, no theatres, no TV.' Ana turned back to the stove. 'There was not even much sex,' Ioana continued, 'or at least not much satisfying sex, because there was no contraception and few could afford more than one child. Some people did try to get some knowledge of the outside world by learning languages, but it usually didn't last long. What was the point?'

'What about drink?' I was thinking of the Russians.

'No, surprisingly that was kept to a minimum. To be honest, I can't remember what we did. The great question, of course, is, why did we let it go on so long? As a foreigner you must be wondering why, and it's time we all faced up to our guilt. We are to blame. We got the government we deserved. The result is that we have lost our youth, and brought the country to its knees.' It was the first time I had heard anyone blaming themselves. Ana, understanding most of it, nodded agreement as she heated *sarmale*, stuffed cabbage, on the gas stove.

'The cliché of Romanian literature seems to be this spirit of resignation,' I said. 'That you have bowed your heads before your destiny – the supple branch that bends in the wind, rather than the thick trunk that gets blown over.'

'Oh, I don't know all this stuff about destiny. I think "destiny" is really oppression in disguise. But there is a Romanian spirit, more a belief that things will come right in the end, a faith in the country and in the people. And after everything we've gone through, that spirit hasn't been destroyed. I heard the most extraordinary story recently. As you know, when the Communists arrived they took everything. Land was communalised. They even took chickens, turkeys – everything. Nothing belonged to anyone any more. They turned us into nobodies. But one man owned a tractor and when he saw the Communists coming he took it apart, covered it in oil and buried it in the garden. Now, forty-five years later, he has dug it up. Not only that, he has put it back together again, too. Of course it's years out of date, but apparently it works. Imagine that, after all these years.' Behind her glasses, Ioana's eyes were wet, and she turned her face to the window. 'I find it so . . . marvellous, so . . . incredible. For all those years he kept alive that faith that one day the horror would end. I think he was a true patriot. I have no use for that word really. Patriot! It was forced down our throats. But that's what he is. It's a pity our leaders don't have the same spirit. They should be patriots, but are not. They are concerned with one thing only, and that is themselves. Oh! You're off to bed are you, my darling?' Niculina submitted to a smacking kiss; it had been decided, despite my protests, that she would sleep with her parents on the brown fold-out chairs, while I had her room to myself. The sheets and pillow cases were so stiff with starch that I had to tear them apart like paper.

Ana washed up, then settled into a rocking chair, sipping coffee. She looked exhausted, but insisted she wasn't.

'Ana, promise you'll kick me out when you want to sleep,' Ioana said. 'So, Helena,' she continued, 'what brings you to Vîlcea?'

I explained about George. I had not yet mentioned him to Ana, being unsure of her political allegiances, but of Ioana I felt confident.

'I'm interested in discovering something more about the Securitate,' I explained. 'Why George was so frightened in the hotel. What would have happened to him if he'd been caught with us.'

'Hmm. You know that by law it was his duty to report your visit to his house to the Securitate? It was monstrous. What you do in your own house is your own affair. And what did they think the foreigner was after? State secrets about rocket installations? Even a simple conversation should have been reported. So if he didn't do that and then went off with you, he could have had problems. Perhaps he recognised someone in the hotel here?'

'It seems unlikely, when he came from so far away.'

'Yes, but he had been in the army, hadn't he? And it was soldiers you saw around the reception desk? And then there was the restaurant manager who chatted to you.'

'Yes. I have never in my life seen anyone as frightened. What intrigues me is who were these people who had such secret power? Where are they now?'

Ioana stirred her coffee. 'I can tell you a few things. I also had a brush with the Securitate.'

Ana nodded. 'Ioana had a very bad time.'

During the early 1980s Ioana had been arrested for being too outspoken in her criticism of the regime. She was questioned for six days by the Securitate; they held her in their town-centre headquarters. These were more like offices than cells. The officers were even kind, in their way, Ioana said. They chose her as a scapegoat because she had no family, and they were clever in their questioning, relentless yet polite. But that only increased their power; they terrorised, but in such a *reasonable* way. Shortly after her release, Ioana was given a show trial in front of several hundred workers from the factory where she was employed in 'protocol'. Having been publicly humiliated, she was then forced to leave and make her living teaching English.

While Ana and Niculina attended their respective schools I revisited the Hotel Alutus. A tongue of concrete protruded over a Seventies porch. Nothing evoked what I remembered – the layout, the restaurant, the shape of the staircase, the colour of the carpet. It was disorientating. The receptionist insisted that the décor had not been altered since 1979, but it was hard to believe that memories could be so distorting. I glanced towards the park but it was . . . just a park. Revisiting it seemed pointless: it recaptured nothing. I was thankful to return for lunch to a family, to real people rather than vanishing recollections.

Ioana had insisted that Ana show me the sights of Oltenia. Ana was nervous – she could barely drive – but those were Ioana's orders. We set off in a battered Dacia, Ana on her seat-edge, gripping the wheel, Niculina sprawled with a book in the back. Ana apologised for the state of the car, so old and uncomfortable. Camil had asked her to wash it that morning, but she had had no time, what with teaching, cooking, caring for Niculina and me. For all the egalitarian principles of Communism, and the forthright way in which women tended to voice their opinions, Romania was still a macho man's world, a Latin man's world. Although she had her job, Ana was expected to be full-time mother and wife too: this was unquestioned. She pumped the accelerator and we lurched out of the parking lot, past Camil's factory (part of a string of chemical plants, cooling pipes, chimneys belching yellow smoke) and into the countryside. Niculina slept, the sun silver on her black hair, and Ana and I sat in silence.

'I'm sorry,' she said, 'I'm not very communicative. More introverted.'

'I'm OK. I like looking at the view and thinking.'

'Ioana's very talkative. She makes so many jokes. When I'm with her I lose my nerve.'

'It's easier for you when it's just the two of us.'

'Yes. We get along fine, don't we?'

Villages were strung along the road. Wooden seats invited people to stop and watch pedestrians and the few cars pass by. Houses painted ice-cream colours had arched porticoes and windows in the Brâncoveanu style, so called after the great Voivide of Wallachia, and fruit trees blossomed white and pink. But for all that, there was a seedy atmosphere, without pride. Fences were collapsing and people looked dour under their headscarves and astrakhans.

We reached Hurez, Brâncoveanu's great monastic foundation, in late afternoon. It was even more beautiful than I recalled, the white walls with their turrets and cupolas enveloped in forests behind, fields in front, the perfection of the cloisters with their carved Italianate pillars silent and unspoilt. Niculina, who was Orthodox, kissed the icons and dropped a coin in the offertory box, while Ana, who was Catholic, talked to a nun. There was something restless and incomplete about the church; Brâncoveanu had planned it as his final resting place, but his tomb had been left unfilled; after he and his family were brutally executed in a public square in Constantinople in 1714, his body had been flung into the Bosphorus.

I thought of other unfinished business. It was here that I fell in love with George, but there had also been some misunderstanding at Hurez. It transpired in the letters that when, in Bucov de Sus, I had asked him why he was not married, he had taken this as an indirect proposal from me. *I thought it was a good opportunity to begin a new life. First I believed that you were joking, then I wanted to ask you if you wanted me only for a night. At last I supposed it was my chance to find my kind of girl.* Unknown to me, he had been mulling over this throughout our time together; marriage had seemed an increasingly tempting solution. That, I realised now, was why here in Hurez he had probed me about my life in England. But at the same moment I gave him reason to doubt me. *You said in that monastery called Hurez: 'Excuse me for what I said about marriage, you see, when you are nineteen, it is easy to make mistakes. . . .' 'OK, OK,' I replied, but it was striking news for me.* My flippancy against his seriousness. It seemed that my enthusiastic letters had then rekindled his hopes. I remembered Roxana's advice that this time I should make my intentions clear.

Camil appeared that evening. He had Greek looks with swarthy skin and dark-rimmed eyes. At first I found him intimidating: he still wore the traditional Communist garb of long leather coat and collar-length hair, and I feared he would resent the arrival of this capitalist foreigner picked up on a train. But he was welcoming and his slightly stern expression was transformed by an impish smile. Over the next few years we were to become the greatest of friends, and in retrospect I understood that he had been stressed with overwork and anxiety; he was hoping that a French company would go into partnership with him to rescue his factory, while also being forced to convince the old guard of Vîlcea that he was not, as they suspected, selling out Romania's industry to foreign exploiters. We strolled to a neighbouring block for dinner at Ioana's, but Camil found an excuse to leave. He and Ioana did not get on; she teased him about being Mr Gloom, Mr National Salvation Front, and he found her abrasive, unfeminine.

We sat on corduroy seats – orange versions of Ana's – with two of Ioana's friends, Valeria and Rodica, one a fellow English teacher, the other a physicist. Valeria was in her forties, chic in white suit and high heels, although like other Romanian women she left her legs unshaved, a curious sight under white tights, like wriggling black life-forms. She was bright, brittle, excited by recently becoming the owner of an orchard which had been 'liberated' from her family forty-five years ago and which under new laws had been returned. It was the first Valeria had heard of this orchard, but now she planned to sell apples to her friends at special prices. Ioana ruminated about some share certificates she still had in gold mines in a forest near Cluj. Might they be worth something?

'Go for it!' Valeria urged her.

'I don't know. My family owned vast tracts of forest, but we'd only get back a few hectares, and presumably not those with the gold in. I'm not sure I can be bothered with the whole thing. Besides, it could go on for ever. Who owned what *before*? What about the land the boyars stole from the peasants? Come to that, what about the land the Romanians stole from the Hungarians?' Ioana grinned as she verged on difficult territory. 'No, don't worry. I'm not going to get into one of those tedious arguments about the rightful heirs to Romania. It bores me stiff.'

'Hear, hear,' said Valeria.

'OK, so it's used to justify Romanian domination of Transylvania, but who cares?'

'I was only talking about an orchard.'

We laughed. Ioana raised her glass. 'I propose a toast. To all of us. To change.'

'To change!' we chorused.

'To think that sixteen months ago we could never have sat together so freely, and with a foreigner in our midst, and talked about whatever we wanted.' Ioana had tears in her eyes, and I did too, though perhaps it was the *ţuica* which burned my throat. 'Before the revolution a group of us, five or six women – you used to come, didn't you, Valeria? We used to get together every two or three months. The idea was to escape from home and have some time to ourselves. We used to meet in each other's houses. We tried not to talk about our families, and of course we couldn't mention politics.'

'Come to think of it, what did we talk about?'

'D'you know, I can't remember. We used to pretend we were enjoying ourselves, didn't we? Having a good time.'

'But we weren't.' Valeria laughed, a hysterical laugh which teetered on the edge of taking off on its own around the room.

'No, not really. How could we? It was all such a strain. Now we can be free, and really enjoy ourselves, so let's have another toast to that!'

Rodica was a morose-looking woman in brown. She had buck teeth. I imagined wrapping wire around them and reining them in. She said, 'What's such a pity is that we've left it all so late.'

'Rodica! No politics!' cried Ioana.

'You see,' I said, 'nothing's really changed.'

Ioana laughed. 'I mean, no complaining!'

I spent the next morning with Ioana, back on the squidgy orange chairs, going over her imprisonment and trial once more. I was moved by her courage and integrity, but her story was important not just for her sake: it also gave me an insight into what could have happened to George. I might be able to ask him about it myself, but then again, I might not. Even if I could, I wanted to be able to place him in the broader picture.

'What's become of the Securitate officers who interrogated you?' I asked.

Ioana was patient with my questions. 'Most of those people were genuine criminals, but there were also professionals. Intellectuals. Doctors and teachers. It was a good opportunity for them. They were well paid and they had access to special shops and other privileges. I expect they've probably washed their hands of the whole thing and gone back to their original jobs. But there are others – those criminals and other people – who are making use of all those original contacts and other advantages to start up their own businesses.'

'At least someone's doing something.'

'Ough! These aren't the right types to begin the regeneration of Romania's economy. They are dishonest. That's why all the new businesses are so hated by the intellectuals. You know something? When I came back from England last year I noticed something about the Romanian character which I had felt before but never put into words. It's a sense that if I have a piece of cake, and someone else has a piece too, I enjoy it less than if no-one else has a piece. It seems mad, I know. But when I went abroad for the first time I suddenly noticed its absence. That this wasn't something universal. That sort of selfishness was particularly true of the Securitate. You could tell who was a member by the children who came to classes with a banana or an orange, something special, when the others had nothing. Their parents relished those privileges. Everyone wanted to be friends with them because they knew they had access to the food and clothes. And medicines, of course. So when the need arose they could beg the Securitate for things. Oh yes, people were forced to humiliate themselves just to survive.'

'So all that's changing.'

'The one change is that we are no longer afraid. They've been shown up for the straw dogs that they are. It was fear that kept us under. I suspected after my interrogation that my flat was bugged. I was an obvious target. I had to be terribly careful of what I said.

Even if you weren't bugged, you thought you were, and the effect was the same. Silence. Fear. Paranoia. That's how this country was controlled.' Ioana leaned towards me and lowered her voice, as if still wary of hidden microphones. 'You know how they used to bug us?'

'How?'

'Through the telephone receiver. It recorded not only what was being said down the telephone, but what was being said throughout the room, all the time.'

'How do you know that?'

'I saw it in a film called *Gorky Park*.'

She'd seen it in *Gorky Park*, so that made it true. It seemed absurd, but I could understand it: there was no other frame of reference, no access to anything outside except films like *Gorky Park* for analysing what might or might not have been happening. In the years of silence images grew inside your head; there was no-one you could trust to bounce ideas against. No wonder Ioana clung to her belief in herself; she had nothing else. But that self was not as rooted and confident as it appeared. Like everyone here, Ioana inhabited a world of half-truths. Living in Romania meant having to believe everything – or nothing – as you chose. Facts, rumours, lies – take your pick. There was no proof either way. History was class struggle, Ceauşescu was a great leader, Alex was a spy and Ali and I were his bait, your house was bugged, *Gorky Park* was the reality, Ioana was a traitor – or not. In a country where transcendental meditation is banned for fear of mass exodus, where a medical professor receives seven hunks of lamb for Easter, where women who queue for bread drink champagne and wear no tights, it comes as no surprise that Dada was invented by Tristan Tzara, a Romanian. No surprise that Eugène Ionesco was originally Eugen Ionescu, a Romanian, before he left for Paris. Parody, sarcasm, nonsense, madness: Romania itself was a Theatre of the Absurd.

George was just another member of the cast: no wonder his letters were so confusing. Their contradictions, their doubling back and hints were finding a context. Was he being persecuted by the Putna monks or not? Was he at risk from the TB doctors or not? What was paranoia and what was truth? Did it matter? Even now no-one really knew what was happening, but they were used to not knowing, almost resigned to it.

I counted four dead dogs on the road to Craiova. Shepherds with pack donkeys drove herds of sheep, like swarms of maggots. Ceauşescu and his wife were born nearby, a presence far more haunting than that of Dracula in Transylvania; how appropriate that this bleak earth should have spawned such a couple. By the time I reached the sprawling industrial town, its old heart torn out by Ceauşescu himself as part of his megalomaniac reconstruction, I despaired. What was I doing here? I could find no answer. I listened to my own shoes echoing through the art museum; I longed for my husband and dreaded the next stage of the journey, the effort of plunging into the unknown.

I used my travelling time to study a copy of *Româna cu sau fără Profesor*, trying to make the unknown less so. Surprise surprise: I found a beautiful, easy language. A Latin island in its sea of Slavs. Each Romanian sentence was illuminated by pinpricks of light, like lamps along a dark road, which were the Latin or Romance words; these enabled me to guess at what lay hidden in the shadows between. Lost one day in Bucharest, I had been directed to the *fluviu*, even to the *ripa* of the *fluviu*. Running my finger down one page of my *lexic general* provided: to see – *a vedea* (goodbye, i.e. see you again, being *La revedere*); the sea – *mare*; the seaside – *litoral*; to seem – *a părea*; self-service – *autoservire*; September – *septembrie*; serious – *serios*; to smoke – *a fuma*; to speak – *a vorbi*; stale or old – *vechi*; station – *gară*. And so on. *Lună* means month; *primăvară* means spring; *dată* means date. In the second century AD Dacia, which occupied most of present-day Romania, was colonised by the Romans, and the colonists, who came from all over the Roman Empire, used Latin as their *lingua franca*. When at a loss I thought of the Latin word (when I could) and was often understood. *Casă* means house. *Cameră* means room. *Da* means give (and yes). Whole phrases sound almost identical to the Italian. *Cum te cheamă?* means *Come ti chiama?* (What is your name?).

Romanians are proud of their Latin origins and give their babies splendid Roman names. I met people called Caius, Titus, Tiberius, Justinian, even Virgil. To emphasise the purity of their Dacian blood, Ceauşescu's historians had played down the effect of the successive invasions of Goths, Huns, Bulgarians, Slavs, Hungarians, Jews, gypsies, Ottomans and Tartars, and during the nineteenth century much of the invaders' vocabulary was replaced in an attempt to 're-Romanise' Romanian, often with French or Italian supplying the basis of the word. But plenty of borrowed words remained, words I was to come to know later. Like *bolnav*, meaning sick. Like *slab*, meaning weak.

There was little to look at from the train to Turnu Severin – until we climbed an embankment and an old man prodded his granddaughter and announced, 'The Danube.' At last! A silver ribbon winding through the distance, not only a great river that spans half of Europe, but until the revolution a symbol of freedom. This was where we said goodbye to George and crossed the bridge into Tito's Yugoslavia, into the relative political *détente* which to Romanians seemed a haven of liberal well-being. This was where Alex had promised to help George to escape from Romania, should the need arise. This was why I was here.

I wanted to discover what it meant to escape from Romania. What it involved. How often it happened. George's attempt was of course aborted, but perhaps his plans were not as ludicrous as they seemed. Perhaps other people had had similar ambitions. Perhaps even George, during the years of silence, had tried again. Perhaps he had succeeded. For most people dreaming of escape, the Danube was the obvious choice. Yugoslavia was known to be sympathetic to Romanian refugees, had villages of ethnic Romanians beyond the border, and provided a gateway to the West through Italy. A river busy with boats would be less easy to police than no-man's-land.

But as I quickly realised, I was unlikely to meet anyone who had escaped, since they would now be living abroad. My morning depression returned.

I lingered beside the river. Here, at Turnu Severin, the Danube's silver was tarnished. Slowed by the dam further upstream at Djerdap, the river was no longer fecund or vital but weary, polluted. It slid between Romania and Serbia torpid as a slug. A few dredgers were tied up nearby, but there was no other traffic. An oleaginous, lazy-looking river. But to the Romanians it was a messenger from the free world, from Regensburg, Vienna, Budapest, Belgrade, the towns and cities it threaded together. The far bank was fringed with the woods of Serbia, with red-roofed houses drifting smoke, and a road with cars on. Normal life. It was tantalisingly close, a vision of freedom that until sixteen months ago must have been almost unbearable for the imprisoned Romanians. But that vision of freedom was a mirage. Dangerous currents swept between the banks, and border patrols used power boats to police the river.

In the Museum of the Danube I tried to concentrate on the fish and birds unique to this river, but it seemed increasingly irrelevant. It had nothing to do with George. A tour group filed past, and when I heard them speaking English I tagged along to listen to my own language. They were Baptists from Kansas City, and I got chatting to a straggler at the back. I explained that I was concerned with the Danube primarily as a means of escape. My, that's interesting, one of them said, because only yesterday we met a fine lady who swam the Danube and escaped but came back and is now working as a missionary. He produced her card: Veronica Filip, Turnu Severin. I could not believe my luck. I rushed around the building in search of the exit, but in each room the lady guards smilingly insisted that I saw every exhibit. They switched on every light, guided me from case to case. I stared impatiently at Trajan remains, at diagrams of medieval trade routes, at maps of sweeping hordes of Jazyges, Roxolans, Avars, Cumans, Pechenegs and Huns, until at last I could flee.

I rang Veronica Filip and she met me in the road, reassuringly Western-looking in a pink sweater, jeans and trainers, but still with a strong Romanian accent even after eight years away. She was pretty, slim with dark curls, in her late thirties. She led me into one of the few old houses left in Severin, single-storey with large, high rooms which she was redecorating. She complained of the scarcity of honest builders. One had ripped her off, and now the water from her bath flowed not down the drain but all over the bathroom floor. As for the kitchen, it was a damp hole. I envisaged the lifestyle she must have sacrificed to return, and could not help thinking she was a fool. Not only because of the material discomfort, but because of the suspicion she said surrounded her.

She was friendly and I sensed that she wanted to trust me, but was not yet sure; so I made it clear that I trusted her by telling her about George.

'I think he lied,' she said at once.

'What do you mean?' The word was brutal, offensive.

'I mean that he never joined the police. He was forced to say that. He was lying.'

'I see. Maybe. But why?'

'Threats. Promises. Who knows? Possibly because of his correspondence with you. Because he tried to escape from the country. They would certainly have read that in his letter. You would have been caught, by the way.'

'You don't think it was a trap, then, asking me to come with the British passport?'

'I don't know. It could have been. He could have been forced to write that, after having been beaten or tortured in some way. But from what you've said of him . . . I don't know. How can I judge? I can only talk about my own experiences. But from what you say, he sounds as if he was desperate. Desperate for freedom.' She was sympathetic to George, and I was grateful to her for it.

We were interrupted by a stream of visitors: builders, Baptists, beggars. She apologised and explained that it was important for her to take trouble because she was still 'bridge building'. She had come as the single representative of an evangelical mission whose aim was to plant churches in Oltenia.

'Why Oltenia?'

She explained that Oltenia, particularly the south, seemed to her an unholy, devilish place. I had to agree. There was a dank joylessness in the way the people looked and walked. She was trying to exorcise a girl who was invaded by devils, and although she suspected the girl of exaggerating (mysteriously, the devils visited her only in public), Veronica nevertheless felt that this region suffered from a moral and spiritual decay which she had been 'called' to arrest. She expounded to her visitors her plans for taking over an old synagogue. Only five or six Jewish families remained in the town – the rest had fled during the war, or in the 1970s when there were opportunities for resettlement in Israel – so it was empty, and a perfect focus for an interdenominational Protestant church.

'What about the Orthodox church?' I asked. 'Isn't that enough?'

'I don't consider the Orthodox church to be a church. It has not taken care of the people and their spiritual needs. It is corrupt and dead.'

Under Ceauşescu, every form of religious 'propaganda' except Orthodoxy had been condemned, and Catholic and Uniate churches had been handed over to the Orthodox church. Now they wanted their churches back, and accused the Orthodox church of having collaborated with the regime. But surely George would not have been training to become a member of a community that was corrupt and dead?

I sat on the sofa listening to the talk, so still that my body seemed to evaporate, leaving me weightless to fly around the room. I alighted on a crucifix on the wall, on her framed inscription from Proverbs 3 verses 5–6 ('Trust in the Lord with all thine heart . . .'), on black and white photographs of Veronica with a tall young man, on girlish stuffed toys, chairs draped in tartan rugs, the big old white ceramic stove, a cushion embroidered with a religious text, a guitar and vases of flowers.

'OK,' she said when after an hour and a half we were at last alone, 'now we can talk. But first I'm gonna feed you.' While she heated some sour *ciorbă* soup we leant companionably against the windowsill and she said, 'You may find it difficult to get any information about your friend, especially if he did attempt to escape. Speaking from my own experience, the people he left behind would have suffered because of him. They might have lost their jobs.'

'I'll have to tread very carefully.'

'Yes. But you may also find that people just don't know. So much went on and people had to keep their heads down and get on with their lives. I myself still have no idea why my husband died.'

So young, and already a widow. 'How did he die?'

'I don't know.' She paused. 'He was found hanging in an attic in Bucharest.'

We sat with our *ciorbă* on our laps in the sitting room. Veronica said grace. She prayed that our talk would be edifying for both of us, and that the Lord would be present and help us to speak the truth. Being a doubter I could not bring myself to echo her Amen, but I respected her honesty in expressing her anxieties about our meeting, and was touched by her suffering and bravery.

We were interrupted again, this time by her brother, Radu. 'I've brought you a present,' he said to Veronica, waggling a salami. Surprised to find a foreigner in his sister's house, he courteously kissed my hand. It was a gesture which never failed to move me with its old-world *politesse*. I often stuck out my hand to give someone a manly shake, only to have it twisted to their lips. I liked Radu. His well-shaped black head, hair pressed to scalp, and his neat features combined to express dignity and gentleness. He had been an officer in the Romanian army, a vet, Veronica explained, concerned with animals rather than with fighting. He had lost his job when she escaped and though his career was ruined, in a way he was relieved to leave the political pressures of that world. Now, eight years on, his job had been restored.

When Radu heard I was a writer he expressed a passion for literature, and asked eagerly if I wrote epics or lyrics.

'Neither,' I confessed, hating to disappoint. By now I had grown accustomed to 'writer' meaning 'poet'. It was the norm in Romania. Poetry was no marginal literary form or closet hobby, but a part of daily life. Poets like Ana Blandiana had helped to bring about the revolution and formed part of the first post-revolutionary government; poets were respected. A Romanian friend in London had dismissed the Romanian love of poetry as a sign of emotional infantilism, of an inability to express anything except in fragments. It was, he claimed, an escape, a couching of disorder in the fake order of metre and rhyme. But I was not so sure. To me it suggested a sensitivity and a yearning for beauty in all this ugliness, a love of landscape and music, which was partly what had attracted me to George and to Romania in the first place and now had drawn me back.

It was also more subtle and more discreet than clumsy old prose. And discretion was necessary in Romania.

A young woman burst in, all of a dither. The three of them conferred. 'Don't tell Helena,' Radu said. 'It's embarrassing for Romania.' I pretended incomprehension, but I had already seen a notice on a wall: a PA system had been stolen from a group of American evangelists who were beginning a Romanian tour, and 100,000 lei was the reward for its return. Now it had been 'found' by the leader of the local mafia, and the girl had come to collect the money from Veronica, the only person in town likely to have such a sum. I did not feel too sorry for the evangelists; I disliked the way a mass of religious groups had descended like vultures on the newly opened East European countries, snatching up the convertible before any other group could claim them. Romania, in its innocence, was prey to all kinds of oddballs. So I did not blame the Romanians for stealing the PA system: they had probably heard enough.

Veronica was different; she belonged here, and besides, she did not proselytise to me.

While still a student she had become a Protestant, which was illegal, and married a fellow Protestant who worked for an underground organisation smuggling Bibles into Romania. In due course they were both arrested and interrogated, and in order to escape prison they fled to the mountains, where they searched for some way of escaping from Romania altogether. But they could not agree on a method. She would suggest a plan, and he would point out its flaws; he would make a suggestion and she would pick holes in that. They discussed the Danube but he could not swim and, although she had been brought up beside it, neither could she. The banks were too steep, the current too swift. But it was the only way. Her husband had seen a sort of submarine in a magazine and decided that this was the solution. He was a metal worker so thought he could build it, and in this submarine they would slip across the river. Theatre of the Absurd! What if it filled with water and sank? They would certainly drown. How would they transport it? Power it? Veronica's objections were limitless, but he grew more determined. Eventually they decided to escape separately; each would keep their plan secret from the other for fear of losing faith in it themselves. She would leave first, and he would try to join her.

Risking her life – endangered not only by the currents but by the border guards who shot to kill – she paddled across the Danube on a lilo. Absurd! After several weeks in a refugee camp outside Belgrade she made her way to Italy and thence to Chicago. Her husband never joined her, and in 1984 she learned through the underground church that he was dead. To this day she had no idea whether he was murdered by the Securitate, or whether he committed suicide, unable to tolerate his life of fear and subterfuge any longer. Although devastated at the time, she had come to accept that she would never know.

What of George? As I listened to Veronica's harrowing tale I was haunted by an image of his black eyes. Had he suffered something similar? Had he come face to face with despair, desolation, martyrdom? Not if he joined the police. I hoped for his sake that he had compromised and saved his skin, but Veronica was adamant that this was impossible. She had more faith in him than I did.

Suddenly I woke up. It had been folly to embark alone on a quest around this volatile and often brutal country when life and love were so fragile, so precious. Here I was, adrift in the middle of nowhere, my husband hundreds of miles away, and George himself so close. I could procrastinate no longer. I left Veronica and Turnu Severin and Oltenia as soon as I could and took the train north, via Timişoara and Arad, to Suceava. Back to Bucovina.

Three

Cutting into the hills we time-travelled from spring back into winter. Early leaves shrivelled into buds, fields sucked back their sprouts of green. Then the hills levelled up into the plains of the Banat, an empty expanse of collectivised black earth. It flicked past bleak and treeless. Last year's maize lay dead, waiting to be raked up. Our desolate train stopped in the middle of nowhere and waited . . . it was hard to remember the reality of home, of my husband, our house, our sycamore, when I was stuck here in the reality of the brown plastic seats, the dust along the window ledge, the metal teeth. It was always like this. When I was at home, nothing else existed; now it was hard to imagine that home existed at all.

How would I fill the next fourteen hours? I studied my fellow-passengers. We were five adults: a tired woman with haunted brown eyes and a drab skirt, a loud-mouthed worker, an elderly peasant couple, and me. All the women were called Helena. They argued politics and prices. The worker thought life was better before – *before* – and when I asked him to point out a station on my map, I saw that he was illiterate. They were worried. Prices were rising, wages were not. Where was the milk that should have been in the shops? And the cheese? The problem was that no-one wanted to get up in the morning to milk the cows without milking machines, so they didn't have cows. It was that simple.

A buzzard hovered over the prairie, and a hare searched in vain for a place to hide; the only other signs of life were herds of sheep, then a lonely house made safe in this emptiness by its enclosed garden of flowering fruit trees. Eastwards into the Mureş valley the plain crinkled into hills, and the fields on their sides reverted to human scale, fringed with trees. It was mid-April and here, beneath banking clouds and shafts of sun, the empty deciduous woods filled up with green, each species taking its turn. The willows had come first, trailing roadside fronds, followed by silver birch.

Cosmin, a solitary fat boy in a woolly hat, pressed his face against the glass, also looking out.

The sun blasted its last rays on to the crest of a hill and then vanished behind it. It was 8 p.m., another eight and a half hours to go. I was excited about seeing George again, yet dreaded it too. So many mistakes. So many years. So many unknowns.

Passengers slid open the carriage door and went into the corridor for a smoke. They stood together, breathing fumes out of the window. But several times the door opened on gypsies and cripples who whined for money and waved their stumps in brutal rebuke of our able bodies. A woman with no eyes. A man with one leg. Another with deformed hands. If they saw a passenger eating they demanded their share and someone always gave them something.

I was thirsty, and it seemed that everyone else was too, because I had to fight to fill my bottle on Cluj station. Picnics were unpacked on the seats; grey bread, grey meat and grey boiled eggs, rough meals but eaten neatly, with endless hand wiping, crumbs swept off the seat. Cosmin was ticked off for touching the curtains with his greasy hands. I had searched for a similar picnic but although I found bread, I found nothing to go with it except a tin of 'Crap'. This turned out to be the Romanian word for carp, but I thought I could live without it. When Cosmin whispered to his mother, apples and ersatz crisps were produced from a plastic bag and generously pressed on me. I recalled Ioana's remarks about Romanian selfishness, and wondered at how different my own experience was.

'Do you have children?' asked Cosmin's mother. She was the drab one with the furrowed forehead.

'Not yet,' I said. 'No time.'

Everyone in the carriage burst out laughing.

'And you?' I asked. 'Do you have others than Cosmin?'

'Six others,' she said. 'Too much time,' she added, ruefully. *Epoca Ceauşescu*: nothing else to do. I remembered some piglets George had laughed about, his prediction that one day I would resemble the sow, like Ceauşescu's Heroine Mothers, breeding for Socialism, with their litters of fourteen, fifteen, sixteen children.

The night cleared, the moon bleaching the ghostly fir forests of Transylvania. It was darker inside than out (the train's light sockets were broken, dangling wires) and we moved like a black snake up and over the silent mountains. There was nothing to do but sleep, but as there was no heating it was too cold for that. We stretched out across the seats, struggling to get comfortable. I wedged myself along the shelf under the window, my head twisted on to my camera bag, trying by the light of the stations to read my watch every half an hour. The exhausted mother apologised for Romania's discomfort. But the convivial atmosphere evaporated when I unrolled my sleeping bag: its downy pink luxuriousness emphasised the difference between us, my enormous wealth; Cosmin's mother eyed me without friendliness now.

At 4.30 a.m. we reached Suceava, yellow lights fizzing on the cold platform. The presence of a few other disembarking passengers reassured me that there might be a taxi into town, even at this hour. I worried about being ripped off. After all, these were Romanian Romanians, not Hungarians or Germans, and I had been warned.

Mist wreathed the industrial outskirts, then a bridge, a church, a tower block. None of it was even faintly familiar. The tower block was the Class 1 Hotel Bucovina, all marble lobby and grossly over-priced. The sleepy receptionist snapped that I was lucky to have a room at all, since everywhere else was full of Russians. She smacked a key on the desk and watched me stumble across the lobby, backpack swaying, and into the lift. There were no lights in the passage, so I had to feel my way to each door in turn, and read each room number with my fingers, as if it were braille, afraid of opening the wrong door and terrifying some sleeping guest.

I unlocked my door to find the light on. Peering hesitantly around like one of the three bears, I saw that the bed had recently been slept in, and used coffee cups and cigarette butts lay strewn about the table. From the bathroom I could hear a tap dripping. I shut the door quickly and made my way back downstairs. The receptionist was puzzled, though not apologetic. It must have been a policeman or an electrician who was around during the day, she said. He must have had a quick kip. She shrugged and gave me a different key.

I was woken by fear, wanting to scream and yet suffocated. Something evil, some fluttering evil spirit, had landed beside me. Bed, table, chair. I lay back, heart pounding. It was connected with George, and I realised that by an odd coincidence this was 23 April, St George's Day. I was filled with foreboding. George had written, *If accidentally I die, my soul will pay a visit to you, firstly to frighten your enemies, and then to wipe a possible tear from your eyes*. But I was getting morbid; I had been upset by Veronica Filip and her talk of witches.

It was lunchtime when I braved the hotel dining room. Avoiding the eyes of the single men in their black leather jackets wreathed in cigarette smoke, drinking *ţuica* and eating slabs of meat and chips (what carnivores they are!) and the inedible but ubiquitous pickled cabbage, I sat close to the wall, out of the way. Net curtains shrouded the room in speckled gloom and voices were absorbed by the dark nylon carpet; the décor was all pine panelling and swirly textured walls. A flotilla of pink linen napkins sailed across the blood-red table cloth. A stout waitress took pity on me – buttressed bosom, heart of gold – and stomped over with an omelette and a slab of white sheep's cheese. A cocktail glass stood at my elbow with a tea bag floating on top and an inch-deep silt of sugar settling on the bottom. I chewed Sunday bread with chemical-white 'butter'.

The closer I came, the more qualms I had about meeting George

93

again. It may not be better to travel hopefully than to arrive, but it is certainly easier. Why rekindle things? Because I needed to know. Simple as that. Why not let things alone? Well, I could hardly retreat after coming all this way, could I? And what would he think about me being here, so close, and not making that last effort to find him? I had to go on. How would he look? Bad diet and poverty aged people here, so I envisaged grey hair and a stoop, although he would only be thirty-six. As for me, I looked much the same – older, obviously, but my hair as it had been, long and dishevelled.

I imagined a variety of meetings. He has settled down to the happy life of a policeman. He politely introduces me to his peasanty wife. Then I go away, wondering why I bothered. Or I go to Putna and request an English-speaking guide. We look at each other for a long time – he has a beard – before he realises who I am. We sit on the museum steps and he holds my hand and we exchange the stories of our lives. Or he is a teacher. I open the classroom door and stand on the threshold, watching him finish an English lesson, unaware of me. Then he turns, is overcome by astonishment and joy, and leads me away down the school corridor. Or he stares at me vacantly, genuinely remembering nothing at all. Or he stares at me vacantly, preferring to remember nothing at all.

But how little I knew about George, and how difficult it was going to be to get him to explain. He had had a way of suggesting things, hinting, staying silent but investing in that silence some deeper significance. And he was so sensitive that pinning him down to facts, and to the clarification of one incident after another in their correct sequence, which was what I wanted more than anything, would be too crude an approach. I would have to allow him to reveal what he chose in his own way.

One of the problems was that my Romanian was not yet fluent. After a month in the country I could get by, but no more. The prospect of turning up unannounced in Bucov de Sus, an alien from another land, made me so apprehensive that I almost turned and ran for home.

But Călin, brother of a colleague of an acquaintance in London, lived in Rădăuţi. This was the next town north, between Suceava and the end of the railway line at Putna, where the road dwindled to a path and vanished into the Carpathians. It was in Rădăuţi that George had spent all those months at the TB hospital; and when I was to have returned bearing a British passport in George's name it was from Suceava or Rădăuţi that I was supposed to have sent him the postcard inscribed 'Success!' followed by an indecipherable signature. So when I phoned Călin's wife and she immediately invited me to stay, I did so. I was grateful for the prospect of company.

The bus dropped me at a block of flats on the outskirts of Rădăuţi. I picked my way across a muddy parking lot. Călin and Mihaela were lucky to live on the ground floor; having to tolerate the parking lot as their view (and this was screened behind net curtains) meant not having to see too much of the concrete stairwell; they had also sound-proofed their front door with padded leather. Mihaela was welcoming, handsome, with rich brown hair and creamy skin. I perched on a stool in her white corridor-kitchen while she spooned coffee granules into a saucepan and brewed them on the gas cooker, black and sweet.

I wasn't sure what to make of her. She had a matronly look, solidly built, yet was girlishly eager to question me about my life in England and to practise her English. She was quick to complain about 'our situation', yet their flat was larger than most and equipped with colour TV, video, stereo system, mostly gifts from Călin's brother in England. Mihaela was friendly but not, I felt, in the totally disinterested way that Ana was, and I missed Ana, brimming like a full bottle with affection. Mihaela was more guarded, less naive.

Of course Mihaela wanted to know what brought me to Rădăuţi, but since meeting Ioana and Veronica Filip I had become more circumspect about telling George's story: I was wary of whom to trust. So I said that I had returned to compare post-revolutionary Romania with its 1979 former self – which was true. This provoked a sigh of troubles from Mihaela. She denied that things had improved. 'Is your job sure, Helena?' she kept asking. I tried to explain that I didn't really have a job, as such.

'But is what you do *sure*? Our problem is that none of our jobs are sure any more.' She was a GP, currently taking a year's maternity leave, and where before the revolution she would have been secure in the knowledge that she had a job to return to for the rest of her life, now she feared redundancy at any time. Chain-smoking, visibly exhausted, she sat over her coffee with one cheek resting on her hand. It was partly the boredom of staying home with her four-month-old baby, but partly 'our situation' – the anxiety, the not knowing, the tough times forecast. 'They say things are going to improve but it will take time we must be patient but we have young children growing up in these conditions we don't have time to be patient things were bad before but at least as far as our own lives were concerned we knew what was what now everything is so expensive and people are out of work.' It was The Conversation that I had had countless times already, and would have countless times more. When Călin returned from work and we squeezed out of the kitchen and into the sitting room, The Conversation continued.

Călin had a black clump of a beard and a voice that boomed. His big, male presence was dwarfing. He flicked on the TV and stood watching *Today in Parliament*, flinging me the occasional question about why I was here, and what my programme was. I explained that I was interested in seeing the TB hospital.

'You won't have to go far,' he said. 'That's the hospital over the road.'

'But it looks new.'

'It is. About five years. Why?'

'I want to see a hospital that was here twelve years ago.'

'That's the only one. It's a general hospital. TB and everything.'

'Abortions mainly,' Mihaela interjected. 'Since the revolution. About twenty a day.' She tutted, disapproving not so much of the abortions themselves but of the ignorance of the people who did not understand, or could not be persuaded to use, contraception. After years of contraception having been outlawed, this was hardly surprising: it would take years of re-education. Besides, there were no contraceptives to be had. Mihaela knew this; as a GP she had worked in the villages with the Heroine Mothers.

If Călin and Mihaela were going to help me, as they had kindly offered to do, I would have to feed them more information. Just a morsel.

'Twelve years ago,' I began, 'there was a TB hospital. It was opposite a girls' agricultural *lycée*.' George had described his evenings with a fellow patient, another young man from his village, serenading the farming girls. I envisaged strapping women with big thighs laughing down on the slender dark-eyed men, men who fancied them but in a charmingly old-fashioned way. No cat-calls and 'get 'em off' but guitars and poetry. That's what I loved about Romania. Now I began to wonder if this hospital had ever existed at all.

But Mihaela said, 'There *is* an old TB hospital down there. On the edge of town.' They were both looking at me oddly. Why on earth should I be so interested?

Călin stayed with the baby, a bulky man cradling his shawled bundle, while Mihaela and I set off in the family Dacia, rattling past the vast 1930s Orthodox church (which Mihaela and Călin attended each Sunday) and past the ancient church of Bogdan, the oldest in Moldavia, boat-shaped with a flat stern and pointed prow, the roof its wooden deck. ('I love this place,' Mihaela said when she switched off the engine, our ears filling up with the hum of doves.) Before it was 'modernised', Suceava must have resembled Rădăuţi, the walls of its single-storey houses decorated with lattice-work and patterns of lozenges and hung all over with skilfully split wooden shingles, like coats of leaves. The roofs sunk low to the ground as if bent double under last winter's snow. Hunchbacked, leaf-coated houses. Here, in 1955, George was born.

I had imagined the TB hospital as a decaying mansion with echoing wards and flagged floors, doctors conferring in undertones, Florence Nightingales in wimples bending tenderly over the consumptive George. A nineteenth-century vision for a nineteenth-century disease. Instead: two cottages in a field, broken windows, a snoozing dog, crumbling steps leading to a tiny office. A man stood and stretched. He wore a white cap and a white (or rather, grey) towelling dressing gown, and I took him for a patient who had gone astray. This, Mihaela corrected me (prickling at my implied insult to her profession), was the doctor. While I installed myself next to the tiled stove in one corner, she explained my mission.

On entering the hospital, George's first impressions had been of fear, emotion and kindness at the same time. Soon, however, he suspected that the workers in the neighbouring beds were being given preferential treatment. *The doctor's first question is: How do you feel? Fine, doctor, I answered. But I was not quite frank. I didn't tell the doctors and patients anything about my past. I'm just a peasant's son who doesn't work in a factory and that's why his cure is not so important as a worker's cure.* I supposed that by his 'past' he meant his sojourn in Putna monastry; the heroic workers would have resided near the top of the social hierarchy (well above the 'intellectuals'), with priests and monks and then gypsies – the useless parasites – at the bottom.

By his 'past' perhaps George was also referring to his time with us. I didn't know.

George was diagnosed as having water on his lungs, but when the doctor tried to remove it nothing was found. He was convinced that the problem lay in his ribs. He referred several times to his ribs having been broken by 'that prior' during 'that beating' about which I knew nothing, and he believed that these broken ribs had received the wrong treatment and were now damaging his lung. *It seems to me that my left lung has not enough place. And they say there is no pleurisy.* He had long mistrusted doctors. That was why he had initially avoided Ali, he said, because she was planning to become a doctor. Now that mistrust was growing into hatred. Not only did the doctors give the wrong treatment, but they were also in cahoots with the monks, or so he suspected.

This small, sleepy doctor looked an unlikely object of George's suspicions, and he for his part failed to recognise George's name. It meant nothing to him, even though he claimed to have been at the hospital for many years. He scratched his head, tied his dressing-gown cord around his waist and called down the corridor. A nurse in an identical dressing gown was dispatched to search the records for George's medical details. Meanwhile we would make a tour of the hospital. Mihaela held up a traffic-stopping hand; she would stay behind. The last thing she wanted was to carry contagious germs back to her baby.

'We have no facilities whatsoever,' the doctor complained to me as we crossed a field to the male wards. 'We have no drugs, an X-ray machine thirty years out of date, and the place is full to bursting.'

Images of elegant tubercular suffering: Munch's ghost-like sister, Keats coughing into a frilled handkerchief, vivid red on stark white. They vanished. TB was no nineteenth-century disease. Here it was commonplace, and people were inured to its dangers. A tragedy, of course, but a mundane one with its drama blunted. TB was rife, the doctor explained, because of bad living conditions, poverty, bad food and bad – or non-existent – sanitation. If it was that common, and that infectious, I mused, perhaps George did have TB after all. Why then should he have denied it? TB was nothing to be ashamed of. He had implied that he was being kept at the hospital against his will, that there was something sinister behind his 'incarceration', but if that was true, this little cottage hospital seemed an unlikely venue. The white and white and white, the false smiles and false smiles and false smiles – George's letters read like a description of an altogether more dangerous place. Here, each small room was stove-warm and, well, positively cosy. Patients smiled from their beds, and head-scarved helpers swept floors, fed wood into stoves, carried in meals on trays.

The mystery deepened when the nurse reported from the archives that she could find no mention of George.

Before returning home we called on Mihaela's parents. The interior of their two-roomed flat was identical to all the others I had visited. The same heavy veneered furniture, the same oddments of embroidery on the walls and tables, the same lack of space. Mihaela's mother was tall and handsome with wayward fair hair, and her father small and nut-brown with a large white walrus moustache. They were both workers, he recently retired, she still employed in a local factory;

she worked the early shift so that she could look after Mihaela's elder son in the afternoons. He was with them now, an eight-year-old just returned from school. Cakes, bread, cheese and tea were provided for the visitor. Mihaela's father kissed my hand, spoke French and emerged from the kitchen with a bowl of freshly washed apples which he presented to me with a courtly bow.

We were joined by Mihaela's sister Teodora, her husband Sergiu, and their daughter Sonia. Teodora resembled her mother – lean with unruly curls. She was less solid and conventional than Mihaela, less placid. Mihaela seemed bovine beside her. But she was unpleasantly short with her husband, who irritated her. Everything he said was contradicted, automatically. He took this well, which only irritated her more. I liked Sergiu for his lack of cynicism and was hurt for him when Teodora managed, relentlessly, to put him down.

Sergiu taught French and Russian in village schools along the Ukrainian border. Some of these villages were Ukrainian, but had been left on the Romanian side when the border was drawn up after the last war; the inhabitants were primarily Russian-speaking; in general, however, there was less call for Russian these days, Sergiu said. He was dark and thoughtful and had eyes so wide apart that I wondered if it was possible to see through both at once. He had recently returned from his first trip outside the Eastern Bloc – to France – where he had been shocked, he said, by the excess: the amount of unnecessary food in the shops, one man he met who owned five cars, and another with a collection of guns which Sergiu considered particularly frivolous.

'With all your prosperity,' he observed, 'you West Europeans have lost touch with the essentials of life.'

I agreed. 'But here you can only concentrate on the essentials because you have nothing else. In fact you barely have the essentials.'

'Yes, but even so, here there is still a spirit. We're still more idealistic and in a way more spiritual – in spite of forty years of materialist Marxist culture – than you in the lazy West.'

This was just what George would say. It was certainly true of him, and probably of Sergiu also, but of all those politicians and informers and bribe-accepting professionals? Hardly. Even so, I did wonder how many workers' families in the West would have greeted a stranger with such aristocratic courtesy. How many workers in the West had such highly educated daughters, one a psychologist, the other a doctor? While we were talking Grandma led Mihaela's son into the bedroom, and Teodora took her daughter into the hall, and instead of shouting around or watching telly these two serious eight-year-olds got on with their homework. *They* were not lazy; their studies were taken seriously, especially by them. We've got a little school here, they joked.

With his worker in-laws, his interest in Russia and disapproval of the lazy West, I wasn't sure where to place Sergiu politically, so was reluctant to mention George even though he was my reason for being there and was constantly on my mind. I managed to wait until we had returned home and were being questioned by Călin about the results of our hospital visit before resuming the subject. We were sitting around an embroidered tablecloth eating cheese and spring onions – a Bucovina staple, they said.

'You're sure your friend was at that TB hospital?' Mihaela asked.

'Yes. He was there for four months.'

'It's just that it is strange. Every patient who has ever been there would have their name in the records, and their medical details.'

'Maybe he didn't have TB or pleurisy. Maybe he was kept at the hospital for other reasons.'

Mihaela looked dubious. 'It seems unlikely.'

'Well, he did say that he was having trouble with the authorities because of his correspondence with me. He said he had trouble with the police and that they demanded to see my letters. He refused to stop writing. It was only months later that he stopped, after people in his village said we were spies. He said that he stayed on in the hospital because he was waiting for the authorities' storm to pass away, and that he would have real trouble if he ever wanted to join the Party. And all because of his foreign correspondence.'

'But those were still the good times, the late Seventies, early Eighties. It was only later that contact with foreigners was . . . more difficult.'

'I guess it depended on what you wrote in your letters.'

'Well! If he wrote some crazy things, what could he expect?'

Călin and Mihaela seemed a world away from the Bucharestians who scented a conspiracy around every corner, or from Ioana. They gave the impression of never having brushed against the Securitate, of never having suspected that their phone was tapped and picking up conversations in the room, à la *Gorky Park*; all that was just too *implausible*. But who was I to know what had really been going on?

Mihaela cleared away the plates, and I nervously filled the hiatus of her absence with small talk. There was something forbidding about Călin, beyond the big black beard. Mihaela, like all the Romanian women I had met, was spiritedly argumentative, but Călin had authority and dignity; he was Transylvanian, not Moldavian, so maybe that explained it. Whatever the cause, he was definitely boss around here. I commented on the paintings, small and Klee-like, and Călin said they were by his brother. It was thanks to this brother that I was here this evening, but I had had no idea that he painted. How could I? I had met him for five minutes in the visa section of the Romanian Embassy in London. I knew nothing about him, and I felt a fraud, enjoying Călin's hospitality through such a tenuous connection.

'Has your brother been in England long?' I chattered, for the sake of it.

'About ten years.'

'So he left long before the revolution.'

'Yes.'

'Why did he leave Romania?'

Călin looked at me for a minute. 'I don't know exactly.'

How could anyone not know why their own brother emigrated, escaped, perhaps suffered like Veronica Filip? It said something either about Călin's relationship with his brother, or about his relationship with the 'authorities'. Or both. Călin's expression was impassive; my own must have shown astonishment and curiosity, because he added,

'I never asked him.' The rebuke was explicit. I inwardly cursed my indiscretion: it was none of my business. And the camaraderie that I had presumed to exist in our English connection was one presumption too many. Remember, I told myself, the revolution was no turnaround; it was far more complex than that. Most people I had met and would meet had made their little compromises.

What I had begun by seeing as complacency I now came to recognise as pragmatism. After all, why should anyone have kept George in hospital under false pretences? They hardly had the drugs to spare. And it was incredible that the monks should have attempted to get rid of him. Why should they bother? When I was alone that night I leafed through my copies of George's letters; in the light of Călin and Mihaela's scepticism they glowed with a rather absurd paranoia, and an overinflated self-importance. If George was suffering from anything I'd have said it was pleonexia, a morbid selfishness. However, the question remained: why should his records have vanished? The answer: perhaps nothing more suspicious than clerical error. I became aware that Călin and Mihaela were beginning to doubt George's very existence, and I must admit that I was beginning to doubt him myself. I teetered uncannily, a split second of wondering if I was slightly mad, and if our meeting had ever happened at all.

Despite their protestations, I attempted to help clear the dishes and we laughed awkwardly as we pressed past each other between the sitting room and the kitchen, avoiding each other's eyes in the physical closeness. When we were settled back around the sitting-room table I broached the George subject again. I couldn't let it go.

'One of the things about him is that he speaks excellent English. Or did when we met.' I had discovered that speaking foreign languages was not just a skill in Romania, but a mark of rank. When I spoke French with her family Mihaela had been unduly impressed: I went whizzing up in her estimation. Foreign languages were a sign of sophistication, education, of having a window on the world.

'But I thought you said George came from Bucov de Sus?' commented Mihaela, frowning.

'Yes?'

'Where did he learn his English, then? There wasn't an English teacher in Bucov then. Only Russian.'

She didn't believe me. I had the solid evidence of his letters to prove it; they were an anchor, and Mihaela was curious to read them. But they were private letters.

'He learned at home. He taught himself.'

'So he doesn't speak well English. Just a little.' Mihaela was a bit jealous.

'No, he speaks excellent English.'

'Better than me?'

Yes, I wanted to say. 'No. About the same.'

Călin and Mihaela looked at me for a while. 'His name's unusual,' Călin said, after a pause. 'What is it again?'

'George Cooper. At least that's the English version. Coopor in Romanian, I think. It's of Ukrainian origin.' I scratched it with a knife on my paper napkin.

'Ah!' Călin boomed. 'Cupar, you mean. There are any number of those. It must be George Cupar.' The 'Gh's were hard.

'Don't say you know him?'

'No, but it's a very common name round here.'

Oh. Just one of many. Nobody special. Călin and Mihaela exchanged glances. It shows how well she knew him, they were thinking, if she doesn't even know his real name. So what is she doing here on this wild-goose chase?

The town's central-heating system had been extinguished for spring. That night I clenched myself into a ball in all my clothes under a massive duvet, and even so could not sleep. I lay watching my white breath huff around me in the dark. The black coffee didn't help, nor the fact that I had stomach cramps and had to tiptoe in the dark up and down the passage to the bathroom. Why, I wondered, were all the flats built with frosted-glass interior doors? Was it part of communal living? No privacy even within the home itself? They were ill-fitting, and every light and sound rattled through them, magnified and echoing, threatening to wake the family with each of my frozen doubled-over excursions.

Next morning Mihaela took me to a TB dispensary in town. From here patients were forwarded to the hospital. Mihaela had been a colleague of one of the women doctors, and hoped she might be able to use that contact to extract some more information. She dressed up in brown – brown skirt, brown shirt, brown jacket, brown felt hat, brown lipstick. She looked forty-five, not thirty-five. The outfit was to impress the doctors, and (although she was too polite to mention this) to compensate for my scruffiness. My clothes-washing efforts were infrequent because:

1. I was always on the move.
2. It was too cold for things to dry.
3. Hand-washing jeans is just so much effort and scrapes your knuckles raw.

'Leave this to me,' Mihaela said, so I sat discreetly in the corner while she chatted to her ex-colleague. They were studiously pleasant. This was Old Europe, Mihaela in her drab but smart brown suit, her sensible brown hair recently 'done', exchanging ritual politenesses.

The doctor leaned against a light box, holding in her right hand an X-ray of someone's chest, and as she gossiped she waved this X-ray around. Each gesticulation was accompanied by a flash of white rib cage, thorax, diaphragm and filmy lungs. I was struck by the doctor's insouciance, this mixture of *politesse* and heartlessness. These were the very intimate parts of a man who was sitting outside in the waiting room, and who was doubtless dying of TB. Those ribs and organs could have belonged to George. They might have been his innards, waved about with such abandon.

Mihaela succeeded in charming the lady doctor into sending someone down to the archives. But again there was no sign of George/George, although we tried every possible permutation of his name.

'I knew a ooman,' George had said. That's why he was forced out of Putna; perhaps that explained the beating by 'that prior'. More than a beating, since it later transpired that he had not just broken his vows; he had also broken the law. He wrote to me, *I think you guessed. What do you think of me now, Helena?* and went on to describe the plot of the film *Detective Story*, starring Kirk Douglas. Kirk and his wife were unable to have a baby, and Kirk discovered that she had had an abortion which had made her infertile, so he left her. *That's why I want you to know everything about me,* George wrote (somewhat disingenuously). *Yes, I had to marry, but I didn't. It was only you that I should have liked to marry. First nobody knew anything about me, but my conscience obliged me to confess and go to the monastery. When I wanted to leave the monastery the church obliged me to a public confession and I did it. Oh Helena, it was an unbearable humiliation. This humiliation destroyed me but it brought my pardon by God, they said. That's why I should have liked to go with you. I should have preferred to be slave abroad instead of staying here.*

It was terrible to imagine George, just twenty-four years old, suffering alone in front of ranks of monks and 'authorities' assembled to witness his disgrace. The monks would have listened with pity, perhaps, but also with a faint prurience. Then he was cast out of the monastery. I thought of Ioana's show trial – another public confession, another ritual humiliation. In a society based not on individuals but on communal living, what could be a more powerful threat than that of public disgrace? What more terrifying than that of being an outcast? This country was like a boarding school on a massive scale: lots of room for power games and bullies; no room for misfits. At least Ioana's 'crime' had been heroic: she had won secret respect. But a monk escaping from a monastery to have sex without love with a local woman, who then – or so I surmised – had an abortion? No, not heroic at all.

What were the implications? The 'authorities' had acquired an American film to use in their anti-abortion propaganda. Be warned! Abortion destroys your body! Abortion destroys your marriage! In fact, abortion was not only held up as evil (a sign of the degeneration of the West), it was also illegal for any woman who had borne less than five children. So unless his 'ooman' had been a mother of five

– which was unlikely – George's lover would have been faced with two choices: to risk an illegal back-street abortion, or to abandon the baby to an 'orphanage'. The former meant possible haemorrhage, septicaemia and arrest. The latter meant that immediately after giving birth in hospital she would have been presented with a document to sign, stating whether or not she wished to keep her baby. If not, it would have been whisked away. But she probably made the right choice for the child, because the fate that awaited most of these discarded children was often worse than death. Siret orphanage. I'd seen the pictures. The hollow eyes, the shaven heads, the naked bodies infested with sores, the head-banging and moaning. The world in which such darkness was possible was the world in which George lived.

The West, particularly the British, had responded with emotional outpourings of aid. For a time every parish church collection seemed to be for the Romanian orphans, and from each village volunteers (lorry-drivers, builders, plumbers, unlikely do-gooders for the most part) set off to brave the vampire-infested forests of Eastern Europe, bearing gifts. On Romanian street corners I had glimpsed convoys of these lorries cruising through – sleek and shiny, obviously not Romanian. Their very presence was a rebuke.

Călin was keen for me to visit the orphanage in Siret; he wanted me to admire the improvements. As English speakers Mihaela had mediated between adoptive parents and their future children, while Călin had liaised between British aid agencies and the orphanage, and when our mutual acquaintance in London had – a month earlier – driven out from London in the Bedford van, Călin had directed him to Siret. In return, the Bedford van appeared to be more or less at Călin's disposal. It came to pick me up, and later brought me back.

In my absence Mihaela would try to telephone the dispensary in Bucov de Sus to see if they knew anything about George.

The orphanage turned out to be a perfectly decent institution not unlike my own prep school – stinking loos, vats of boiling stew, iron-framed beds with horsehair mattresses stained with generations of pee. Leaning on a balcony I noticed a handsome yellow stucco building behind a wall a few streets away. Oh that, my driver said, that's the neurological hospital. Seems an odd place for a brain hospital, in Siret, I said. Yes, well, it's for children, handicapped children. I see, I said. Do you? he asked.

So this was the place. Barricaded behind barbed wire, but unavoidably in the town centre. Ioana had asserted that just as the majority of Germans claimed ignorance of the Nazi concentration camps, so the majority of Romanians were ignorant of the 'orphanages'. But how could anyone have ignored this one, dominating this small town as it did?

In a smaller building outside the perimeter I was ushered into an airy room bleached by light, net curtains shimmering, carpet lush underfoot, a bank of hi-fi equipment from which *Cosi fan Tutte* reached its finale. And behind a desk the suave polo-necked form of Domnul Director. He slid his newspaper under a file, drained his coffee and waved me to a chair. No, no, it was *quite* impossible for me to visit the hospital. He was smooth but firm. The BBC had already been here with some interfering blonde woman and caused a scandal, and he had had quite enough trouble with that. Who was I anyway? Where were my official papers? Where was my letter of introduction?

I had blundered in, unprepared. I hazarded what I hoped were the right things to say, then quickly retracted them when I saw that they were not. The Domnul Director had been here only a few months, so was not personally responsible for the dungeon I had seen on *Challenge Anneka*; even so, he wanted me away. I was beginning to lose my temper when a slender woman slipped in, murmuring soothingly. She was Helen, with a long fair plait and white skin, a soft Indian shirt and a crucifix around her neck, a vision of English purity, a medieval virgin. The Director visibly softened. I was all right, she convinced him; she would be my guide and I would take no photographs but would write a report for him afterwards detailing my impressions. Fine by me, I said.

Helen was calm, quiet, infinitely gentle. She was a teacher, but there was no call yet for her skills. Most of the children had first to

108

learn how to be with people, how to accept and return affection, how to respond to loving voices and being held.

'Before I show you round, would you like to join us for lunch?'

'Yes. Thank you very much.'

We set off towards the main building. It would have made a splendid palace for some Moldavian prince, Roxana's grandfather perhaps, before he was exiled to oblivion on the Black Sea canal. But forty-five years earlier the driveway would not have been bobbing and dipping with loony faces, mangled flailing limbs. Helen! Helen! Helen! They grabbed her hands and slobbered on them and pressed them to their cheeks, then grabbed mine too, tagging along. Helen glided through them, dispensing a kiss here, stroking a head there. She knelt beside a buckled young woman in a wheelchair.

'This is Mariana,' she said to me. 'How are you feeling?'

'I'm depressed,' Mariana said. 'I want to get out of this place.' She knotted her hands together, and I noticed that her nails were varnished red. Helen took them in hers.

'I know. We're seeing what we can do.' Helen turned to me and explained in English, 'The terrible thing is that she's got nowhere else to go. She can't work, she's got no family. She's been here her whole life. She's twenty-four. Look, she's even got grey hairs.'

'Is she . . .?'

'No, surprisingly enough. She's still completely sane.'

'What will become of her?'

'One of the options is an old people's home. There's one called Costina which is a real dump. Even worse than this place used to be.'

'Worse?'

'Yes. None of the aid organisations have even begun on the old people. They're not as appealing as the orphans, news-wise.'

Mariana said something in Romanian that I didn't catch.

'She said, this is a prison, and she wants to escape. She says she hasn't committed any crime. Sssh, Mariana, it's OK.'

Mariana wiped her eyes.

'What can you do?'

'Not much. We can try to get some family to take her on, but that's pretty unlikely. All we can do for the moment is try to improve her life here. We give her make-up and clothes. Not much, I know. Of course the danger is that we raise her expectations and then have to disappoint her.'

Even the kitchen staff – peasant women with hefty bodies and headscarves – welcomed Helen. We were seated in a cell-like room and joined by Alistair, a fourth-year English medic, also pale and blonde and beautiful. The peasant women ladled out fatty sausages which stuck in my throat with the smell of the institution around us.

'Of course this isn't what the kids get,' Alistair said. 'They're mostly fed a liquid diet. They're so understaffed here that there isn't time to feed the kids properly.'

There was mayhem when the aid convoys arrived, they said. A lorryload of clothes was recently set upon by both children and staff. One small boy put on a sheepskin jacket and a cleaner went for him, scrabbling at the jacket, trying to tear it from his back, ending by ripping the sleeve from its socket. The woman stood there, the empty sleeve flapping in her hand, and screamed abuse into the air. Drugs and other supplies frequently vanished.

'These kids are Romania's refuse. They're ugly and dirty and horrible. And now suddenly they're being given all these clothes and toys and attention and stuff. The workers want to know why, when their own beautiful kids are left hungry and badly dressed. They resent these kids for it, and sometimes they take it out on them.'

'What do you mean?'

'They beat them. Not when we're around. At night.'

'How do you know?'

'The kids tell us. Anyway, we can see for ourselves. The bruises.'

'One volunteer hit one of the nurses. He was so angry about a defenceless child being beaten. There was a big scene about that. He was sent home.'

They had to tread carefully because they were here to help the children and wanted nothing to jeopardise that.

At the bottom of the steps a small crowd of children awaited us. *Helen! Helen! Doctor! Domnişoară!* We were clasped by yearning hands, shaved heads pressed against us, wonky lopsided grins, bulgy snotty noses, skins dry and spotty. Shaving, which was indiscriminate – you couldn't tell boys from girls – made it easier to keep the lice at bay. Hands reached up to stroke my long hair, *frumos, frumos, frumos*, usually gently, sometimes tugging more urgently. Our white-coated minder, one of the Romanian doctors, watched impassively from the top of the steps. Helen and Alistair floated past him, two blonde angels dispensing goodness and love to children accustomed, until a few months ago, only to darkness.

'He'll follow us around, but we can ignore him,' Alistair said in English.

The doctor kissed my hand sycophantically and waved us inside.

What had been a dungeon of unspeakable squalor had, in one week, been transformed by the BBC *Challenge Anneka* team into something more humane. White walls, new beds with clean sheets and blue blankets immaculately folded down at one corner, topped by soft clean pillows. But in the corner two beds had been stripped and covered with old grey blankets, and on them were seated the children, forty of them. Half were away at the school in the compound, while the other half sat there awaiting their return. Until we arrived they had nothing to do. Some rocked back and forth, eyes glazed; many were sedated; the alert ones shrieked *Helen Helen Helen*, more eyes dark and wide and begging for affection, more hair stroking. They longed for hair.

'The white beds are for show,' Alistair explained. 'The children can never sit on them during the day. They're shouted at if they so much as touch them. Then at night they're stripped off and the old blankets go back on, with kids three or four to a bed.'

Helen said, 'They haven't got the staff to wash all those beautiful sheets. Or the hot water. They look good, but they're just not practical.'

Toys magically appeared and the children who were able to shook them about and shouted.

'They've brought these out to impress you,' Alistair commented scornfully.

'To be fair, they can't let the kids play with the toys all the time because they destroy them,' Helen said. 'They haven't learnt how to play yet. They don't know what toys are. And still the toys keep on coming. We don't need all those toys! These kids need medicine and money for staff and food, not toys.'

'At least everything's better than it was,' I said.

'Mmm. *Challenge Anneka*, it was a bit like a whirlwind. They flew in, transformed lives on the surface in a week, then flew out again, leaving everyone reeling in their wake. Only when everything settles down again can the real work begin. But of course it was an important start. The other thing is that the stuff they brought out here is pretty tacky. The cots are already falling apart. It looked good for the TV but it won't last long. You know, you wouldn't believe some of the stuff that people sent out here. Not *Challenge Anneka* necessarily, but other groups. Out-of-date drugs, medical samples, even half-eaten packets of sweets. It's outrageous. It was all stuff they would never have given to their own kids. It's insulting to the Romanians.'

'Perhaps, in a way, that's what's intended,' I hazarded. 'I mean, like a punishment, for treating the children in this way. For letting it come to this.'

'Maybe. I must admit, it's sometimes hard to remember that it wasn't really these people's fault. Many of the women are very caring and loving. It was the system, the cruelty which stemmed from the top and filtered down.'

The windows were barred against escape, and the air was thick and sour.

A blonde girl sat on a bed, unable to speak. She seemed alien, unapproachable, until she started to cry and clutch her head; she kissed my hand and pressed it to her forehead, rolling up huge blue eyes until they disappeared into their sockets. Suddenly she was made human by her pain. Alistair sat beside her and tried to diagnose the problem while the doctor watched. At Alistair's request the doctor led her away to give her a painkiller.

'If Alistair hadn't been here he wouldn't have done a thing,' Helen whispered.

A cleaner mopped the floor; she was middle-aged and wooden-faced. Even so, one child, a boy I think, excited by our visit, pointed to her and chanted, *'Mama! Mama! Frumos.'* She remained blank, hard. The boy grinned and bounced up and down on the bed, but she went on mopping.

A room of cots housed the 'babies', the seriously handicapped. Many had not been handicapped at birth, but became so here. One eleven-year-old girl with a large, pale, bald head had sprouted tiny stunted limbs; they had never grown because she had never been lifted from her cot. She was unable to walk, talk, or express emotion, because no-one had held her or spoken to her. Now Helen picked her up and carried her to the window.

'Here, my little one, have some daylight on your skin. Most of them are anaemic,' she said to me. 'They've never seen the sun. They've got every sort of vitamin deficiency, rickets, the lot.'

'Aids?'

'Not sure. There've been tests, but we've not had the results yet. Before the revolution they were dying at the rate of about two a week. Now there's been only one in two months, hasn't there, my little one? That was supposedly pneumonia, but we suspect Aids. Of course they've been using the same syringes again and again, so it's highly likely.'

One of the babies stood up in his cot and as I passed he reached out and gripped my coat with startling strength. His face was clenched with determination; he would not let go. I managed to move one hand but he gripped my finger; his small claws dug into my flesh. Then they moved in a flash and tangled in my hair, tugging my head down towards him. There was something frightening about him, a baby who could be dangerous – Steinbeck's Lennie in miniature – whose own physical strength had outgrown him. But of course he was no baby. He looked about two years old, but that face set with desperation gave it away: he was twelve. Alistair had to prise his fingers off.

* * *

113

Before the revolution, Mihaela, as a paediatrician, had been summoned several times to Siret. She knew the state of things, but I couldn't bring myself to ask her why she had not intervened. I was too polite and, besides, I already knew the answers: fear, revulsion, weakness, inertia, apathy and helplessness.

Mihaela and Călin's flat embraced me, though I couldn't shake off the sweet-sour smell of Siret in my hair. Mihaela seemed distracted. She held open the bedroom door.

'Helena, will you come in here, please?'

Uncharacteristically formal, she had that air of self-importance that accompanies the bearer of bad news. I followed her inside.

'Sit here, please.' She patted the bed. 'Bad news about your friend George.'

'I see. You'd better tell me.'

'He is died.'

Surprised that I was not surprised. Somehow I had known it all along.

'He is died of schizophrenia.'

'Schizophrenia? It's not possible. I mean, he wasn't . . .'

'I rang the dispensary in Bucov. They say he was in Costina. It's a mental hospital about twenty kilometres from Suceava.'

After my day in Siret I had some inkling of what 'mental hospital' might mean. Costina was where Helen had said the crippled Mariana might end up.

'Costina is serious. Nobody go there unless they seriously sick. I never go there, but I heard about it. Paranoid schizophrenia, that's what they say.'

'But George wasn't schizophrenic. It's not possible.'

Mihaela shook her head. 'I think George is crazy.' She was brutal. Besides, she was inclined to give her own profession the benefit of the doubt. She asked to look at his letters, insisting that as a doctor she would be able to recognise schizophrenia if she saw it, and with some reluctance I handed them over. She peered at them, but her English was not up to understanding enough.

'It seems he was not a monk as he say to you, but he worked at the monastery as some kind of guide.' She implied that he had lied to me. 'He had to leave the monastery because of a foreigner. I guess it was you.'

Mihaela ignored my denials. She seemed intent on belittling him, and on judging him. Her mind was made up: George was insane and a charlatan. If he had ended up in Costina mental hospital, he had only got what he deserved. He was a nobody, a mad nobody, and I was a fool.

She left me, and in the privacy of the bedroom I put my head in my hands. I suppose it was the shock of it, but I felt numb. So that's it, I kept repeating, so that's it. That's just it. Then an odd thing happened. Into the emptiness came a vision of George which was much more solid than any I had had before: George in his cheap, indelibly Romanian shoes; George sitting on a grassy bank at Hurez eating plums; George at home, proud and diffident. Confirmation that he no longer existed was the first proof – other than my own – that he had ever existed at all. In his death he suddenly came alive; in his absence he assumed a more vivid presence. George was no longer a memory and some letters, but a friend with cherry-black eyes and a peasanty smell who was capable of *dying*, of all things.

And I had done nothing about it. While I was swanning through my life, leaving Cambridge, doing various pleasant jobs in London, falling in love, travelling, writing, getting married, George had been incarcerated in a mental institution that even Romanians considered bad, and they should know. My roundabout journey through Romania, all the more necessary now that he was unable to talk, paradoxically seemed absurd. Padding. Time-wasting. Mihaela didn't know his date of death – she said I would have to go myself to the dispensary in Bucov – but it could have been last week; it could have been yesterday.

I skimmed through the letters. Where before they had been full of his love of life, of walking in the woods, of his friendship with us, of our holiday together, his love for me, now they were full of prophesies of death. On 19 September 1979 he had written of our prospective return to Romania: *Welcome every time, friends! But I'm not sure if you will find me at home. I'm not sure if you will find me alive.* I had taken this as his romantic literary style, his melodrama; now it read like a warning that I had ignored. Later, after listing the failures of his life: *All that I have to do now is find my death, because an ambitious like me is rejected everywhere.* Later still: *Would you like to see some petals of one of the chrysanthemums you gave me when you left me at Turnu Severin railway station? And all that I wanted was to rush back to you and stay with you. We are sad at parting, we say don't forget me, yet perhaps we shall never see each other again? I've got not much chance, that's why I prefer to shut up, suffer and die.* Rereading them now, his letters became all the more poignant, and Romania all the more dismal.

I was struck not only by the references to death, but also by the number of times he mentioned madness. The word 'crazy' crops up again and again. He had also used it in conversation with us. He was considered crazy for not marrying, crazy for organising a protest in Constanţa, crazy for going off with the woman at Putna. Come to that, it was a word often used by other people here. Before I arrived an exiled Romanian in London had warned me that I would find the people 'schizophrenic'. She had meant paranoid, persecuted, untrustworthy. In Bucharest Nicu had mentioned that after forty years of Communism he felt mentally handicapped. It was almost as if madness was the norm in the Theatre of the Absurd.

Was George just one of many, or was he genuinely certifiable as a paranoid schizophrenic? Was he mad when we met? Even to contemplate it was a betrayal, reducing all he said and did and thought and wrote to mere insanity. But could he have been? What signs should I have recognised? What *is* schizophrenia?

Most psychiatrists agree that schizophrenia means disturbances in feeling, thought and relationship to the outside world. There are considered to be four main types, with the paranoid type being characterised above all by delusions of persecution and grandeur.

Let's begin with persecution. The person most vulnerable to persecutory paranoia tends to be tense, insecure, suspicious, secretive, has few close friends and is addicted to solitary rumination. It has to be admitted that George fitted this description exactly. An atmosphere of tension swirled around him like an aura, repelling Alex but draw-ing me irresistibly towards him. This tension seemed to arise from his intensity of feeling, from his awkwardness in the company of three strangers, from his self-doubt, all of which were oh so appeal-ing. He was certainly insecure. As for being suspicious, it was that very mistrust of his Romanian colleagues that led to his joy in being able to befriend us – the outsiders he could, for once, trust. Was he secretive? Yes, for surely that was why I knew so little about him; and that ascetic cell where he studied, and his command of languages, all self-taught, testified to the extent of his solitary rumination. It was safe to say that George was vulnerable to persecutory paranoia.

The question was: did those suspicions and tensions enlarge into serious paranoid delusions? He was moody, certainly, but so are most sensitive people; the paranoid goes further and regards the world as hostile. He becomes increasingly uneasy and vigilant, watching for hidden meanings and little clues that prove he is the victim of a plot; he is ready to accept the flimsiest evidence to support this belief.

I couldn't help thinking of Rîmnicu Vîlcea, and George's extreme terror at the sight of the army officers lolling around the reception desk. He was frightened enough to spend the entire night – a cold night – hiding in a park. Then there were his letters, filled with fear of persecution by the Putna monks and the doctors, and of the people who called him 'a dangerous and unuseful man'. Over the following year he steadily became more suspicious, convinced that the 'authori-ties' were reading our correspondence and punishing him for it. Were his fears justified, or were they merely the product of a sick mind? Sadly, I could find no answer from him. But his doctor, his family, his monastery, his friends; they would have to tell me.

And what of delusions of grandeur? Most psychiatrists would agree that a firmly held notion by the patient that he is Jesus Christ or Napoleon would justify a diagnosis of schizophrenia, but did George belong to this category? He did not consider himself a great poet, but he wanted to be. Nothing odd about that, especially in Romania, and he did not fool himself that he was a reincarnation of Mihai Eminescu even if he would have liked to have been. But in his long

117

hospital letter/journal there was one section that made me uneasy. *I forgot to tell you about three prophetic signs.*

1. I dreamt that I slept with my mother. And they say it means I shall be master of the world. Then Helena and Ali will really be princesses.
2. On a night last autumn I was forced to stay for a night in a nut tree and I saw a brilliant throne. Only I didn't know if it was prepared for me and who offered me this throne. Have you got a rich imagination? To imagine me a king or an emperor? Time will prove if these presumptions are true.

What had read as playfulness now read like delusions of grandeur. However, a delusion is not – as this was – a fantasy, or dream; a delusion is a completely unshakeable belief in the truth of a proposition which is idiosyncratic and incorrigible. A psychoanalyst might be interested in interpreting George's fantasies, but would be hard pressed to classify them as delusions of grandeur.

The third sign is a religious one. An old and unmarried man told me to open the Psalms with closed eyes. What page do you guess I found, and what was written there? Be master among your enemies. God is with you during your days of power. Psalm 109.

Many great men of history believed in natural signs and I must believe too. Psalm 109 is a psalm of desperation and vengeance, in which David exhorts his enemies to let their children be fatherless, their wives widows; it is full of fears of persecution. *For the mouth of the wicked and the mouth of the deceitful are opened against me: they have spoken against me with a lying tongue. They compassed me about also with words of hatred; and fought against me without a cause.* Later: *Let mine adversaries be clothed with shame, and let them cover themselves with their own confusion, as with a mantle.* This was how George felt about the 'authorities', the monks, the doctors. But I doubt that David was diagnosed as suffering from paranoid schizophrenia.

Even if George was not a paranoid schizophrenic when we met and corresponded, he may have become one later, although if schizophrenia has not emerged by early adulthood it is unlikely ever to do so. The simplest explanation was in the September 1979 letter/journal. *A light wind blowing on my face and my hair. I begin to feel better. In fact I feel better since I met you, dear English friends. It's important for me to not lose your friendship, for you are my last connection with the formal world. If you leave me, I shall be really crazy.* And perhaps that is what happened: we left him, and he went really crazy. That was that. But then again, perhaps that was not that.

What Mihaela had not mentioned was that no-one dies of schizophrenia. You commit suicide, perhaps, or inner voices propel you towards some terrible end, but schizophrenia itself is not a cause of death.

Four

I met nothing but kindness on my journey to Bucov. Călin attempted to buy my train ticket, and peasants returning home after the Friday market, loaded like pack animals with woollen bags of vegetables and chickens, welcomed me aboard. It was a 'personal' train, the slowest variety and the scruffiest, but such a pleasure to sit high above the fields lining the dried-up river beds, and to rock through them. I got off at the wrong station but a couple drove me several miles to the right one, refusing payment. It was often like this: just when I was feeling most hostile I met with simple generosity, and was disarmed.

What I remembered as a tiny hamlet turned out – disorientatingly – to be a town of 15,000 people that straggled up the Suceava valley. These were linear settlements, like Celtic villages, sprawling along a road and without any clear centre. The odd block of flats sprouting from fields of wind-blown litter were the already decaying attempts at modernisation, far shabbier after five or ten years than the old single-storey wooden houses around them that they had replaced. As usual, poplars and willows and pollarded limes made all the difference.

The dispensary's hallway was shadowed with sickness, huddled patients hawking and limping. From somewhere beyond them resonated the seismic shocks of heavy metal music. I was led towards its epicentre. The door was open, and a red-haired woman sat on the edge of a bed, staring at a black and white television. She wore the regulation grey towelling dressing gown, which she hugged around her knees in excitement at the heavy metal stars flayling their matted locks and smashing at their guitars. She glanced up, eyes glazed with violence and irritated by the interruption.

'Cupar George?' She was expecting me; Mihaela had phoned.

'Yes.'

'It's dead.' She turned back to the TV. 'Beautiful,' she breathed, and increased the volume. A cigarette stub burned low between talon-like nails. Her hair was too ginger, her fingernails too pink, and smeared over her eye sockets like lurid bruises was eyeshadow that was too green; like her dressing gown, she was no longer young.

'I know.'

'Too bad,' she shrugged. 'Schizophrenia.'

I stood in the doorway with my rucksack. If I waited around perhaps at least a snippet of information would come my way. Sure enough, the matron waved me impatiently inside, and when she could tear herself away from the screen she summoned a nurse to bring her the book of *evidenca*. It was a wide, brown volume, like an old photograph album, and she turned the pages until she found what she wanted. She jabbed it with her fingernail. Smudged ink and that curly, old-fashioned, continental handwriting like George's own: Cupar George; born 18.7.55; first ill 14.4.85; first in Costina 06.85; died 6.10.87. So there we had it, the bald facts of George's life and death. Odd how one minute death is resplendent and operatic, grand in its tragedy, the next minute something so banal, a snuffing out and quick forgetting. Switching off the gas.

George had died three and a half years earlier, aged only thirty-two, just a year older than I was now.

Mihaela had assured me that dispensary staff knew most about the local population since they were responsible for their physical welfare, but the matron said she couldn't recall George. No, she simply couldn't put a face to him. She quickly changed the subject; she preferred to complain about her life – the poverty, the lack of facilities, the lack of foreign exchange. Her husband was the dispensary doctor, and he folded on to the bed opposite, hair skull-plastered, shoulders slumped; he had a seedy, collapsed look; they were waiting to see if things would improve in Romania, and if not, they were off to apartheid-ridden South Africa. Good riddance, I thought, brutalised as they were by hardship and failure.

Sandwiches were ordered, and sweet black coffee, and neat *rachiu*, the local hooch, which the matron tossed back. They invited me to join them; I was hungry, and besides if I abandoned myself to them they would have to find some way of getting me off their hands. The *rachiu* helped, and with each swig the matron mellowed, until she found herself remembering that George's mother was still alive and living in the village, and that one of the dispensary cleaners was a friend of the family. This cleaner, she added, would take me to see them.

A dirt track stretched out of the town and straight to the USSR. *Frontiera 1km*. That much I recalled, along with the narrow roadside ditches into which last time, having only recently passed my test, I accidentally drove a small girl. The smallholdings were more substantial than I remembered, with their yards and wooden barns, and the carved and roofed wooden gateways were bigger; it was as if the years had acted as a temporal perspective, diminishing things in size as they receded in time.

The full-sized reality of Rodica, the cleaner, was reassuring. Yes, she repeated as we wobbled companionably up the track (each with one steadying hand on the handlebars of her bicycle, the other balancing my rucksack on the saddle), yes, we were talking about the same George Cupar, who died in Costina; yes, George's mother still lived here; yes, she would be at home. Without Rodica I might have turned back, nervous as I was of intruding in the delicate matter of George's death and possible madness. I hoped to be greeted with the unquestioning warmth of twelve years earlier, but I couldn't count on it. George had written to me from the TB hospital: *Still, I don't regret at all having met you. Your presence lighted me and made me happy for some moments of my life. Yes, let's be satisfied with that wonderful night!* But George's mother may not have felt the same; after all, if George had been punished for his foreign correspondence, then I was to blame. No traveller can be a silent witness, leaving no trace; their very presence, watching and listening, changes what they see and hear. But I had done more than that; I had blown through George's life like a breeze, stirring things up, and his family had no reason to welcome me back.

Perhaps – and this was worse – when George wrote of 'people' who suspected Alex of being a spy and Ali and me of being his bait, he was referring to his own family. Such primitive hostility and mistrust was what I dreaded most.

Women in sturdy skirts and rubber boots looked up, startled, from sweeping their yards or drawing water from their wells. I suspected them, too, of suspecting me, but their greetings were friendly. *Bună ziua Bună ziua.* Rodica fended off their questions: who is the young woman? where is she from? where is she going? This was a small, gossipy place, and I didn't want the news of a foreigner visiting Doamna Cupar – an extraordinary event – to reach her before I did.

The houses petered out as we neared the forest-padded frontier. There were still no crossings made here, except by gypsy smugglers. Their encampment lay – a cold shoulder's distance from Bucov – to one side of the track. To the other side, a rutted lane. We turned down it, and stopped in front of a gate. A concrete path crossed a yard to a small white house with a shingle roof. It had grey-painted windows and, at right angles, a wooden barn. George's house. My heart was beating uncomfortably.

'Wait here,' Rodica suggested with tact.

'Yes, why not ask if she wants to see me? Explain that I was here a long time ago.'

Rodica smiled: she understood perfectly. She leant her bicycle against the wattle fence, into which, I noticed absently, sprigs of winter-flowering jasmine had been twined; they were wilting now. Rodica knocked on the door and disappeared. I sat in cool spring sun on the edge of the well. This had thoughtfully been left outside the fence, on the roadside, so that passers-by could help themselves to water, and as if to sanctify this act of generosity the well had been turned into a shrine, with an icon embedded in its shingled cap. There was beauty here, in such attention to detail, and in the neatness of it – the way geometric patterns were carved into the walls of the house between each window, and the way the stupa-shaped haystack beside the barn was fenced with carefully woven branches. A garden (striped rows freshly marked out for vegetables, fruit trees recently pruned) dropped gently from the house down to a willow-fringed stream.

I might have recognised it, but the angle of house and barn, the lie of the land, the colour of the light, all these had changed, and where were the chrysanthemums? But of course it was too early for them.

This was a civilisation based on wood. Carved wood, shingled wood, planked wood, woven wood. Against the barn and beneath the shelter of its eaves, newly chopped logs were carefully stacked, ready to be split and burnt. Unlike the apartment blocks in the village centre, this house could have been built any time – last year, a hundred years ago. It belonged here, built from trees, and situated amongst trees.

Beyond the stream, brown and gurgling, the fields rose to distant pine-clad hills. They were busy with women raking, and a pair of roan horses dragged a plough. '*Tcha! Tcha!*' the ploughman called, driving them on, red tassels on manes and tails bouncing and keeping off the evil eye. In another field a man trod slowly back and forth, reaching into a chequered bag at his side and letting fly a spray of seed in a white arc. Horses stamped, and snuffled into nosebags under a still skeletal oak. Further downstream two women were washing clothes by beating them with a wooden bat, like a ping-pong bat, against a wooden stool. The smack smack of the bats mimicked the rat tat tat of a woodpecker. The women stood in the stream in rubber boots and rolled their sleeves up. One of them called to the ploughman, and he raised his felt hat in reply. Then the clothes were trailed in the stream, the current washing the soap away, and beaten again. A hard life, yes, but a sociable one, a pastoral idyll. Less wooded than Gainsborough, less visionary and secret than Palmer, less suburban than Stanley Spencer, more a jewel-like scene from the Duc de Berry's *Très Riches Heures*.

For many Romanian poets the village was a mythical ideal, a landscape of the Romanian soul. George's beloved Mihai Eminescu eulogised the archaic peasant world, the houses raising to the moon their old roof beams, the tired men with scythes returning from the fields, the smoke weaving through the valley. For the contemporary poet Ana Blandiana the village was more a smell than an image or sound, the smell of smoke in the evening, the smell of frothing milk, of wet straw, of self – of long hair in the sun. I could never imagine George leaving this rural bliss for exile abroad.

A young woman wearing a cotton headscarf and a dark flower-patterned dress emerged from George's mother's barn and stood in the doorway of the house staring at me, then turned abruptly to go in. I waited.

No, this was not a scene from a Book of Hours, this was a Flemish landscape glimpsed behind a Pietà, with peasants toiling in the fields and living their lives unaware of the tragedy taking place in their midst.

Uphill behind me was Vasile's house, where Ali, Alex and I had spent the night. It was unchanged, still with the separate summer and winter house, the winter one with its broad, low roof supported by corner posts, the summer one like a potting shed, immaculate behind its picket fence. Our night there with the burly Vasile and his family – so friendly, so hospitable – had been one of our most magical.

'You can come in.' Rodica was standing at the door, her hand shading her eyes. I opened the gate and walked up the path towards her. The young woman came out behind her and set a spinning wheel down on the ground. She looked at me silently, without expression. She shook my hand, gravely, then pushed open the door and stood aside to let me pass.

The room was bare, with a cold stone floor, a basin of water on a sideboard, and piles of coats and boots.

'In here,' Rodica said, opening a green door. Behind it, sitting up in a bed that filled half the room, was George's mother. She reached out and wrapped her arms around me, then pushed me back and studied my face with her hands clasping my cheeks. Then she kissed me twice, four times, six times. Tears were streaming down her face.

'George, George,' she wept. She shook her head and pulled a handkerchief from her sleeve to dab her eyes. Rodica signalled farewell. Doamna Cupar pulled up a stool beside her and I sat while she held my hand. 'George. Dead. Dead and gone.'

'I know,' I said. 'I'm so sorry.' I couldn't stop my own tears, and it was a relief to let them flow at last. She pressed her hands to her heart, then let them flutter upwards, a wonderfully expressive gesture. Her eyes were gentle, and as she looked up at me from under her black headscarf, her few remaining metal teeth glinting, I thought again of Northern Renaissance paintings.

'Thank you for coming. You've come because of George. Thank you. All the way from England.'

She didn't blame or accuse me, nor did she express surprise, and she recalled every detail of my previous visit. 'You stayed the night with Vasile, and you visited us in the morning. We had cakes and apples!' She particularly remembered that she and Ali and I had posed together for a photograph, and that we had promised to send her a copy. We did as we promised, but it had never arrived. 'Stolen by the authorities,' she whispered knowingly. She had also not received my last letter; for unknown bureaucratic reasons the house numbers had been changed, and as most people in the neighbourhood appeared to be called Cupar, the letter had never been forwarded.

The young woman was summoned. She was George's youngest sister, Viorica, now nineteen years old, the age I was when I came here last. She must have been seven then, and a memory of a shy child having her hair tousled by George did float murkily to the surface.

'This is a friend of George's, from *England*.' Doamna Cupar's eyes shone with both sadness and excitement. Viorica expressed interest, but only out of politeness. Doamna Cupar gave her some instructions from the bed, and she silently obeyed. She fed sticks through a metal door in the side of the green-tiled stove which stood at the foot of the bed and filled that end of the room, and then lit them; once they were blazing she closed the door and cracked eggs into a frying pan on top, brewed tea, laid an embroidered white cloth on a table beneath the window, sliced a loaf of bread, and went out for a bowl of apples. She did all this with her eyes lowered, never uttering a word. I was disappointed to find no trace of George in her round, soft fairness; she also lacked his animation. She had cold, pale eyelashes. She had been married just three months.

At Doamna Cupar's insistence I sat at the table; she and Viorica had eaten already. Our conversation continued in bursts, punctuated by Please! You must eat more! More eggs! More apples! More bread! More tea! You have hardly touched anything! No, no, thank you, I couldn't. From her vantage point at the head of the bed Doamna Cupar directed Viorica in her chores, then smiled weepily at me, sighing and fluttering her hands heavenwards.

I wasn't sure how much she knew about my relationship with her son. She couldn't fail to have known of our correspondence since in the beginning he wrote to me most days. As to the contents of the letters, she did not speak English, so she can have known only as much as George told her. He wrote to me sometime after Christmas in 1980: *In your first letter you asked me: Did your mother miss you when you came travelling with us? Well, so-and-so. She was worried about what happened to me. When I showed her your pictures she was thoughtful for a while and said then that you deserved to be accompanied across Romania. She added, 'They were pretty girls after all, especially the long-dark-haired one. . . .' 'Would you like her to be your daughter-in-law?' I asked her. She didn't reply, she was just smiling.*

She was just smiling. Did that mean yes? Or did that mean she was wise enough to know it would never happen? I wondered what sort of a mother-in-law she would have made. Hanging above the door was a hand-tinted photograph of her and her husband on their wedding day, both in traditional Bucovina dress; she was pretty then, with large black eyes and narrow features, but now she was old, a withered crone. When she said she was only fifty-seven, she must have seen my surprise; all my troubles, she said, holding up her hands in a gesture of defeat. Even so, she exuded kindness, gentleness, goodness. She and I were worlds apart, but perhaps qualities like hers could have overcome our differences. If I had married George I might have lived in this village, even shared this very house with her, like Viorica and her husband Ioan. But I would never have married George: not in a million years.

As for husband, he died in 1984 aged sixty, killed off, she said bitterly, by all the problems with George.

Remember that if I ever recover my health, if I ever get the chance to meet you, I shall not lose you again. Unlike me, he had remained true to his word, and had never married. *Darling Helena, I gave you so much trouble with my troubles. Still, you are the best lady I'd really like to marry. Any other marriage will be simple formality . . . simple formality. . . .*

Doamna Cupar pointed to my wedding ring. 'When did you marry?'

'In 1987.'

She nodded significantly. 'So you waited.'

'What do you mean?'

'1987. That was the year George died.'

'But I didn't know George had died.'

'Yes, you waited.' She seemed to think that the bond between us had been so strong that only with George's death had I been released to marry someone else.

'No,' I said. 'I would have married my husband at any time, whenever I met him. It had nothing to do with George.'

She shook her head firmly. 'You waited.'

I gave up. This was what she wanted to believe. It made me ashamed to have even considered the possibility that he might have forgotten me; how could I have doubted him? My shame deepened when Viorica was asked to fetch a photograph, a copy of which he had sent me. It was a black and white picture of George in the traditional Bucovina waistcoat of embroidered sheepskin, moustache trim, eyes olive-black and soulful. On the back he had inscribed, grandly: *Taken in the year of Our Lord 1979 for my English friends, hoping they will someday return to Romania.* On the back of mine he had written: *My true love hath my heart. Have I got her?* I had imagined him rummaging around in a drawer and finding some old snapshot to send to me; only now that I was here could I appreciate what it cost him even to have this photograph made. He must have dressed up in his traditional clothes (normally reserved for Sundays and festivals), then walked the several miles to the station (an hour's walk), caught the train to Rădăuţi (an hour's journey), had the photograph taken in a studio (expensive), waited in Rădăuţi while it was developed, paid for the stamps, posted it to me, then travelled all the way home again. *Helena, please give me your blessing to write you some more lines. The stamps cost money and I've got not enough money. That's why my letters are so long.* Then with his romantic sense of drama he had written these words on the back of the remaining photograph and tucked it away in a drawer. Only now did I see how much my return would have meant to him.

Here I was at last, but too late.

George, Doamna Cupar whispered, was not interested in Romanian women. He didn't even look at them. All he ever wanted was to go to England. 'He used to go on about it all the time,' she said. 'England, England, England.' As she spoke, more things about George fell into place. His letters were full of his efforts to improve his English; flights of poetic prose and declarations of undying love interrupted by '*So you see I have just used the past conditional!*' Knowing of his passion for languages I had doubted his love and suspected him of simply using me to practise his English; only now did I understand that the language was not an end in itself, but proof that he was capable of living in England. *If we were meant for each other I don't know. All I know is that an old man from Bucovina used to call me 'the English'. Perhaps this name was a prophetic one, who knows?*

I produced the tiny picture I had of George, the one with the anxious, clean-shaven face that he had sent me for his 'possible passport'. Doamna Cupar gazed at it for a long time, her fat tears dripping on it. She handed it to Viorica, who can barely have known George in his prime. Again, only now could I imagine the efforts involved in sending me this picture, and in keeping it secret, and only now did I see how very serious had been his desire to leave the country. It was no whim.

Doamna Cupar asked Viorica to lift from the wall a frame of black and white photographs. There were pictures of her six other children – Maria, Georgeta and Irina getting married, Constantin studying engineering in Iaşi, Andrei in a felt hat – and amongst them were pictures of George. There he was as a boy dressed in a miniature version of the embroidered sheepskin waistcoat, already serious, with a long jaw and that romantic expression. There he was in uniform doing military service, his chin thrust determinedly forward, his eyes with a wounded, hurt look even then. He lasted two years, patrolling the Soviet border at Sighet. Then there was a happier one of him in monk's robes at Putna, with a small pointy beard. He spent two years there, his mother explained, studying theology and training to become a priest; because he was so clever he had been given special dispensation to study at Putna since his father could not afford to send him to the seminary at Neamţ, although that was where he went to take his exams. He was never a monk, but lived as one and took monastic vows, and, she added proudly, he worked as a monastic guide at the same time. This meant making use of his languages.

'Seven! He spoke seven languages! Didn't he, Viorica?'

Viorica nodded. Doamna Cupar mopped her eyes.

'He was so clever. What did he speak, Viorica?'

'He spoke English, French, Italian, German, Spanish, Russian and Latin.'

'Yes, he did. That's right. What was it again?'

'English, French, Italian, German, Spanish, Russian and Latin.'

Doamna Cupar closed her eyes to listen to the litany.

'Where did he learn all this?' I asked.

'He learnt Russian and French at school, here in Bucov, at the *lycée*. But the rest he taught himself. Viorica, get his dictionaries.'

Viorica produced two mini dictionaries, one Italian–Romanian, the other Spanish–Romanian. On the outer edges of the pages George, in a childish way, had scribbled his name. He had no other language books or tapes, and he had simply sat down and memorised the dictionaries from A to Z. These books had been lovingly preserved in a cupboard on the end wall; George had parted with his Romanian–English phrasebook, and Ali, Alex and I had accepted it lightly, unaware of its preciousness. In fact we had lost it.

'He studied in that end room, didn't he?'

'Yes! You remember. Viorica, show Helena the room.'

Viorica obediently opened the last of the three doors in the house. The study-cell had been transformed into a bridal suite, the bed banked with embroidered pillows, every available space stacked with newly woven green and red blankets, Viorica's dowry. Beneath the window, where George had had his desk, rose piles of starched napkins and tablecloths run up by Viorica and her mother on the sewing machine for sale in local craft shops. No sign of George here now.

'He never stopped reading and writing,' Doamna Cupar called.

I returned to her bedside. 'What happened to his other books?'

'Some I gave to Putna library. Others were taken by the *miliţia*.' Her eyes widened at the word *miliţia*.

'They came here?'

She nodded.

'Can you tell me a bit about what happened?'

'Sit down here.' She patted the stool and lowered her voice. 'They came from Suceava, and took him away. Three men came, in uniforms. They took my husband too.' She pressed her hands to her breast and shook her head, miming the shame and fear. Sometime in 1980 – she couldn't remember when – George and his father were arrested. I imagined the neighbours watching the car arrive and George and his father being bundled into the back, and I imagined the shock of such an intrusion on the life of a simple family who had no connections with politics or even with the city. These were simple, good-hearted peasants who meant no harm.

George and his father were taken to Suceava, where George was questioned. Domnul Cupar was released the same day, but George was retained overnight. He was beaten and given an injection, although of what Doamna Cupar did not know. From then on, she said, his character changed and she blamed this change on the mystery injection. From then on he was angry angry angry. She used the word *supărat*, a word I had come across only in the context of politely interrupting a stranger on the street to ask the way or the time. '*Nu vă supăraţi*,' I would say, 'Don't be angry', and always receive a polite smile in return. Doamna Cupar said it bitterly, and incomprehendingly: *supărat supărat supărat*. Was George's anger really caused by a drug, was it the beginnings of a mental illness, or was he simply angry, as he had every reason to be? His attempts to escape from his Romanian prison, both mentally and physically, had been thwarted; he hated the place; he was being prevented from communicating with someone he loved: no wonder he was angry.

George never had TB, Doamna Cupar added quietly, only internal injuries caused by the beatings. That was why there were no records at the TB hospital.

'And this arrest was because of our correspondence?'

'Yes.'

I am still in the hospital because I'm waiting for the authorities' storm to pass away. I hope their anger is only simple dew. They said they were prolonging my stay only because I felt ill and I was enough cursed by the fate. But they said I would have real troubles if I wanted to become member of the Party. And all that because of my foreign correspondence. Never mind, I continue to write in order to improve my English.

'He refused to stop,' said Doamna Cupar.

'How did the *miliţia* know about it?'

Doamna Cupar hesitated, as if afraid that even now someone might be listening. 'Vasile,' she murmured.

'You mean Vasile, his friend? Your neighbour? The one we stayed with?'

She nodded. Vasile had gone to the authorities as soon as we left Bucov and reported the fact that we had stayed the night with him. He was obliged to do this: it was the law. But he had volunteered

132

the extra information that George had left Bucov with us. A few weeks later Vasile had returned to the authorities to report our correspondence.

'But he was George's friend. They live just there.'

Doamna Cupar shrugged: that's how people are. They want to get on in the world.

George had so often mentioned his joy at our being his 'true' friends. I saw now what that had meant to him. 'You were better off here without friends,' I observed. Viorica, passing in her slippers on another errand, agreed with more vehemence than usual. She was a solitary person, maybe because of the troubles with George.

In 1982 he burnt all my letters and his own writings and anything that might have incriminated him, and left for Arad, a handsome Austro-Hungarian city in the Banat, near the Hungarian border, where I had spent a few days on my way to Suceava. From here, George attempted to escape from Romania. So he did try again. I knew from Veronica Filip what that might mean: the weeks of preparation, the subterfuge, the fear, the aloneness. Unlike Veronica, George was caught. That meant beatings, questioning, more beatings. He was returned to Suceava and, Doamna Cupar said, beaten again. From then on he did a few odd jobs, but nothing much.

When her husband died in 1984 Doamna Cupar was no longer able to cope. She had problems with her other children and no money to support them as well as George, and when the *miliţia* came and told her about Costina she thought it sounded a good solution. They said it was a comfortable place with a pretty garden and television in the rooms, and that George would be well cared for, so she agreed that he should go. At first she was even able to visit him. But she soon realised that life at Costina was not as it seemed. The clothes and food that she took for him were immediately stolen by the hospital staff. He then escaped from the hospital. He came home to collect his things before attempting to cross the border again, but he was caught by the *miliţia* before he could leave the house, and was returned to Costina. Doamna Cupar's voice was barely audible. 'He was punished by being kept in a bath of ice-cold water.' Within three weeks he was dead. She moved her hands up from her breast, like two birds fluttering away.

'How did he die?'

She shrugged, tears coursing down the crinkles in her cheeks.

'You don't know?'

She shook her head.

'Don't you have a death certificate?'

She shook her head again. I waited.

She burst out: 'In fact it was many days before I was even told of his death, and by the time I got to Costina I was told it was too late to see the body. That's why he was buried at Costina and not brought home. The priest at Costina said that was better.'

'Where is his grave?'

'In Costina. Beside the hospital. One day – when I have the money – I will bring him home.'

I left the house for a walk, slithering through the mud between the smallholdings. I wanted to be alone, but for all the unspoilt rural beauty there was no hiding from people here. A dog alerted a woman, who hurried out to ask me – in the friendliest way – who I was. I escaped from her to search for somewhere to sit in private, but the fields were full.

A pastoral idyll, perhaps, but with dark roots embedded in oppression and suspicion. Now I knew that cruelty hid behind the twitching curtains. The warm cowshed community was chilled by poverty and violence. Only now did I recall the rape. It happened here, in this village. George's uncle and a group of friends had gang-raped a girl, and when the *miliția* forced her to marry one of her rapists, it was George's uncle she chose. I remembered how matter-of-factly George had told this story. Then there were his letters to me. *You remember when you said, 'I don't want to'? Perhaps I should have forced you this way to be my wife, if I had had more courage, if I had been more decisive. But I could have destroyed this way your life, your future. Perhaps your parents would not have agreed their daughter to marry a Romanian, although I am a man too after all.* I had glossed over this when I received the letter, but now those words – courage, decisive – made me retrospectively afraid.

And there, just above Doamna Cupar's house, was Vasile's. I could see his mother crossing her garden. She and her son and her house were defiled; it was a wonder that they could continue to be neighbours. She was peering down at me, curious about the stranger in her neighbour's garden – or perhaps she already knew my identity. News travelled fast here.

What induced Vasile to betray his friend? Fear. Greed. On the train to Suceava I had read a poem of Ana Blandiana's, written, bravely, over ten years before the revolution:

> Asleep
> I happen to cry out,
> Only when asleep,
> And frightened by my own daring
> I wake,
> In the well-disciplined silence of night,
> And try to hear
> Cries from neighbours' sleep.
> But the neighbours are wise
> Crying out only when they're sure
> That they dream they're asleep.
> In the sleep within sleep
> Where no one can hear,
> They give way to cries.
> What free uproar
> Must be there,
> In the sleep within sleep.

Vasile was the enemy, the indirect cause of George's death. But even he must have had his sleep within sleep, his secret life. After all, he was a victim too, though I didn't see it like that at the time. As for George, he let the neighbours hear his cries, and that was where he went wrong.

When I returned in the late afternoon Mama had vanished. I sat on the stool beneath the window, wondering where everybody was. Then I heard a sigh. High in the gloom, somewhere near the ceiling, was Mama. She had moved a rug up on to the stove behind the chimney and was keeping warm on the tiles. Like an old blackbird in her nest, her eyes round and brown, her nose beaky, she studied me, then sighed again.

Our companionable silence was punctured by the return from work of Viorica's husband, Ioan. He was hefty, sullen, good-looking in a macho, brutish way with a ruddy face and black moustache. Viorica introduced us, but he refused to look me in the eye; he had never known George and did not welcome me. Viorica was even more subdued in his presence, fearful even. Doamna Cupar directed her from her perch and Viorica dutifully scrabbled for money in a drawer, then left the house. The silence was now uncomfortable. Doamna Cupar climbed down and resumed her position in bed, while Ioan sat in the corner, frowning at his shoes.

The door burst open and in came Andrei, George's youngest brother, cross-eyed, and narrow as a weasel. He sat opposite me and peered into my face (or so it seemed), then shrugged and turned to Mama.

'Talk to her,' she urged softly. 'She speaks Romanian.'

'Aah. Good. That makes life easier.'

Viorica reappeared with an unlabelled bottle of *rachiu*. Andrei poured small glasses for me, Ioan and himself, and raised his. 'To George!'

'To George!' I replied. We clinked glasses and tossed back the raw alcohol, my throat scorched. Andrei noticed the passport photo of George on the table; he snatched it up and studied it closely.

'He was brilliant,' he shouted to Ioan, thrusting the photo at him. Clearly Ioan knew nothing about George, which I found strange. 'He could have been a millionaire if he'd wanted. He spoke seven languages. Imagine! Seven! But kaput.'

Ioan grunted. Andrei shared none of George's sensibilities, but I warmed to his pride in his brother. What a prodigy George must have seemed, what a miracle, what a step up for this peasant family, and in the end what a disappointment. It was the hothouse *lycée* education that had produced him. Andrei himself was just one of the herd; he earned his living through 'business', he said, in other words smuggling; there was little else for a landless peasant to do.

'*La mulți ani!*' Another clink of glasses. I took genteel sips, but Andrei, increasingly excited, urged me on. Even Ioan began to relax, and Viorica was sent out for another bottle.

Andrei pressed me to tell him more about my trip with George. 'You went camping!' He raised his arms in mock amazement. 'George danced in Rîmnicu Vîlcea?' He was incredulous. 'Do you hear that?' he asked his mother, who marvelled. 'George dancing!' He slapped his leg and guffawed. What a time-out-of-life it was for George, what golden days. I don't believe he had ever danced in his life before. I produced the typed copies of George's letters. Andrei was impressed by how much George had written, and asked me to translate. I struggled as best I could through one of George's poems which he himself had translated from Romanian. It wasn't a good poem, but I liked it and it went like this:

> I had in my life a deception in love
> I loved a pretty girl but she didn't want that
> Because she decided to marry a rich man
> O my God, but she broke my heart.
>
> I felt after so lonely I had no sleep
> I was like a poor reed in the wind
> People told me that there are other girls
> But I gave up love, and in a monastery I went
>
> Bad men forced me to go from there
> And now I wander through the world
> I had no hope, waiting my death
> But all my life changed when I met you, my dear
>
> I liked singing birds but I can't any more
> No more sunsets and sunny days no more
> I can't even look at the stars in the sky
> For now the star of my life is only you, darling

> I should go on foot round the earth for your smile
> I should fight with an army for your blue eyes
> I should break my oath right now for you
> Our God is good and will forgive
> But I'm not sure if you agree.

George said he had written this for me at the *cabanăs*. At the time I ignored the detail that my eyes are green, not blue, but now I wondered again if he had been more in love with the sound of the words than with me.

Andrei seized the sheaf of letters. 'Mine. Please.'

I hung on to the other end. 'No, no. They're private.'

'I want them. Please.'

'But they're mine.' They referred to 'that wonderful night'. Only copies of course, but all I had with me. They were my only connection with George, and I wanted to reread them when I was alone.

'Please. I'm his brother. They took everything else.'

I had brought the family no presents, not even copies of photographs. This was all there was of him now: two dictionaries, a few formal black and white photos, and some typed letters, neither in his own hand nor in his own language. I could not refuse. Andrei bowed formally and kissed my hand, then turned and whispered to his mother. She nodded, and he got up and went into the end room. He returned with a leather waistcoat which he dropped into my lap. 'George's,' he said. It was the embroidered sheepskin from the photograph, stitched with intricate patterns of bright coloured thread, probably an heirloom. 'For you.' I was touched by their generosity, and also by the value they gave to the letters, but I refused it without hesitation and they were secretly relieved.

Viorica stoked the stove and fried more eggs. Meanwhile Doamna Cupar questioned me about my family.

'What sort of place do you live in, in . . . where does she live?'

'England, Mama, England.'

'Yes, yes, England. What sort of place do you live in there?' She had no idea where it was. How can George have developed his passion in such isolation?

'I live in London.'

She looked blank.

'Mama, it's the capital. Like Bucharest.'

'I see. And your husband?' she asked. 'Is he a good man? He doesn't drink? No? He doesn't beat you? Then you are lucky. He is a good man.' I wondered about Ioan and Viorica; Ioan had the red face of a drinker, and looked as if he could get mean. But mostly Mama sat silent, smiling her watery smile, sometimes shrugging with despair, sometimes weeping. I often caught her watching me, wondering about me, her dead son's English friend, and sometimes she caught my eye and again moved her hands from her heart upwards.

Viorica laid the table and politely urged me, Andrei and Ioan to eat. She and her mother would not join us. Andrei reached past me and dragged over a fourth stool. 'For George,' he said, now a bit drunk, and we both burst out laughing and toasted the chair. 'George!'

Andrei wobbled his head sagely. 'Ceauşescu is dead, and George is dead.'

'Yes,' I agreed, 'it's true.' And that was the pity of it. If only George had hung on for two and a bit more years. What was it he had written to me? *They steal everywhere and I don't like it. What does it mean? It means I'm not a man of the times, and I'm not strong enough to change the times. Yes, now if you want a good life you are forced to have a dirty consciousness. But the lie, the stealing, the soul murder, all that must have an end.*

It had ended, but only for George.

Andrei stood suddenly, kissed my hand and strode away, banging the door behind him. Our conviviality ebbed in his wake, and Ioan reasserted his authority: he was now the man about the house. He bored me with questions about salaries and prices in Britain. As for him, he worked as a driver for a factory making lights in Rădăuţi. It was a hard life. He left the house at 5 a.m., walked to the station in time for the six o'clock train, reached Rădăuţi at seven, then reversed the journey every evening: four hours travelling, five days a week. Once home he helped Viorica and Mama to draw water from the well and to feed the animals; no wonder he looked so much older than twenty-seven.

Outside with the animals Ioan and Viorica seemed happier. They leant on the wooden stalls in the barn, laughing down at three piglets that were squealing in their pen. Viorica lifted a hen off a bed of straw to show me her chicks, all thirteen of them – breeding Romanian-style – and then cried with delight when she spotted two eggs, on which she pounced. Above us clouds of hens roosted in the rafters. They also had two cows, which Viorica milked each morning. She was the perfect peasant wife: strong, quiet, respectful and endlessly hard-working.

Viorica protested when I did as she did and left my mud-clogged shoes at the door. I was used to leaving my shoes at the door in other houses, a lingering Turkish influence which protected the carpets, a sensible custom if you could stand the smell of people's feet. But here, as honoured guest, I was permitted to spread filth about the house, and Viorica considered it degrading for me to slip about in my socks. When I insisted, she lent me a pair of her slippers – our feet were the same size. A sort of bond had been formed with the two of them in the barn, and now Ioan and I sat contentedly at the table for an hour or so. I was surprised to see they had a television. Running water no, but electricity and TV yes. It was black and white and crackled high in the corner opposite the bed. Ioan watched adverts for things he could never have, and asked me to come back next year with a colour one.

The room was cosy, lamplight enriching the already deep purples and reds of Mama's floral weavings which lined one wall, and the black and white ziggurat-patterned cotton which lined another. Every surface was decorated. Ceaușescu had encouraged the folk element, particularly to emphasise the Romanian – as opposed to Hungarian or German – heritage of Romania. On my last trip I had bought a book called *Sweet Bucovina* with photographs of dance troupes in folk costumes (the men ridiculous in tights), flashing white teeth and posing incongruously in front of the modernist blocks of Suceava's Republicii Square, entitled ' "Idyll" – a symbol of youth and love'. But at the Cupars' house there was nothing folksy or twee; this was simply how they liked to cover their walls, as their families and neighbours and neighbours' families had done for centuries. Viorica whizzed along the sewing machine making more napkins. At her mother's suggestion she gave me one, and another for 'the husband'. There was talk of me returning the following summer and Mama said that if I brought the husband with me we wouldn't mention George, as if he was our secret. She was disappointed when I assured her that the husband knew all about George already; to her that belittled our romance, and she was even a bit shocked: in her world women did not go around kissing every frog to see if he would turn into a prince.

There was a bright moon and a pallid TV and, underfoot, scuttling mice. Only I took any notice of the mice, though I tried not to.

When I asked for the *toileta* Mama and Viorica exchanged glances, and it was with reluctance that Viorica gave me a torch; I didn't wish to embarrass them, but I had put off the evil moment long enough. The cold night caught my throat. There were no street lights and for a moment the darkness was so thick and velvety I could almost put out my hand and stroke it. I slithered across the mud and cow shit towards the pile of logs, whose cut ends glimmered, and skirted the wall of the barn to where I had noticed a wooden cabin, the latrine. It consisted of a plank with a hole in it over a pit, and some torn-up sheets of newspaper; I would have preferred to switch off the torch, but I needed to see where I was going, and my eye was caught by maggots seething in the pit, which had not been emptied for years. Things had gone to pieces here. Even so, it seemed less squalid than the half-hearted attempts at hygiene in the hotels, decaying and light bulb-free with black beetles skittering across the floor. I like my hotel bathrooms a sanitary white, preferably with a loo seat wrapped in a sheet of paper stamped with the reassuring word 'disinfected'. But this latrine was so basic it was animal, and therefore natural; and it didn't smell. It was hard to equate George's peasant background with

141

his high-minded learning and romance, but I could almost hear him saying, 'I am a man too, after all.'

Before going to bed no-one bothered to wash, so I didn't either. The bucket of water was kept in the room beside the front door, which was too bitterly cold to linger in, let alone undress. Ioan and Viorica said goodnight and closed the door on the end room. The walls were thin, allowing the newly-weds virtually no privacy; how Mama had managed to conceive and raise seven children here was hard to imagine. She had returned to her eyrie on the stove. She invited me to join her, so I stood on the bed and levered myself up; the stove had gone out but the tiles retained a lingering warmth. I sat on the edge with my legs dangling over the side while Mama sighed and stroked my hair, murmuring '*Frumos*.' She planned to spend the night up here, leaving her bed to me, but the tiles were hard so I begged her to share the bed, and she agreed. I slid down and she watched me undress – her son's lover, however innocent – and I hoped she didn't notice the holes in my long-johns. '*Frumos*,' she repeated. Her mouth dropped open in undisguised astonishment when I took out my contact lenses. I kept on my T-shirt and the holey long-johns and slid under the quilt; the mattress was hard, and lumps dug into my ribs and hips.

'Turn the light out,' Mama said, and she slid off the stove and down into the bed bedside me. She patted the blankets around me, but we kept a good distance apart. I dreaded her rolling over.

It was a terrible night. I was rigid with cold but could not bring myself to get up and put on more clothes because:

1. I would wake her
2. I was too cold to move
3. She might have felt criticised
4. I might have trodden on the mice.

The mice kept me awake, as did her snoring, which was loud.

Viorica and Ioan had been too poor to pay for wedding photos, so I shot a roll for them the next morning. They spent an hour preparing. Viorica tried on different outfits (Mama proffering advice from the bed) and when they eventually emerged on the doorstep Viorica was smart in a dark blue dress, white scarf and white high heels which flattered her shapely legs, while Ioan was stiff and unsmiling in a grey suit. They posed side by side, but did not touch or even look at each other; in fact, Ioan indicated that he preferred to be photographed alone. This time he changed into matching blue jeans and jacket recently brought back from Poland; he preened in front of the mirror, fancying himself in the denim look. I wondered what kind of life Viorica had in store with him – he was selfish and did not care about her – and I insisted on photographing her alone as well. She changed into her traditional dress which she wore every Sunday, a hand-woven wrap-around skirt like a warm northern sarong, dark blue shot with gold and edged with red, and held tight with a scarlet cummerbund. She wore it with a shirt of translucent cotton embroidered with black, and a little black and white sheepskin waistcoat. She looked dignified and strong, but she tucked her hands into the armholes of the waistcoat and bit her lip; she wasn't used to being made a fuss of.

When we went inside I asked Doamna Cupar about the forsythia branches woven into the fence and sticking out of the gatepost. She had put them there, she said, on St George's Day, in memory of her son.

My plan was to stop by the market in Bucov and then to make my way to Putna. Mama said, 'George had so many friends in Putna, they'll be happy to tell you about him. They know more than I do. Speak to the Father Superior. He'll tell you all about George.'

Before leaving I slipped an envelope of 2000 lei on to the table near the front door. It was two weeks' wages, not a huge amount, but all I could afford. Ioan noticed the envelope and got excited. 'Dollars?' he breathed. He tried to look inside to see how much, but I repeated that it was a small present for Mama, and only for her. Ioan became much friendlier now.

He and Viorica took me to the market. It was a long walk and we picked our way over ruts of dried mud in the lanes between the houses. People were returning from market on bicycles or on foot or clopping along in horse-drawn carts with apple-tree saplings wobbling on the back and a piglet and bags of chicks and potatoes.

'*Hristos a înviat!*'

Viorica would respond, '*Adevărat a înviat!*' But her nod was tight; she had no spontaneous warmth, kept herself to herself.

The lane led to a patch of ground squared by poplars. The market had nearly ended but stragglers milled around tables mounded with badger-striped pumpkin seeds. Ioan was concerned that I should have supplies for my journey to Putna – from the back of a van he bought flat grey bread, sheep's cheese and Russian chocolate which tasted of plastic. As it turned out I was grateful for them later, but he would insist on barging in front of me and paying for everything himself. He became the grand host, flourishing wads of blue notes and refusing to let me reimburse him, then even trying to force me to accept money for the wedding photos. Perhaps he felt rich with the prospect of the hundreds of dollars he thought I had left behind. I found him overbearing and was relieved when he left me and Viorica to make our own way to the station.

'You go home too,' I urged her. But Ioan had told her to accompany me, and she dared not disobey.

Wooden planks raised six feet off the ground and strung along cables swayed into the distance: it was the longest suspension bridge I have ever seen. It traversed a mile-wide valley, a myriad of streams, shingle, grazing sheep and reeds clotted with flood detritus, and it swung dangerously as other walkers clumped towards us and squeezed past, many wheeling bikes. I gripped the sides of the bridge, top-heavy with my rucksack, afraid of being bounced over.

Only when we reached the railway did I understand that there was no train, and that we would have to walk the remaining ten miles to Putna. Again I tried to persuade Viorica to leave – I could manage alone – but again she refused, and instead tried to drag my pack off my back so that she could carry it. We had a tussle in the road. I won and kept the pack, but then she tried to thrust the photograph money into my pocket, and I tried to run away.

'Either I go with you to Putna, or you take the money,' Viorica bargained.

I preferred her company to her lei.

'Ioan will be angry with me if you don't take the money too,' she said. Again she tried to thrust it in my pocket, again I evaded her, so she threw it in the road. Blue notes fluttered to the ground. 'If you won't take them, we'll just leave them there,' she announced.

'OK.' I walked quickly away, not turning round to see if she picked them up. Viorica puffed after me, genuinely concerned.

'You can always tell Ioan that I took the money.'

She looked shocked. Then she asked, shyly looking up from under her headscarf, 'What do you think of Ioan?'

I said I thought he was handsome, not a complete lie. He did have a certain presence. She agreed. She loved him, even if he did not love her.

'And my mother?'

'She's a wonderful woman! So warm and gentle and good.'

'You think so?' Viorica looked dubious.

'Yes, I think she's wonderful.'

Viorica shrugged and turned away. I was surprised by this reaction from the dutiful daughter and wondered if there was something I didn't know, perhaps connected with George. But I couldn't bear to doubt Doamna Cupar, of all people; she had been so genuinely torn apart by George's death and was one of the few people I felt I could trust absolutely. Perhaps Viorica had something she wished to tell me; for the moment, however, I chose not to hear it.

In September 1979 George had sent a postcard to Ali, 'Princess of Cornwall', written on this road between Bucov and Putna:

A young man is looking for the foot marks of his true friends
But they left no rut, no trace behind.
It's autumn time now but the leaves are still green
Today he's free, tomorrow who knows what could happen to him?

Now he's alive and kissing fanatically their pictures
He's weening to write a letter to England.
Your friend and obedient knight.

I was excited about returning to Putna, and also about being amongst people – soul-mates in a way – who shared my concern for George and all he stood for – learning, sensitivity, romance – in this otherwise brutal world. The Cupar family loved him, but only his fellow monks, educated as highly as he was, could have understood him. Anticipating the warm greeting I would receive, the camaraderie with George's friends, I enjoyed the walk. When the sun got high, my pack heavy and our feet sore, we flagged down a car and sped the final mile to the village.

Apart from the name and address of a renegade priest who lived 170 miles away, I left the monastery with nothing. The monks had refused to speak to me, had given me no information, no solace. The only glimmer of light was shed by the red-bearded Brother Gregoriu, who had barely known George but did at least treat his memory with respect.

'Was George taken forcibly to Costina?' I had asked him as he steered me towards the gate. 'Against his will?'

'Yes, most certainly.'

'Do you mean that he was a political prisoner?'

'It's difficult to say. Perhaps.'

'But I understood that political prisoners were not taken to Costina? A doctor told me Costina was only for the seriously insane.'

Gregoriu stopped and answered softly, choosing his words with care: 'Listen. If George went mad it was because he couldn't accept the situation he found himself in. Leading a double life. All those lies. That's what drove him mad.'

'How did he die?' I whispered too.

'No-one knows.'

'Did he have TB?'

'No. He had no lung trouble at the end.'

146

'Was it suicide?'

'It's an enigma.'

On checking into the hotel near the monastery I discovered that I had left my passport in Suceava. Although the receptionist was kind and rang the Hotel Bucovina to establish its whereabouts, this was almost the final straw, though not quite. I humped my pack around the ground floor. The terrace was deserted and had an unprepossessing outlook over a few rotting *cabanăs*, yet this must have been the sun-gold setting for my first meeting with George. Gone was the throng of drinkers, gone the brown felt hats, gone George.

It was here that George would have waited for me day after day in August 1980, sitting over a bottle of wine, watching the road, dreaming of escape.

The entire restaurant had been block-booked by a wedding party so, I was informed by a forbidding-looking waitress, there was no dinner. I retreated to my attic room. Here there was no hot water – or indeed any water at all. No food, no water and the loos clogged and unusable. There was also no heating, and the attic was ice cold; my breath huffed over the window as I leant on the sill and stared miserably out over the tree tops and back towards the monastery. The view was exquisite – the white self-contained monastery, the sprawl of black mountains – but it was swamped with grief. It was the pity of it, the wasted life, the suffering. Now that I was here again George revived so vividly in my mind – I could almost see him pacing the monastery, black robes billowing, face in a book – but he was dead. I could have helped him but did not. Yes, George had been important to me, but not important enough – or at least not as important as he should have been. I wept against the window, pity for George wrestling with self-pity. Odd how grief, unlike joy, often has an echo of narcissism. I wept, but at the same time watched myself weeping; I almost exulted in being able to feel such delicious sorrow.

I lit my primus and warmed my hands over the flame; fortunately there was enough water in my water bottle to brew a cup of hot chocolate, which I drank in bed. The bed was piled high with every blanket and duvet (all dirty) which I dragged off the other four beds in the room. Downstairs the wedding party got underway, friends shouting and banging doors and calling to each other whilst dressing for dinner; their jollities increased my loneliness. I would have reread George's letters and tried to feel close to him, but now I couldn't even do that.

The next morning – a Sunday – I returned to the monastery and spread-eagled against the church wall in the sun, thawing out after a freezing and sleepless night. The church was blinding stone without, a chill cave within, and against my back I could feel the resonating voices of the faithful. I felt myself uncoiling, and removed some of my six layers of clothing before going inside.

Unlike many of the Bucovina churches, little remained of Putna's frescoes, but this gave it an unusual purity. Arches divided the church into intimate chambers. It was early and the priest, splendid in blue and gold robes, chanted prayers, while a younger novice swept the floor. George would have done that: this was his church, his Sunday. He too would have cleared the old stubs out of the candle tray in the naos, then led the prayers and read the day's texts from a leather-bound Bible. I lurked in the pronaos, out of sight. Older monks, standing, sitting, collected in the apses on the north and south walls. As they rattled through the prayers the priest opened the gilded doors to the inner sanctum and closed the curtains behind him. His rites, too sacred for us to witness, were flung up against the curtain in gigantic shadow play by a diagonal of light. His high hat bowed to the chalice before he raised it to his lips. Still hidden, he began a sonorous chant, echoed by the monks. Then he swept aside the curtain, pushed open the doors and sent billows of sanctifying incense towards the icons and over the bowed heads of the faithful who knelt and made the sign of the cross. He disappeared again, to re-emerge with a Bible between his hands. He processed around the church with ancient dignity while the bearded monks bowed and crossed themselves once more. The monks moved forward as one and knelt, their faces tilted, and the priest emerged yet again. This time he held a golden chalice and a dish of bread draped in a gold cloth, not unleavened bread or hosts but white bread baked that morning, and white wine. Each monk dipped a morsel of the bread into the wine.

In from the fields, an old monk stood in the pronaos, his habit hemmed with dried mud, rubber boots caked in it. His long white hair hung in a cue down his back, straight as a plum line.

A dark corner beside me was occupied by a nun who had spread out a mat on which she knelt and prayed, her body bent forward like a Muslim's. In front of her was a stern icon of a haloed saint, flattened against a dark background. Her prayers were reserved for him alone. I wondered if she saw the icon as a portrait of a man – there was his face, firmly delineated, stern, yet passive, and his well-moulded hands – or more as an abstract representation of holiness. He had no individuality. His features were familiar from every other icon: heavy-lidded Byzantine eyes, long nose, rounded chin and shapely lips. His identity would have been indicated by his saintly attributes, like a soldier's badge of rank, but they had vanished under layers of dirt. Even so, the icon was charged with a spiritual intensity, and this was what drew the nun so close. Perhaps she saw him as both individual and symbol, a real man who had been transfigured by holiness, a man who occupied some mysterious space between abstraction and reality, not yet God but poised between godliness and humanity.

George, as a priest, had attempted to occupy such a space. He expected so much of himself but in the end his human frailties dragged him down. *I'm a man too, after all.*

He would have prayed before this very icon. George was different, but was there something in the general Orthodox make-up, I wondered, that felt safe with the icon's conventionality, its lack of individuality, the *we* as opposed to the *I*? Western art has always sought to break with convention; icon painters have done the opposite, maintaining the same basic language of images year after year, century after century. Did this represent some inherent Romanian will to conform, which could help to explain the last forty years of history and, in the sacrifice of the individual to the community, George's death?

Perhaps. Perhaps not. They conformed, yes, they had raised their arms in sycophantic union, but in some ways they are great individualists, the Romanians, each with his or her own opinion.

Was there another connection then between the Orthodox reverence for the icon and recent history? After all, Ceaușescu became an icon for the masses, his portrait paraded on billboards and banners and on the front pages of books, even emerging (people joked) from under the iron on your shirt. He too occupied the realm between holiness and reality, a man and yet not a man. That he was so physically unprepossessing was immaterial; what mattered was that he represented the abstract qualities of – what? Not spirituality, certainly, but paternalism, leadership, intellect, power. Perhaps (I mused) the Romanians' Orthodox background gave them a *tendency* to hero-worship. . . .

Two hours later I was blinking in the sun.

At dawn I had slipped in and out of dreams peopled by George, and now, as I lingered on the steps, I was disconcerted by a cluster of four young monks who closely resembled him. They each had his dark hair and white skin, the same narrow features and eyes black as Marmite. One of them turned towards me; I half expected him to break into a smile of recognition, and for George's death to turn out to have been just another of the dawn dreams. But his eyes flicked blankly over me and passed on. Another was the novice from the museum who had been kind to me the evening before; he kept his head turned away, yesterday's intimacy embarrassing today. Besides, he had his monastic duties to attend to, and probably found my presence a bore.

The monastery became surprisingly busy. Voices lowered, feet tapping purposefully on pavings, black robes, black beards and black mortar boards cutting out silhouettes against white buildings. The four novices conferred in an undertone, then dispersed on unknown errands. Others, doubtless hoping to impress their superiors with their assiduous attention to duty, only just restrained themselves from running criss-cross the courtyard, their skirts entangling their feet, their genuflections as they passed the church hasty.

Putna must have seemed very like the Cambridge college that George yearned for, an enclosed haven of learning, an intellectual's refuge from both the grossness of peasant life and the pressures of Communism. Like a Cambridge college, Putna had been founded as a centre of learning, intended to attract monkish scholars to its workshops. Here George had his private cell, studied, and took care of the museum. Only now did I see that with this experience he might have settled into Cambridge life much more easily than I had anticipated at the time.

Lay people attending mass bought candles in the church porch and planted their stalks in two beds of sand, one for the living, the other for the dead.

The archives! I ran after the novice as he climbed the museum steps. He turned, faintly irritated at being bothered by me again, and began saying there was nothing more he could do.

'Please,' I said, 'isn't there someone with a record of my friend's time here at least?'

Yes, there was an archivist. Unwillingly, the novice accompanied me back down the steps and into a wing of the monastery. A red-tiled corridor was slippery with polish. Beside each door was a low oven door into which logs were fed to warm the monks in their cells without disturbing them. One door was ajar. The novice knocked and a cadaverous man with long grey hair bundled loosely into a knot peered around a curtain. He stood there, wiping his hands with a smacking sound while the novice explained what I wanted. The old man was deaf.

'HIS NAME WAS GEORGE CUPAR,' the novice bellowed.

'GEORGE CUPAR? WHICH ONE? THERE WERE TWO GEORGE CUPARS,' the monk, attempting to hear himself, bellowed back.

'HE CAME FROM BUCOV DE SUS.'

'THEY BOTH CAME FROM BUCOV DE SUS.'

'THIS ONE DIED AT COSTINA.'

'COSTINA?'

'YES! COSTINA.'

'OH YES, I REMEMBER HIM. HE NEVER BECAME A PRIEST BECAUSE HE MADE A MISTAKE AND HAD TO LEAVE THE MONASTERY.'

'Did you hear that?' the novice asked me. I smiled. That was the right George Cupar, I said. The old man agreed to open the records book, and there were the details of my George Cupar. He came to Putna as a brother on 20 April 1976, aged twenty-two, and stayed on and off until 14 May 1986. By chance, the other George Cupar joined Putna the very day he left, almost as if he had been reincarnated.

The old monk remembered him but knew little. He himself had often been away at the monastery of St Ioan in Suceava, and he recalled George and the other seminarians stopping there to pray on their return from taking exams in Neamţ. One day he received a message to tell George that he had failed his exams. Failed his exams? I found this hard to believe but the monk insisted it was true. After that, he added, George began his 'foolishness'. He made a 'mistake', though the monk did not wish to speak about that. Then he abandoned the monastery. He went off around the country, goodness knows where, and was altogether very ill and crazy. The old monk coiled his long hair around his fingers and apologised for remembering so little.

'HOW MANY MONKS HAVE YOU GOT HERE NOW?' I asked him.

'MORE AND MORE. SIXTY-FIVE NOW.'

'AND THEN, WHEN GHEORGHE WAS HERE?'

'ABOUT TWELVE.'

'SO FEW, AND YET YOU REMEMBER SO LITTLE ABOUT HIM?'

He wiped his hands, smack smack, as if wiping his hands of George. 'I AM VERY OLD. SIXTY-TWO. BLIND IN ONE EYE. MY MEMORY'S BAD.'

'DO YOU REMEMBER FATHER IACOV?'

'IACOV... IACOV... WAS THAT HIS OWN NAME, OR THE NAME HE TOOK?' He leafed through the records book, suddenly seeming dotty, unable to concentrate, flicking through the 'f's and 'g's.

'Look under "I",' I suggested, but he ignored me, carried on flicking.

'NO, THAT NAME MEANS NOTHING.'

I wondered if this was the old monk who Father Gregoriu said had Costina hanging over him. He smacked his hands together again and wandered off behind his curtain. The novice looked at me, shrugged and led me out into the courtyard.

Up the valley the river tightened into a mountain stream; I had intended to cross the mountains on foot to Suceviţa, but George's mother had been so vehemently against the plan, warning of vagabonds and wolves, that instead I made do with crawling through a gap in the monastery fence and up into the dark forest, pine needles crunching underfoot, to sit in a meadow on its edge. From here I could admire Putna's square-walled symmetry. How often George must have walked here and extolled the wonders of nature. I was struck – not for the first time – by how beautiful Romania is, but how tainted. Hidden from the monks, I wept again, and on cue, as if prompted by my mood, the sky thickened and reared towards me over the mountains; thunder reverberated and hailstones drummed on my head, caught in my hair, sprang up from the ground. A streak of lightning: thunder banged overhead. From far below, almost drowned out by this torment, there rose a dirge. A dismal troupe waving banners straggled behind a horse cart which made its way to the village church. It seemed too absurdly appropriate for this to be a funeral, but it was. Later I saw the planks wrapped in blankets which served as a bier, and the wreaths propped against the church wall.

I caught the 'personal' slow train back to Mihaela and Călin, where I was grateful for the comfort, and for being comforted. Although Mihaela had been unsympathetic to the idea of George, I could at least unburden myself to her – and in English. She was motherly and kind, saying she had been anxious about me and insisting on feeding me at once.

Teodora, Mihaela's sister, and her husband Sergiu called in on their way home to Suceava, and when they offered me a lift I accepted that gratefully too. We drove the straight road through leafless poplars which had suspended between them a yellow light-bulb moon; it lit up Teodora's gaunt face and turned her hair silver. We were alone on the road, and the interior of the Dacia created a space in which I felt it was safe to talk about George; I sensed that they would sympathise more than Mihaela did. I had begun to predict by people's clothes what their response would be: suits believed he was a madman, while jeans believed he was the victim of conspiracies. Teodora and Sergiu wore jeans. Sergiu immediately came up with a story about trouble he had experienced with the Securitate over a foreign correspondence. That was different, snapped Teodora, you didn't try to escape. She always contradicted him. OK, so it was a bit different, he conceded. But like George, he had been questioned by the Suceava Securitate and then ordered to terminate the correspondence. Unlike George, he had obeyed. No wonder George was hounded for such flagrant defiance, said Sergiu.

Teodora stared out at the moon. It was bisected now by a cloud which had the peculiar optical effect of elongating it from a circle into an egg. She muttered something and turned her back on her husband. When I went to see them a few days later, Teodora had stormed off after a row. I often wondered if she ever came back.

Sergiu said he knew a major in the Securitate who owed him a favour, and he offered to telephone him on my behalf. I was amazed that Sergiu should be on such intimate terms with a major that he could call him up to discuss a case. Odd to imagine the proximity with which ordinary people lived alongside the Securitate, the way these 'Majors' and 'Colonels' were so feared, yet lived so openly in the community, sharing lifts with neighbours in blocks, looking exactly like everybody else, exchanging polite greetings on the stairs, borrowing bits of this and that. I was to call Sergiu tomorrow.

They dropped me at the Hotel Bucovina. What a pleasure to be back! The hideous low-lying veneer chest of drawers and bedside tables, the stained curtains that no longer met in the middle, the plate-glass windows that no longer slid apart, the sand-blasted plaster walls painted shades of algae green: the room was big and my own and it seemed like a palace. There was a telephone, too, and after only a short wait I managed to get through to London and speak at expensive length to Richard. I told him about George's death and asked him to relay the news to Ali. Only two or three wires linked Romania with the outside world, but that tenuous link hauled me into my own life: it was Richard who mattered, along with our house, our families, our cat. George paled back into a story, a sad but not a real person. In the silence after the call I sat for a long time on the edge of the bed, missing home. Then I wallowed in a bath and strewed my possessions around what was, briefly, my private space, and for the rest of the night tried to preserve my own illusion of escape.

Reality returned when I called Sergiu. The major was not prepared to meet me in person. I was disappointed, but it did seem appropriate that this shadowy major – hear-all-evil, see-all-evil, speak-all-evil – should remain an anonymous voice in the ether. Sergiu relayed that he remembered George's case. In the old days he had been in the habit of going to Putna for meals. The Securitate had access to the monastery's wine cellars, and thus the church kept the Securitate sweet. George had served at table, and his intelligence and courtesy had impressed the major. After being expelled from the monastery, George had had 'medical problems', so was picked up for questioning by the Securitate. The interview took place in the presence of a doctor and was intended to ascertain whether he was politically suspect or simply crazy. They decided on the latter and released him (no mention of any injection). Later, when he tried to escape from the country, he was investigated again, and again found to be mentally disturbed. He got crazier and crazier. The monastery allowed him to do odd jobs until he became too depressed even for that, and the monks persuaded his mother to have him committed. The monks

155

were then gathered together and ordered not to speak to anyone about what had happened.

How brave then was Brother Gregoriu for speaking to me.

Although he remembered so much about his life, the major remembered nothing about George's death. That remained as much of a mystery as ever.

The major added that the Securitate kept no records of cases of this sort. Sergiu explained this bureaucratic blip. It looked bad for the authorities if people tried to escape from Romania. Why should anyone want to leave the Socialist paradise? Attempted escapes like George's simply did not exist. Likewise murders and robberies; they happened in the decadent West, not in Romania. The crimes were hushed up and the criminals enrolled to spy for the Securitate and act as their bully boys. Sergiu had encountered this wilful blindness with regard to backward pupils. He had to pass them, however badly they performed at their lessons, or risk being condemned as a bad teacher. The marks meant nothing – some of the pupils could not read – but still Sergiu had to pass them. Backward children did not exist in the Theatre of the Absurd.

Slowly – it was always slowly in Romania – I made my way to Iaşi. On the train I sat opposite a medical student who addressed me in Romanian in a tone that was curt, almost dismissive. It was a tone I had heard before. In Turnu Severin I had been mistaken for a Romanian interpreter for the Red Cross. 'Translate! Translate!' a Romanian woman had commanded, waving an impatient hand in my direction without bothering to glance my way. I had struggled as best I could – and my Romanian was improving – but eventually I had been forced to admit to my origins. At once the woman became obsequiously polite. Now the medical student did the same. My long dark hair could have been Romanian, but that alone was not enough; after several months I had obviously acquired the ill-fed East European pallor, the tired clothes that had travelled too far and too often. I like to metamorphose into a fly on the wall, to observe without being observed; but that desire was misplaced, I now realised, since Romanians tend to distrust their compatriots.

These days I distrusted them too. Beside the medic sat a stout woman. I hated her old suit which she had moth-balled for fifty years, and the fox fur round her crepy neck, the hat perched on her newly set grey curls, the rings on her fingers hedged in by fat, the gold-lined teeth. She looked the collaborating type, the sort who would have disapproved of George and told tales. Once she discovered my foreignness she probed me, wanting to know where I had stayed in Suceava so as to assess my wealth, something difficult to do with a foreigner since she could not read the language of my clothes.

'I was staying with friends,' I lied.

'Where?'

'I don't know the name of the street.'

It must have been the paranoia in the air that I was breathing since she turned out to be a kindly old soul off to Iaşi to see her grandchildren. There was a child on board and she offered him sweets, then offered me some too.

I was sorry to come down off the mountains of Bucovina, although as a princely seat and capital of Moldavia, Iaşi promised nineteenth-century boulevards and a mass of museums. I was to be disappointed. Iaşi was being torn apart, the streets pitted with rubble and hoardings and nascent modernist blocks. Building sites and dust. I wondered if news of the revolution – supposedly the end of Socialist reconstruction – had failed to reach Iaşi; after all, I was now in the Communist heartland, tucked away up the far eastern side of Romania a few miles from the River Prut, its border with the Soviet Union. Here satellite TV was beamed in from Kishinev in Soviet Moldavia, and trains and buses made regular forays across the frontier. This was where ex-Communist President Iliescu and his National Salvation Front picked up most of their votes.

Lower than Suceava, Iaşi's main appeal was its climate: it was warmer and spring more advanced, the chestnuts sagging under

157

candelabra. But my peripheral vision was blurred: all I could focus on was George and what he had gone through.

I walked straight down Strada Ştefan cel Mare in search of Father Iacov. At the entrance to the Metropolitan church I moved like a somnambulist through a cluster of beggars who waved disfigured limbs and shook crutches at the less generous passers-by. Their pleas and blessings and curses merged into a continuous hum, like the droning of bees. It was May Day, a public holiday, and pickings were rich.

I crossed a formal park dotted with municipal bedding and speared with fir trees to an impressive nineteenth-century Metropolitan cathedral, gleaming white. Shoulder-padded women, matrons in suits, students: Iaşi society was out and tripping up and down the cathedral steps. I laid my hand on the arm of a passing nun to ask her where I might find Father Iacov.

'Father Iacov is with the saint,' she replied gently.

'The saint?'

'Inside.'

I followed her up the steps and paused in the entrance, momentarily blinded by the interior gloom. Glinting gold in a long dark barn of a building, broad flat columns, a sheet of marble floor. A small group stood in the centre, under the dome, attending mass, but most activity was concentrated in a corner on the right where a crowd dipped and ducked and jostled to thrust notes – money or messages, perhaps both – at a priest. The object of their worship was an ornate tomb, in which lay a jewelled coffin. Its lid was raised, and inside the coffin, from under a strip of gold chain mail, waved a tiny skeletal hand. These were the mortal remains of the popular seventeenth-century Saint Paraschiva, a young woman who had died in Constantinople but who had been brought back here in 1889. The faithful pressed her coffin with their foreheads, lips and fingers, mumbling prayers, then turned to the priest who laid a hand on a head in blessing, listened to a prayer, accepted hand-written messages which were to be read over the saint, imploring her to revive the sick or help the needy. Was this man resplendent in black beard and gold-embroidered stole Father Iacov? I stood in the church, still wearing my pack, people buffeting around me, and stared at him. He was patient with these people. Then he looked up and for a second I thought he stared back at me as if he knew why I had come.

He was unapproachable for the moment. I left the church. Yes, a monk confirmed, that was Father Iacov. But he would not be free for two hours.

After booking into a hotel I returned to find Father Iacov taking mass beside the saint. The congregation gathered close and crossed themselves, some on their knees on the ungiving floor. Two men in suits, tenors with rich voices – professionals surely – harmonised the responses. Father Iacov was illuminated from above by a single bulb; he held a crucifix in one hand and as he intoned the ancient words he tilted his black beard, cast his eyes upwards to heaven and turned into a Byzantine mosaic, dignified, melancholy and decorative. His voice resonated with genuine belief. At the end of the service I queued with the rest to speak to him. When I got close I murmured, in English, 'Are you Father Iacov?'

He looked at me, surprised. 'Yes, it is me.'

'Are you free? I mean, can we talk?' My voice came out wrong, hoarse, what with people pressing up behind and listening in. 'When will you be free?'

'What is your name?' He searched my face, perhaps thinking he ought to recognise me.

I told him. 'I'm from England,' I added. 'I'm a friend of George Cupar.'

He did not react to the name. 'Ten minutes. Can you stand ten minutes?'

'Of course.'

I wandered around the church, beneath the colonnade and away from the expansive centre into the dark recesses at the side where wooden fold-down seats lined the walls, the mysterious retreats for contemplation. Here a private form of worship went on. In the unlit gloom the elderly, bow-legged and frail in slippers, kissed the icons and pressed their faces to the walls, whispering prayers.

Saint Paraschiva's tomb was the only concentration of light, and the only church furniture were two ornate bishops' thrones, the gold candelabra hanging low on its golden chain and swinging with ostrich eggs, and a vast gold iconostasis, a wall of saints which soared to the roof and hid from the unworthy eyes of all but the priests and bishop the altar in its sacred, secret place at the east end. Furnishings were sparse yet the church was opulently decorated, grave and ceremonious but not depressing.

Father Iacov was still hemmed in. He would take longer then ten minutes, so I went out into the sun. He must have seen me leave, for he broke through the crowd to follow me.

'Don't go away,' he said. 'Ten more minutes.' He had kind eyes, a beard streaked with grey, and hair shorter than usual, not tied in a ponytail. I had an impression of largeness, although in reality he was not much taller than me; it was bulk, exaggerated by his robes, and, I sensed, a largeness of spirit. I liked him instinctively.

Eventually he joined me on the steps.

'We have a couple of hours until I'm back on duty. Shall we go to my room?'

We crossed to one of the white Metropolitan buildings that overlooked the church. They were modern-ish and institutional, a monastery for a city, very different from the intimate spaces of Putna up its bud-like valley. We paused for a nun to kiss Iacov's hand and give him a brown paper bag, its sides translucent with grease. He thanked the nun warmly, without the usual priestly hauteur.

Father Iacov's quarters consisted of a tiny bathroom and a small bed-sitting room. No ascetic's cell this, but a study encrusted with stalagmites of books. They grew from every surface, from the floor, the table, the bed, the bedside table, from the top of the cupboard and even from the windowsill. Teetering columns: we edged round them, Father Iacov lifting his skirts out of the way. He apologised for his English and said he preferred to speak French; we ended by shifting between the two and occasionally into Romanian.

'Now, let's see. Another chair.' He lifted a stack of books off a seat and peered around him for a space to put them; he eventually pushed them under the table. Then he settled his robes around him and smiled benevolently at me. 'So, here we are. From England, you say? Well, well. Well, well. Let's see what we have here.' He opened the paper bag and unwrapped a parcel of bread and meat. 'For you. Please.'

'No, no, it's your lunch. I couldn't.'

'Well, if you won't, then I won't either.'

'Please don't mind me. I expect you're hungry after standing there all that time beside the saint.'

'It is tiring,' he admitted. But he refused to eat, even though I heard his stomach rumble. The food sat between us, smelling delicious, until we left the room.

'So you're from England,' he repeated. 'That means you could help me get some books.'

'I'd be happy to.'

He was interested not only in modern languages, but in ancient ones too and had undertaken the massive task of teaching himself the languages of every great world religion: Greek, Hebrew, Sanskrit, Chinese, Japanese, Latin and Arabic. But he also wanted medical books and dictionaries, encyclopaedias of religious texts, and a biblical concordance translated from the German. What he wanted above all was an *Encyclopaedia Britannica*. And how about a book of early religious poetry? His voice dropped, so excited was he by the prospect, so hungry for knowledge. He didn't mind if the books were second-hand. 'I am a scholar, not a bibliophile,' he said. 'We can't get any of these books in Romania. I just want to read them and have them in my library.'

I weakly offered to see what I could do.

'And could you get me an invitation to visit England? To see Cambridge, and the British Museum? I've heard it's more difficult to get into England than into any other occidental country. I'm fed up with humiliating myself at these embassies and being told that I am not wanted in your country. But you could tell the officials that I don't want to live there or be a refugee. I simply want to see.'

'Of course.'

'Thank you. You are very kind. It's so terrible for me to have to ask you these things when I can offer nothing in return. Won't you take this painted egg?'.

I shook my head.

'What about this icon? And this?' He pressed on me a crude modern icon on glass, and another on wood.

'No, but thank you. I can't carry any more.'

'Please. What else can I do?'

'Don't feel you have to give me anything. I'd like to help you. And you are giving me something when you tell me about George.'

'If you can send me these books I shall be eternally grateful. I've heard that you can get the *Encyclopaedia Britannica* on microfilm now, little diskettes.'

He had no conception of the costs. 'I'll see what I can do. But I wanted to speak about George.'

'George who?'

Not a good start.

'George Cupar. That's why I came to see you.'

'Ah . . . George!' His face softened, his voice hushed. '*George. George était une case unique . . . unique . . . et fantastique.*' His eyes gleamed. '*Une intelligence fantastique.*' Iacov studied me for a moment, suddenly suspicious. 'You know he was very ill?' He tapped his head.

'Well, yes, that's what I wanted to talk about.' To encourage him to trust me I revealed how much I already knew. He listened, nodding from time to time, and shaking his head sadly.

'He was really a friend of my brother's. I didn't know George as well as he did. But the stories my brother used to tell me about the times they spent together!' He laughed. 'Amazing stories. Amazing. They were students together. I was a few years older.'

'When did you know him?'

'I knew him at Putna between about, let's see, say 1976 and when he left, in 1979. Then on and off after that. I was there fourteen years. I was the official guide at Putna and I ran the museum, but I let him help me because he spoke such excellent English, even though he wasn't qualified. He took this work very seriously. He was

162

still training then. He wasn't a monk. Don't say he was a monk because it wasn't true. He was still a student, training to be a priest. Like me. I am a priest, not a monk. It's an important difference. I can marry and have a family. But at Putna, and here in Iaşi, we live according to monastic rules.'

'About George . . .'

'Oh George, George. He studied and read all the time, and wrote. I encouraged him to write. Wonderful poems, and prose.'

Iacov veered off to talk about his own studies. He was nervous and overexcited and I kept having to steer him back to George.

'I used to hear him writing late into the night, and reading. Sometimes he would come to me and read me what he had written, or recite it.' He peered at me and whispered, '*Il était un génie. Un génie.*'

'What do you mean by that?'

'George was a poet. A true poet. I mean that he looked for the true names for things. He tried to speak the truth.'

I explained that I had travelled with George around Romania, but Iacov was too agitated to listen. 'George desperately wanted to come to Cambridge to study,' I added.

'Of course, the great dream! The great dream for all of us. You know the trouble is that we lost touch after he left Putna. He used to come back and do odd jobs when he was in and out of hospital, and he used to come and see me, but we didn't talk that much. Then his death . . .'

'How did he die?'

'Nobody knows. I remember about four of us from Putna went to assist at his funeral, but nobody talked about the manner of his death. It was a dismal affair. Pathetic.'

'I want to see Costina.'

He drew in his breath. 'Costina! You do? That place! Hell. Hell on earth. Worse than Auschwitz! If you aren't crazy when you go in you certainly are by the time you get out – if you ever do. Or so I've heard.' Costina's reputation was as a dumping ground for outcasts, a snake pit.

163

'I want to go there,' I said. 'I've got to find out what happened to George.'

'You realise it's basically a prison?'

'But surely times have changed? The revolution . . . they've got nothing to hide any more.'

'That's the point. Times haven't changed.'

'So you mean I can't just turn up.'

'You'll need permission. And if you do get in you'll find it very hard to discover anything about George.' He leaned towards me over the table and said in an undertone, 'I myself only narrowly escaped the same fate. I was due for it. If it wasn't for the revolution that's where I'd be now.'

'About George . . .'

'George! I find it hard to talk about him. It takes me by the throat each time.' He clutched his throat and stared at the sky. 'It was such a tragic case. He was taken by the Securitate again and again. When he was guiding tourists around Putna he refused to toe the Party line. We both spoke the truth about religion, about the monastery, the buildings, not the Socialist nonsense they expected of us. We spoke the truth about life in Romania. But there was always a Securitate man around, in the car parks, in the church, listening.'

'I imagine that some of the monks themselves were Securitate agents, or informers?' The monks were resplendent in their beards and robes, but some, I now suspected, were hypocrites, little more than curators of a monument, who accepted veneration which was not their due. The Patriarch himself, enthroned in Bucharest, was despised by many people for having willingly collaborated with Ceau-şescu and for having joined the revolution only once its success was no longer in doubt.

'No,' Iacov said. 'Not the monks themselves. I am convinced of that. But outsiders, hanging around. I also had many warnings from the Securitate. They used so many different methods to frighten us. One day, for instance, I was contacted by the police to say that a group of English tourists were on their way to Putna, and that I was to watch out for their guide because he was a suspect person. They

164

called me several times, stressing their worries about this guide. The tourists arrived and they were the usual scruffy bunch with long hair and tatty clothes, like tramps. Odd this, when they had so much money they could have looked like royalty. Anyway, they went ahead into the museum and while they were looking at the embroideries and icons I whispered to their guide that he had better look out because the Securitate were after him. "Oh?" he said, drawing a card out of his breast pocket. "That's strange." On the card was written: "Lieutenant Colonel of the Securitate." It was all a horrible trap. So you see, we couldn't trust anybody. Anybody. Not even ourselves. That's what tore George apart.'

'Did you know about this injection?'

'He was certainly injected, yes, though I don't know what with. It was one of their methods. George's problem was that he became more and more moody. Depressed. Perhaps it was connected with the moon. About once a month, and I think it was always during the full moon, he had a sort of crisis. He closed in on himself, became utterly silent. Then it was impossible to get any sort of response out of him. He was locked.'

George a lunatic? I remembered 'that wonderful night', our last together in the mountains. There had been the most magnificently full moon, and he had been far from 'locked'. He has been passionate, dangerous. But the point was that Iacov did consider him to have been mentally disturbed. He said: 'George's problem was that he was never supported by his family.'

'What do you mean?'

'They didn't help him. They had him interned.'

I couldn't bear to blame his family. I explained that the mother was bringing up seven children, had no money, had been convinced by the *miliţia* that Costina was lovely, but Iacov looked sceptical. I said, 'It's so terrible what I am hearing because you see George asked me to marry him and if I had it might have been all right and he would still be alive now.'

Iacov stared hard at me. 'So it was you!' He laughed. 'George spoke to me so often about his English friends and I sensed with my personal radar that he wanted to confess something, but he never did. Then he gradually closed in on himself and it was too late.'

'I think he had some other trouble with a woman?'

'Ah. You know about that too.'

'George told me something.'

'It was when he was still at Putna. Before 1979, I don't remember when. George got drunk and smashed a window at Putna and escaped to a bar in the village. Then he drank some more and went off with some woman. That was really the start of his problems. He had broken his vows. You know, I think it's possible that the Securitate set the whole thing up to disgrace him.'

'How could they do that?'

'All sorts of ways. They got him drunk, they provided the woman – or at least put temptation his way. It would be their sort of thing. It's possible even that the woman invented the story, came to the monastery complaining "look what he did to me".'

Neither of us mentioned the word 'abortion'. It was too indelicate.

'Isn't that a bit far-fetched?'

'Nothing is far-fetched here. You've got to see things in context.'

Iacov explained that the monasteries were a particular worry for the Securitate as they could have become hot-beds of unrest. The church was always held in the deepest respect by the Romanians, who were naturally religious people, and the monks and priests were invested with an authority – and of course with the possibility of preaching to an audience – which could have been used to incite revolt. As it was, eventually, in Timişoara. Monasteries could have become cells of discontent, and they held enormous potential power. They were to be watched with special care.

The church was too entrenched in Romanian life to be abolished altogether. Though discouraged – religious teaching was forbidden in schools and dismissed as propaganda – it was allowed to exist. Above all, the church could be made use of: priests, for example, could be used to report people's confessions to the Securitate. The church was kept in a stranglehold by the state. The two had long been linked. When Iaşi's elected prince, Alexandru Cuza, united the principalities of Moldavia and Wallachia to form Romania in 1859, the church was found to be richer than the new state, so in 1863 monastic land was duly expropriated. As the monks could no longer support themselves, they were given specific jobs with salaries which were paid by the state. The monks became monastic guides – like Iacov – or monastic chauffeurs, shepherds, gardeners. The result was that they had no time left for the real work of an Orthodox monk, which was contemplation and prayer.

When Romania was declared a People's Republic in 1947, this system continued. The respect that Party Secretary General George Gheorghiu-Dej held for the church was maintained during the early years of Ceauşescu in the mid-1960s, although mainly with an eye to public opinion in the West, necessary after Romania had fallen out with the USSR.

' "Look how marvellous we are! We not only allow the church to continue to exist, we even give the monks and nuns a salary," ' Iacov mocked. 'Of course the effect was to control the church and to influence decisions taken in the monasteries. There was always someone watching. In fact the state made it as difficult as possible for monasteries to take in new monks. As they all had to have specific jobs, if there were no jobs available a young man could not be taken in. George was enrolled first as a guardian, and under cover of this he enrolled in the seminary at Neamţ.'

The Communist Party set up a commission to restore the country's historical monuments, both secular and religious. But while they preserved the outside they were destroying the inside, the hearts and souls of the nuns and monks themselves.

'We were in a stranglehold. We had no outside help, unlike the Catholics and Protestants. Think of the Poles,' Iacov said. 'They even had their own Pope.' But the Romanian Patriarch owed his allegiance to nobody. Since 1882 the Romanian Orthodox church had been autocephalous, and once the church was abolished in the Soviet Union there was little connection with the outside world.

'We were on our own,' Iacov said.

'But the Orthodox church was never persecuted like the others. Baptists were not allowed to exist at all.'

'That's true. It was easier for the Orthodox church, but it was not all easy. You see, no-one outside knew what was going on in the Romanian church. Few cared. The Romanians in exile did almost nothing to help because they rarely got together, they were all too suspicious of each other. So the state was able to squeeze us to do certain things or else be destroyed. I tell you this so that you do not condemn us without understanding why things happened as they did. You see, Ceauşescu was on the point of closing the churches. Imagine! The plans were on his desk when he was shot! That was the next thing he was going to do: abolish the church. Remember, it had happened in the USSR.'

'So the Securitate was used to destabilise the church?'

'Precisely. And someone like George, who was young and vulnerable and perhaps a bit unstable himself, was a perfect victim. He could have been set up to discredit Putna. Or else to turn informer. That's what tore him apart.'

'Do you think he did? Turn informer, I mean?'

'I don't think so. But the pressure was appalling. When George used to come and visit me in Putna afterwards, after the incident with the woman, I used to say, "George, why don't you come back to us?" and George would reply, "They don't want me." So I would say, "Wait here, I'll go and see the abbot." But the abbot always refused. By then George had had some other trouble with the police, so the abbot couldn't risk having him back. You can see why, under the circumstances. But I was so fond of him!'

'But he wrote to me that the abbot sent some people to invite him back into the monastery, but he refused to go. He didn't say why.'

'Perhaps the people who came to him were from the Securitate. Perhaps he was afraid of what he might be forced to do for them if he was in Putna.'

'To spy.'

'Maybe.'

168

Iacov was as loose as George's mother about dates: they kept conflicting. It was also an effort to keep him to the point: like so many people, he was desperate to tell me his own story. I decided for the moment to give up the struggle and allow Iacov to flow. I had probed him enough for today and he was like a jug, full to the brim, unable to restrain himself from spilling over.

Like George, he was repeatedly visited by the Securitate, who warned him about his 'attitude' and eventually arrested him. He knew what to expect: Costina. He had seen George disposed of there; now it was his turn. Prison would have involved a trial, which might have prompted protests or dissenting speeches, and the blatantly trumped-up charges might have had political consequences abroad. A mental institution, on the other hand, did away with the right of appeal and access to legal counsel; all that was needed was a psychiatrist's diagnosis, and by then even that had been dispensed with, since at Costina there was no psychiatrist. Iacov, like George, would have been abandoned there, impotent and without hope.

'But I had contacts, you see, unlike George,' Iacov whispered. 'I had studied at the Theological College in Bucharest. I knew people. George was alone. He had no-one to stand up for him, no strings to pull.'

Iacov's friends saved his life. He fled to Iaşi, where he was given sanctuary, but he was warned that his safety depended on his remaining day and night within the church compound and not speaking to anyone other than his closest associates. For sixteen months, until the revolution, he remained under house arrest.

I was enthralled by Iacov's story, but it had its oddities. He had been driven to the Securitate Headquarters in Suceava, where he was interrogated by a tribunal of six or seven uniformed men. They were polite, but menacing, and feeling endangered he became ever more alert to their cunning. So when his inquisitors gave him a cup of coffee, he viewed this cup of coffee with the deepest mistrust. As they left the room, he looked around him, saw a pot plant, and tipped the coffee into it.

'Do you know what happened?' Iacov whispered dramatically.

'What?'

'The plant died instantly. *Instantly.* I promise this is true.'

That familiar feeling of the ground shifting under me. A sceptical voice in my head saying, 'Oh, come *on.*' What had seemed solidly believable was no longer. The image of the *instantly* wilting pot plant was ludicrous. The films Iacov had seen were lower budget than *Gorky Park.* His childish need to exaggerate cast doubt over everything he had said. I even wondered for a second if he himself had been a Securitate informer and if *he* had been the one to set George up. Then I remembered the red-bearded Father Gregoriu in Putna, and the young novice, both of whom had confirmed Iacov's integrity and his persecution by the Securitate. Perhaps Iacov believed it was true; like Ioana, he would have been unable to bounce stories like this off outsiders to assess their veracity. But perhaps – and this was the most absurd idea – perhaps it *was* true. Who was I to doubt anything here in the Theatre of the Absurd? Or anywhere else for that matter?

'Why would they try to poison you? Why not just shoot you and be done with it?'

'The Securitate were much too subtle for that. I would not have died there and then, but I would have been weakened. Perhaps there was something in the coffee that was similar to the injection George was given – and of course it was administered by the same lot of Securitate, in the same place. The idea was to rot your brain or your insides. It was to do with creating a climate of fear. Terrorising the public, intimidating us. Breaking us down. It was clever. We Romanians *are* clever.'

'Yes, I know. But why not just put you in prison?'

'Because it was much more effective to leave people in the community where they could talk about the awful things that had happened to them. It was much more effective than removing people from circulation altogether. And with a bit of pressure, offers of the good life, it was easy to turn informer, which was what they were after. I was offered books, scholarships abroad, you name it. Women, drink, food. That's what they were doing to George. He just couldn't stand it. And now I'm convinced that the Securitate is moving back into place again. I can sense things closing down again.' Iacov's eyes were round. 'For a while the old faces vanished, but now I'm seeing them on the streets again, they're coming out of their holes. We've had about a year without them. But do you know something?' He sat back. 'I don't think about politics any more. That part of my life is over. I just want to stay here and study. I've also found solace in religion.'

There was something very human about this confession, a priest hinting at previous doubts.

'Like many people, I suppose.'

'Oh yes, there are far more people in church these days, since the revolution.'

'Why is that?'

'Why? Partly because it was forbidden fruit, it's still a novelty. But also because people are suffering so much they will turn to anything. I have people coming and asking me to pray for them to get money so that they can have an operation. Imagine! One man came with a prayer because all his money had been stolen and he wanted God, or at least Saint Paraschiva, to help get it back. I know these are stupid material requests, but it shows they are desperate. And I have seen extraordinary miracles performed by that little coffin. But people are suffering so dreadfully! This country is going through an economic catastrophe and there's a spread of anarchy and confusion, I can feel it. The problem is that no-one knows exactly what's going on. But that state of confusion is endemic to Romania. It's always been like this. The mix of East and West here – we have the religion of the East, the language of the West, then we were ruled by the Turks but always felt European. It creates a kind of turbulence, like the meeting of two contraflows, or two seas. What saddens me is that there are fewer young people in church nowadays. It's disappointing, I fear for their future, I really do. They are getting involved in these spurious Eastern religions which they know little about – they have so little information – but it's spreading like a disease. They should make the most of the religion they have! Do

171

you really think you could get me those books?' he asked, disconcertingly. 'You see, what fascinates me so much is the history of the church, and the church fathers. Look, here,' he plucked a book off the floor, 'I'm reading John Chrysostom in the original Greek – it's got the Romanian translation down the side. That's what I'm especially interested in, and in physics.'

'Just to go back to George for a minute . . .'

Iacov looked at me curiously. 'Why exactly do you want to know all this about him?'

'Why? Well . . . because I'm curious, because I want to know who he was . . .'

'And because you loved him!' Iacov clapped his hands in triumph. 'You were right to love him. George was a romantic, like all great geniuses.'

What a splendidly Romanian remark. The sweeping generalisation, the exaggeration, the theatricality, the grandeur. And Iacov was himself a romantic. He wanted me to have loved George: it gave George dignity.

'He was always speaking about his English friends, always, and there was one in particular. I remember it well!' Iacov laughed, delighted. 'So it was you. Oh, Helena!' He leaned over and clasped me to his broad chest, his beard prickling against my forehead. He released me and sat back. 'Do you know what romanticism actually is?'

'The opposite of classicism,' I answered flippantly.

'I'm being serious. It's something I've been looking into lately. It's absolutely relevant to you, you see. Romance began with the Romance language, which is of course what Romanian basically is. Don't you think it extraordinary that Latin imposed itself so strongly on this region when there was already a multitude of different tribes who had established themselves perfectly well here? And when the Roman state had no particular desire to spread the language through their possessions? The Romans were not linguistic missionaries. So don't you think it is extraordinary that so many Latin words have been retained? This is still a Romance language.'

172

'But the word romance goes much further than that.'

'I know! That is what I was coming to. A romance was originally a composition written in a Romance language. I'm referring to the dark ages now. Then it began to acquire certain characteristics. It had to be a narrative story. Well, it had to be like the *Odyssey*. A prolongation rather than an evolution of a story. A mix of supernatural with natural. The juxtaposition of farce and tragedy. Of course above all a quest, although the quester is often led astray, called off on interim adventures. Did I mention love?'

'Not yet.'

'How could I forget love? Of course there have to be love affairs! There must be love. The love interest is usually intricately connected with the quest. Perhaps the cause of it. And religion plays an inseparable part. The love is pure, never coarse. Never. You had the *Morte d'Arthur* in your country, the Germans had Gottfried's *Tristan and Iseult*. There were the *Arabian Nights*. We had folklore, and the lives of the saints. We had Ovid!'

'Here?'

'Yes!' Iacov clapped, applauding my surprise. 'Ovid lived by the Black Sea. He romanticised a great body of classical mythology. The point, or one of the points, is that in Western Europe you had the Renaissance. That killed off romanticism for a century or two. A romance came to be seen as a jumble of ill-told stories – extravagant, outrageous, improbable, childish in their appeal to adventure, totally distorting historical evidence. Goethe made what I consider to be a very crude distinction between classicism and romanticism. He said, "Classicism is health; romanticism is disease." So hard-edged! What one *might* say is that one tends to order and proportion, while the other tends to poetry, the imagination and caprice. Don't you think?'

In his enthusiasm, he did not wait for a reply.

'But you see, we never had a Renaissance as such. Our folkore always flourished. We had our *doine*, our *cantece*, our lyrics and ballads. They never died. Lyrics, above all we had lyric poetry! Love and longing. And it was never flattened by any Age of Enlightenment, any Age of Reason. We never experienced that, so romanticism

173

flourished. Then along came our galaxy of nineteenth-century poets – most of them lived here in Iaşi – and they simply developed that romantic heritage. They enriched it. Our poets were deeply rooted in our ancestral traditions, inspired by our history and by village life. We've never been great novelists. But lyric poets! Oh yes. Always romantics, you see.'

'I'd have thought romanticism and Communism were opposites. The Communist era was your Age of Reason.'

'Not really. Communism has its own romance, the ideal of equality, the self-sacrifice, the hero-worship.'

'Do you mind me asking why you are telling me this? Excuse me, I don't mean to be rude.'

'Don't you see? Your quest for George! Love and religion, interim adventures, much of it improbable? Farce and tragedy? George himself a lyric poet? Don't you see?'

I was laughing now. 'Yes, I do see.'

'You are even conducting most of your quest in one of the purest of the Romance languages.'

'But George was a real person, not a myth.'

'Can you be so sure? No, I'm sorry, I shouldn't say that.'

'Do you mean that I am in danger of romanticising him?'

'Possibly. Maybe I do, too. But that may be a good thing. A necessary thing.'

'Just a pity it's too late for George to enjoy it.'

'Ah yes. Well, there we are.' He sighed, looked at his watch and put his hands flat on the table. 'Three o'clock. I'm afraid I have to go back.' We stood up. 'What about this?' he said suddenly, eyes alighting on a book on the shelf beside his bed. 'I insist you have it. I insist!'

At last he had found something I was prepared to accept: a copy of *Poesii* by Mihai Eminescu. 'You'll find Hindu thought in there, Schopenhauer, folk tales. He is the guiding star of our cultural life, our national poet.'

'Thank you,' I said, very moved. We walked together to the church.

At the bottom of the steps he said, 'Until the same time tomorrow, then?'

'Until the same time.'

'Oh, Helena!' He enveloped me in his reassuring bulk. His robes were perfumed by incense. Then he returned to his sentinel beside the little saint.

I paced the streets, all fired up by the meeting with this burly man brimming with passion, in some ways naive, but also full of sincerity and courage. Above all, he restored George to his status as Special Important Person. I was totally convinced by what he had told me about George, and if there were outrageous and improbable elements, then that, as Iacov had pointed out, made my quest all the more romantic and Romanian.

Iacov was George's father figure; he would have inspired George's interest in the history of the monasteries and Moldavia, and also fanned his doubts about the régime. Perhaps on that score Iacov could be accused of irresponsibility; he was old enough and worldly-wise enough to take care of himself, while George was an innocent, idealistic and unsophisticated. Iacov should have been more circumspect. But who was I to judge? I knew nothing of their late-night discussions in their cells at Putna.

Sitting on the remains of a park bench, I whiled away the hours before I could decently go to bed. The grass was long, dandelions and nettles poked through abandoned flower beds, the benches had been vandalised and ponds had dried up, stray dogs shat and scavenged: it added to my desolation. I felt like crying all the time. That made Iacov's kindness all the more affecting. I turned the *Poesii* over and over in my hands. No present could have been more apt. It was a facsimile of an edition first published in Bucharest in 1884, republished as a centenary edition just before the revolution. The new version was a shadow of the old, a grey paperback decorated with a print of what had originally been an embossed art nouveau cover, but it was still a pleasing object, pocket-sized. The letters danced across the page, the accents over 'a's and 'i's like raised eyebrows, giving the text a surprised look. Sadly, by the time his

Poesii was published, Eminescu had developed syphilis and was going mad. He died five years later, aged thirty-nine.

I wondered how much George had identified with him. Like every Moldavian schoolboy he would have been brought up on the Eminescu myth – the 'Last Romantic' – and learned the poems by heart. Born near Botoşani – not far from Rădăuţi – Eminescu was admired above all because of his nationalism: he was used to impart to schoolchildren a love of their country. But his writing was ambiguous, his symbolism open to interpretation, and since his work was so widely known, that symbolism could be used by Ceauşescu's critics to express their feelings surreptitiously, and to communicate indirectly with each other. I was beginning to realise that this was how George had tried to communicate with me.

The most famous of the poems was *Luceafărul*, 'The Evening Star', which Eminescu himself described as an allegory for genius. Like Hyperion, genius knows no death but shines into perpetuity. On earth, however, the genius is incapable of making anyone happy or of being happy himself; he is immortal, but lacks good fortune. This 'evening star', this 'genius', could also be interpreted by contemporary Romanians as a symbol of the *individual*, the *I* as opposed to the *We*, the uncompromising non-conformist – anathema to Communist society. An English translation published at the same time as the facsimile, during the worst of times before the revolution, was prefaced by a Romanian academic:

> *Cultural history supports the theory that the Romantic genius has always struggled against time. Rising above the contemporary world, his sincerity, lofty thoughts and aspirations inevitably bring him into conflict with society's conventions and prejudices, with philistinism and non-values, with misunderstanding and envy. Therefore posterity cannot help but view the Romantic artist as a hero whose fight and fall acquire tragic significance.*

Brave words! Philistinism and non-values, misunderstanding and envy! The tragic significance would not have been missed in 1989.

George's own honest and revealing words kept coming to mind: *There's such a great difference between papers and reality . . . What does it mean? It means I'm not a man of the times. And I'm not strong enough to change times.* But he added, 'A lot of people say I am a dangerous and unuseful man. But they could be wrong and that's why I don't lose my hope. In fact if I want to be the first, naturally I must be alone and in a manner of speaking the enemy of everybody. He saw himself as the lonely evening star.

Was Eminescu George's role model? The noble, pure, 'heroic' outsider at once proud and uncompromising, the genius facing madness and a young death in an asylum: this was how George saw himself, and was seen by others – by Iacov at least.

'Come on,' said Iacov, taking my arm outside the church. His smile failed to disguise his weariness. He had been at his post since 6.30 a.m., keeping vigil beside the saint for six and a half hours. 'I may feel I'm badly off, but it's nothing compared with what I hear from these people,' he said as we crossed the square. 'They pour out their troubles. There's so little I can do, but I offer prayers and benediction. And when I'm tired I feel the Holy Presence descend and bring peace.' His large brown eyes and soft white scholar's hands were warm; he held my hands in his. 'Oh, Helena,' he sighed, and hugged me against his broad face.

We resumed our positions at his table.

'Listen,' I said firmly. 'I beg you to tell me all you can about George. I have to know.'

Iacov patiently repeated some of what he had said yesterday; I could have heard it a hundred times, like an invocation that might bring George to life.

'I did love George,' Iacov said. 'I saw him as a sort of wayward adolescent, even though I was only a few years older than him. I found myself wanting to protect and look after him, I don't know why. It's funny, isn't it?'

'He had a sort of innocence.'

'Yes, something like that. And he was such a writer! Believe me.'

George, Iacov explained, had a rather unusual status at Putna because he had not arrived there through the usual channels. After he left the *lycée* in Bucov his parents had come to see Gherasim, the Father Superior, to ask him to take George.

'Gherasim saw that George was exceptionally gifted, but the problem was that George needed his freedom. He simply could not cope with being tied down by monastic rules, by being restrained in any way. It was terrible for him. A monastery was not really the right environment for him. So that's why, well . . . now and then he drank.' Iacov was unwilling to betray George's vice. I remembered how he mellowed after a few gulps of wine. He wrote that he felt so exhausted after doing any hard physical work that he had to drink. 'It was just occasionally,' Iacov explained. 'But even a little drink seemed to make him crazy. He had quite a few problems. The main thing was that he desperately needed his liberty. He wasn't strong enough to survive the system.'

'Was he beaten by the Securitate? Did you ever see any evidence of that?'

'Yes, I did once see him with a swollen face. But normally it was invisible. They were clever. The injuries were mostly internal, you see, from being laid out on the ground and beaten with sandbags. It was also rumoured that they had a machine that you were strapped to and which beat you, and when you were unconscious they poured water on you and beat you again. Imagine! Man's inhumanity to man. Imagine what George went through! Beaten until he was broken, threatened. That was all the time he was writing to you. He would have been forced to write that he had joined the police. That was the ultimate horror, being coerced into becoming an informer, then sent back into the monastery to spy on the others. They did all they could to break his spirit. They were like dogs, after him all the time, snapping and yapping at his heels. It was especially bad when he was in that hospital in Rădăuţi: what did you say to whom, what have you written, what did she reply?'

There had been hints of this, hints I had ignored. *Why do I write what's happening every day? Well, it's rather delicate. Perhaps you have*

the possibility and the pleasure to come next year and visit again Bucovina.
Welcome every time friends! But I'm not sure if you will find me at home.
It was that word *delicate* that I, in my clumsiness, had missed.
Abruptly George had launched into page after page of a Communist
history of Romania – victorious proletariat, fighting in a loyal spirit
of self-sacrifice for the common revolutionary cause, a blow to the
imperialistic system, productive forces, working-class movement,
bourgeois landlord, reactionary governments, outstanding patriots,
protest actions of the intellectuals – the language was that of a Party
automaton. I now suspected that he had been forced to write this.
The only glimmer of George came at the end. *But now we live peacefully*
and we don't have territorial pretensions. So they say. Yes, at least so they
say. What, I now wondered, had that last sentence cost him?

'They broke his spirit, and eventually his mind.'

'So you think he was mad in the end?'

'They sent him mad.'

We sat in silence for a while.

'George took me to Neamţ,' I said.

'To Neamţ? You mean you travelled together?'

'Yes!' I had told him this several times.

'You mean you went with George around Romania?' He was
incredulous. For a priest or monk this was unheard of, even with a
fellow Romanian. 'You stayed together in a tent? Oh yes, he had to
have his liberty, that was George all over. He should never have been
incarcerated at the monastery. He was too wild.'

'Can you tell me anything about his attempted escape from
Romania?'

'I didn't know there was one. I knew he wanted to, but I didn't
know he had actually tried it.'

I told Iacov what I knew.

'You see,' he said after a while, 'the problem was that during the
Eighties, after George left Putna, we really lost touch. He used to
come to the monastery sometimes, but we would have to walk past
each other as if we had never met because we knew we were being

watched. We couldn't even speak in private because I suspected that my room was bugged.'

When he begged me to ask my 'authorities' to 'call' him to England (urgently), he said, *'Don't tell them that I have extraordinary qualities, just tell them that I am a man who refused to accept his fate and decided to restore his honour.'* His 'fate' I now understood to be that of collaborator with the Securitate, his 'honour' that of resisting the pressure.

'Did he become an informer then?'

'I don't know. Honestly. Maybe. Under this terrible pressure. But George had to go through it, right to the end.'

'He never told me about this pressure in his letters. Maybe he hinted at it, but I didn't know what to look out for.'

'That's because he was very discreet, and because he loved you. He didn't want you to suffer on his behalf. You see, in the Eighties there was this terrible isolation to add to everything else. And I had troubles of my own to think about.' Iacov's brother, also a priest, had been so badly beaten by the Securitate that his body was broken and he was unconscious for two weeks. 'It was so terrible for my brother that I can't talk to him about it,' Iacov whispered. 'It's too painful. The point is that I was so preoccupied with all this that I lost touch with George. And he closed up anyway.'

'I could have helped him.'

'Yes, you could have. The tragedy is that he could have done marvellous things with his intellect, marvellous things. He was so utterly sincere, so intense, so intelligent.'

'I should have brought him to England.'

'Yes, maybe you should. He would have done marvellous things for England. He could have survived there, or anywhere for that matter, as long as it wasn't here.'

'What would he have done? How would he have survived? I couldn't have supported him.'

'He could have worked at the BBC Romanian Service, in journalism, as a teacher, as a driver – it didn't matter, he could have done it all.'

I had feared that although he said he wanted to escape, in fact he loved his country. He would have left it and in its absence he would have grown fonder of it, and fitted in less and less in England. So one day he would have returned home, only to find that while he had been away his country had changed beyond recognition. He would no longer have fitted in there either.

'That is the fate of the exile,' Iacov replied. 'Stateless. But you see he was a poet. He didn't fit in anywhere, and wouldn't have wanted to. The poet will always be an outsider. At least in the West he would have been allowed to be himself.'

All too soon it was time for Iacov to return to his post. We stood up.

'I'm leaving for Neamţ today,' I said. 'I can't afford to stay in Iaşi any longer. The hotels are too expensive.'

'I'm sorry to hear that.' Iacov held my hand. 'I really am. I really am. But wait! Why didn't I think of it before! You could stay here. Why not? You can stay in my bed and I will stay with a friend.'

'No, no. I couldn't do that. This is a monastery. What if someone caught me here? You might have trouble.'

'Then you can stay in one of the guest rooms. Yes! I can't imagine why I didn't think of it before.'

'But is it allowed? For women, I mean?'

'Wait.' He patted me back down into the chair. 'Wait here. I can arrange everything. You can read a book while I'm away. Here, read this.' He put one of his few English books – a Complete Shakespeare – on to the table and rushed off.

I leafed through it, not sure I had the strength, but my attention was caught by *Timon of Athens*. When George had suddenly changed his mind about leaving Romania, he had blamed his previously angry mood on the influence of his 'former teacher and Timon of Athens'. At the time I had dismissed this as absurd; I knew nothing about his teacher, and had never read or seen Timon of Athens. Now I wondered if the former teacher was Iacov himself, and if, by mentioning Timon of Athens, he was hinting at something which he dared not say directly, Eminescu-style, but which at the time I couldn't be bothered to follow up. I read it now. How Lord Timon boils with rage! Having allowed himself to become susceptible to flattery, when fortune turns against him he discovers the true shallowness of his friends' love. 'Mouth-friends', Lord Timon calls them. 'Policy sits above conscience . . . the devil knew not what he did when he made men politic.' George must have meant Vasile's betrayal of him to the Securitate, or the monks' betrayal, and he was telling me of this in a code which I did not choose to break. The play becomes curiously prophetic. The now misanthropic Lord Timon, having seen through the falseness of his ex-friends, is dismissed by them as mad, and is left to die an outcast in the wilderness.

Iacov returned, breathless, robes flying. 'That's it, then.' I was to sneak back between four and five o'clock that afternoon when the office downstairs was closed. He would smuggle up some supper, and we would talk more this evening. 'I'll come and knock on your door later,' he promised. He showed me my room, on the floor above his: not the usual over-furnished dinginess, but a room airy and white with three white beds, a clean bathroom en suite and a view over the church. I needed purity and cleanliness in this soiled country.

'It's perfect,' I said. We were both lit up, him with excitement about his escapade, me with joy. I had a friend here now, not a 'mouth-friend' but one who was genuinely kind.

At the appointed time I carried my pack upstairs without being noticed and installed myself in the room. When dusk drew in I left the lights off so that when I leaned against the window-sill, looking out, I would not be noticed from below. The open square in front of the church emptied, just a few women tapping in high heels back home; it turned citrus yellow in the evening, lit by distant house lights and the moon.

As promised, Iacov returned. Enjoying the conspiracy, with a magician's flourish he produced from under his black robes a plate of food which he had secreted from supper. A cliff of golden *mămăligă* towered over a white lake of cream cheese. It was delicious. We talked of this and that. He told me that for all the mystery and splendour of the church in Iaşi, and Putna too, only a few places remained where there was any genuine religious feeling, and these were the little *schits* hidden in the mountains, the hermitages.

'That's where people retreat from the world,' he said. 'Five or six monks or nuns. That's where they genuinely pray and contemplate and avoid all contact with politics and other worldly things. That's where I'd like to end my days.'

When he left I felt happy for what seemed the first time in weeks, sniffing the air that rose from the paving after the hot day, the last few monks flitting over the square like bats.

I packed and left, pausing in the church to say farewell to Iacov; with my pack on my back I felt huge, unmissable. Iacov was already in position beside Saint Paraschiva. When I slipped the room key on to his lectern he smiled a smile of complicity.

'Thank you,' I whispered.

He placed his hand on his heart. 'I am very . . . glad.'

'Me too.'

Inspired by Iacov's talk of the spiritual sustenance to be found in the mountain *schits*, I decided to spend some time visiting them. I needed to get away from the misery of George's story for a while, and Iacov urged me to use the seventeenth-century Agapia Convent as a base before going on to Neamţ; Agapia was more healing and cleansing, he said. Trustingly, he gave me some money to deliver to the Mother Superior in payment for a rosary she had sent him, and he also wrote her a letter of introduction.

At the tip of the valley at Agapia Nou my journey ended. The road, which led straight to the convent, was lined with wooden clapboard cottages, like plantation houses. Some were white, others pale blue, each with living quarters upstairs and storage below. Fresh flowers in vases on window-sills, white net curtains looped up over shining windows, Agapia was a village in miniature, a nuns' toytown, in which every detail was attended to, a village of spinsters, thrifty and clean.

The convent itself, like Putna, was built as a protective square around a courtyard garden, and from the heart of it rose the church.

The convent's white outer walls were wrapped on two storeys in brown-painted verandahs, as if held together by two strips of parcel tape. The courtyard was smaller and more intimate than at Putna or Iaşi, and the nuns less worldly than those grand monks. Two nuns lugged a wicker basket of onions across the courtyard, stopping to swap ends and rest their arms before going on with mud on their robes. Another squatted in a flower bed, pulling up weeds. Oh for the simple, secure, well-ordered institutional life. No decisions, no choices. Yet that lack of freedom, the sacrifice of the individual to the community, was precisely what George could not stand. In that sense, joining a monastery was not an escape from Communism, but a case of more of the same.

I stayed here for a while, the time measured in the quarter-hourly rendition of the Easter hymn from the church tower.

Hristos a înviat din morţi
cu moartea pre moarte călcînd
şi celor din mormînturi
viaţă dăruindu-le.

Its amplification was raucous and unmeditative, but I grew fond of the tune.

I was cared for by an English-speaking nun called Maica Lucia. She had never known George but she did know Iacov. He was reputed to be a bit 'crazy', she said, and while at Putna was rarely seen in church. He had many . . . problems. But she was pleased that he had now found God through sitting beside Saint Paraschiva all day long. We talked a lot and, when she was not fasting, ate together in her room. Hunks of roast lamb for breakfast, bowls of nettle soup for lunch, tea of dried lime flowers.

Beyond the convent the valley narrowed into a path that clambered into wild pine forests. They coated the hills around Agapia. The green of the trees was so green it was black; it was pierced by fluorescent green beeches that thrust up between the pines to unroll downy leaves. Evening sun penetrated the canopy in gold bars. Last year's beech leaves crackled underfoot, and cuckoos echoed each other across the hills. The loveliness was almost too much, a painful reminder of George, and of more than George, of an undefiled landscape that in England was lost.

Beside the path was a well, deep and mossy, and beside the well an enamel mug left by some thoughtful nun for thirsty passers-by.

Near the summit of the hill lay an enclosure, an island of sun. In this island stood wooden houses: Agapia din Deal, one of the *schits*. It was a perfect relic of the original fourth-century Orthodox idea of monasticism, of hermits fleeing from the world first to their caves but later, under the authority of an abbot although without distinctions of orders, to a settlement in a wood.

The enamel mug implied that visitors were welcome, so in I went. A tiny church was being rebuilt, part of the flurry of post-revolutionary religious fervour; there was a mess of fresh planks that bounced on each other like spillikins and smelt of pine; sap oozed in amber balls. Inside, the completed parts were tiny and shell-like, encrusted with mosaics. An ancient crone, fist full of candles, asked me if we had many believers in my country. I assured her that we had, and she gave her candles a triumphant shake at the heavens. From high up in her secret enclave she and her fellow hermit nuns could survey the entire forest; it loped away, hill after hill, scarred only by a yellow ridgeback path that zigzagged into the distance.

Below the summit was a glade floored with the softest grass and clumps of cowslips that smelled of musk. Here I lay staring at the sky. There was nothing in it, just emptiness. But down below in Agapia din Vale and up above in Agapia din Deal lived some four hundred nuns and novices; before I went any further, before I went to Costina hospital, I needed to spend some time amongst people like these, good generous simple people, to rid myself of the mistrust and paranoia that were creeping up on me.

Days passed gently. I crossed the mountains to visit Lucia's brother in a neighbouring monastery. He had a Father Christmas beard and tattered robes. He had written a history of the wise men of the Romanian church, and had travelled around the country holding dialogues with these sages. 'Why,' he asked them, 'does God cause the innocent to suffer?' The answers were obscurely theological and meant nothing to me.

I visited more *schits*, one clustered under rocks around the cave of the saintly hermit Teodora. A rain-scoured boulder had served as her bath. The monks were wild-looking and I wondered how their spiritual life could cope with the stream of irreverent Romanians who stomped through their retreat dropping litter. Maica Lucia explained that the monasteries and *schits* depended on public goodwill to remain open at all. Before the revolution Agapia itself had had several altercations with the police, but the Mother Superior was a clever woman. Once, the police had tried to close the church, ostensibly to protect the nineteenth-century Grigorescu frescoes. The Mother Superior had argued that if anyone were capable of preserving the frescoes, it was the nuns themselves. But the police had insisted on closing the church all day. This did not prevent the nuns from holding services, they were simply forced to hold them later in the evening and earlier in the morning. They got into the habit of it, so although the church was now almost always open they still rose for morning mass at 4.45 a.m.

I attended mass at a more civilised hour in the evenings. The church was narrow and dark, lit only by candles which burned around the iconostasis with its tiers of smoke-stained icons. The nuns shuffled forwards from the pronaos, then took turns to break from the crowd to stand alone in the naos and genuflect to the most revered icon. It was a Madonna and child in an elaborate frame, draped with curtains and illuminated with oil lamps which hung with censers and crucifixes. The folds of the drapery and the arms and haloes were encrusted in silver relief, but as if allowing for an intimate glimpse of the real mother and child, the painted hands and faces – the most expressive parts – were left uncovered. The nuns bowed and withdrew to the aisles. The priest, splendid in his gold-embroidered mantle, mortar board high and veiled, intoned the liturgy beneath the dome; behind him the door to the inner sanctum was topped by a carved golden sunburst. It was Bonnington or Alma-

Tadema, the tall black-robed women in the shadows against the walls, some facing the priest, others draped against each other, others seated on the ground, languid and exotic. Like the icon, all that was visible, shining in the gloom, were their pale hands and faces.

Lucia taught Classics and English at the newly opened seminary. She roped me in to teach her pupils English songs. Forty black-robed young women squeezed together behind desks, white faces peeping up from under black scarves. Some had come all the way from Soviet Moldavia – Bessarabia – to study at Agapia, and to return to their Romanian Orthodox roots after half a century of separation. I sang to them and they recorded my renditions on tape; I apologised for my unimpressive voice, but fortunately the acoustics in the stone-walled room were wonderful. 'Barbara Allen', 'Drink to me only with thine eyes'. 'Cockles and Mussels' caused some confusion when the nuns assumed I was serenading parts of the body; 'Dashing Away with the Smoothing Iron' was more successful, particularly when they joined in with the gestures. Sometimes I flitted above the class and thought: what am I doing up a remote valley in Moldavia teaching Orthodox nuns how to i-ron of the linen oh, arms working in unison? Then I dropped back into the moment. We were finally defeated by 'Green Grow the Rushes Oh' and my inability to explain the meaning of the lily-white boys cloth-ed all in green-ho, let alone the six proud walk-ers or the A-pril rain-ers.

When I left, Maica Lucia came to the bus stop and said, 'I have this strange feeling that I want to keep you like an amulet.'

Neamţ: back on George's beat. Beneath the entrance tower two monks sat on a wall and swung their legs. They acknowledged me in an off-hand way. One was a guide of sorts, although unlike George he spoke only Romanian. Yes, he said, I could probably stay, and went to check.

I wandered around. I recalled not the buildings but George's mood, so morose. I had blamed it on us, but now I wondered if the cause of his unease was his disgrace at Putna; this was the first time he had visited his colleagues from the seminary since then.

Inside, the church was grim. Its frescoes had been blackened by a nineteenth-century fire, and those still visible or restored were scenes of horrific martyrdoms. Haloes encased the whole of each saint's head like a spaceman's helmet; they flew from decapitating swords of evil Turks and bounced down steps, blood spurting; others were ravaged by monsters.

Was George such a martyr? Maybe he had no glass-bubble halo round his head, maybe he had vices – his drinking, his affairs – but he did seek to fight for a cause, the cause of his own personal freedom. He wrote of his 'social illness' and his need to settle 'the problems' (presumably with the Securitate) so that we would be granted visas to visit him the following year. *If they refuse my wish, my natural and innocent wish, I shall look for trouble. First I shall write a powerful and awful 'J'accuse'. If I shall not be able to receive my foreign friends without being afraid of police and authorities, then definitely I shall look for trouble. There is the possibility that you can't come again. It's natural, and I must accept it too. Then I shall revenge for they didn't allow me to be a good host in my own country this year.* So it was to be revenge and battle either way. *Yes, now I know that I must fight for peace, for a peaceful life, and I'll do it. It's decided.* He felt that a 'real man' would fight the 'authorities', not succumb to their pressure, and that he did not deserve my love until he had become such a man. He fought, not for any abstract cause, but for his self-esteem. *It's decided: no holiday; the honourable death instead of a life of misery.*

The monk returned. Yes, it was all right for me to stay, and would I like some lunch? In the kitchens, over a steaming vat of lamb *ciorbă*, he introduced me to a monk with ginger hair and teeth, who greeted me in German. 'Hello! My name is Tony!' He said this several times. Tony was drunk. When I asked them about their former colleague George Cupar – you remember, he took his exams here and attended the seminary? – they hadn't a clue what I was talking about.

Tony, with his arm round my waist, guided me into the refectory. It was no longer the dark barn I remembered, but a hall light and airy, plastered and painted, walled with icons and supported by pillars. I sat at the end of one of three stretched refectory tables. I was all alone, a tiny speck. Tony urged me to eat as much bread and *ciorbă* as possible and with wicked complicity he unlocked a cupboard and lifted out a slice of pink cake and a bottle of *rachiu*.

'Schnapps!' We tossed down a glass each and he made me promise to visit him that evening. I wasn't so sure.

He showed me to my cell which was above the refectory, a gloomy room shadowed by the verandah. It was bare and cold and not particularly clean. I missed Agapia. There was something else, he said. I followed him into the cemetery; it was unloved, full of weeds, not interesting. But Tony ignored the graves and led me down into a crypt; I felt like a naughty schoolgirl about to be shown some unmentionable body part. 'There!' he said, sweeping his arm proudly around the room. Its walls were lined with skulls. How appropriate. Some were displayed on pairs of crossed bones, the date of death inscribed on each cranium; several were over a hundred years old. Beneath the shelf were piles of the things. At the east end three important skulls bore the portraits of their original owners; they were exquisite miniatures of bearded faces with high black hats and veils.

Back outside, a monk passed at top speed. I greeted him and he stopped, pressed into my hands a bundle of stuff, then hurried on without a word. There was a small print of an icon in a golden frame, and an Easter card. I stood there holding them, and watched him disappear into the monastery.

I was too shy to enter the refectory for dinner. There would be no other women, and at this time no other visitors either. Instead I sat on the verandah at the back of the building looking at the saturated evening light after a downpour. An old woman joined me to do some washing. She scrubbed clothes in an enamel basin, then hung them on a string to dry.

'Are you alone?' she asked.

'Yes.'

'That's a bad idea. Life's better when you aren't alone.'

'Yes. I agree.'

As if he had sprung from her words, the brown-toothed Tony

189

reappeared. He had brought me a book printed in Neamț in laborious English, about an eighteenth-century Metropolitan called Iacov of Putna, a 'kind and industrious hierarch of a meditative nature, with an infinite love towards the callings of the monastic confraternity'. Tony had inscribed the book with kind words and his address. I was touched by his gift; he wanted nothing in return.

Next morning: glittering mountain light, dandelions sun-yellow pools in the vivid grass. I was full of optimism as I walked to the Neamț seminary, excited about meeting George's former English teacher. The seminary was a scruffy white-walled institution in which three hundred boys spent five years studying before going on to the theology faculty at the universities in Iași, Bucharest or Sibiu. George had been the exception, the outsider, since he had returned to Putna after the exams to continue his studies there. Youths in black suits craned from windows and loitered in an unkempt garden. So many males. One of them led me to the English master, Nichita he was called. He was teaching a class but abandoned it at once, proposing a walk.

My doubts arose when I discovered that Nichita could barely speak a word of English. His French was peculiar too. There were no other language teachers here. Then I discovered that he had been teaching for only one year. He had never known George. Loathsome little man! I felt an overwhelming desire to escape from him, and from Neamț, immediately. A wasted journey. The bus passed, tantalisingly, but Nichita bored on, pausing in the road to continue a monologue, interrupting every time I tried to ask about George. In this way we jerked, stopping and starting, up a fir avenue which prompted Nichita to eulogise about Eminescu. He launched into a recital of 'The Evening Star' and I prepared myself for all ninety-five verses.

I drifted off into a conversation with George. We were here at Neamț. We had left the monastery and were returning to the car, our first day together. Tell me about you, I had asked.

'Me?' he replied, gazing with black-fringed eyes into mine. 'Literature is my passion. My biography is a bibliography. What I am is what I've read.' A good line, I thought. He praised Dostoevsky, Stendhal, Thomas Mann, the romantic Romanian poets, above all Eminescu. I said I'd heard that Eminescu was xenophobic, and George explained that he wasn't nationalistic for its own sake, but because the Romanians were searching for an identity within the smothering overlordship of Russians, Phanariots, and Austro-Hungarians. What is that identity? I asked him. He talked about the Latin temperament. We have a Latin language, he said, but our temperament is nothing like that of the Italians. The Romanian spirit is a melancholy one, closed, introvert, but not tragic. Why not tragic? I asked. Romanians can't be tragic, he replied, our landscape is too gentle, not dramatic enough. But we are secretive, he added. Our secretiveness was not created by Communism, but existed already and has helped Communism to survive. Forty-five years of Communism have turned this into a purely materialistic society, he added as we strolled along together, ahead of the others, but in fact Romanians are a very spiritual people.

'They – we – see God in nature, in a pantheistic way. We see God clothed in nature. That's one of the reasons why the only true life of the spirit survives in the countryside.'

A rain cloud cut Nichita short and set him beetling down the avenue in his dapper anxiety to get shelter.

In Tîrgu Neamţ the bus pumped fumes over waiting passengers in suffocating blasts. I turned to the respectable matron beside me and wrinkled up my nose. 'I know,' she said. 'Gypsies. Disgusting.' She assumed I was referring to a drunken family who staggered about, hawking and spitting and shouting and fighting and cursing and pissing, resplendent in their tattered finery. Later, on the bus, one of them was sick down the sleeve of my jacket. There were protests of disgust on my behalf. It was shameful! In front of a foreigner! Kick them off the bus, someone shouted. An older gypsy woman turned on him and shouted back that Romania was now a democratic country, they had as much right as anyone to be on the bus. Meanwhile she dabbed at her friend with her sleeve. Sick was soon trodden up and down the aisle. The respectable matron was mortified. She had crossed herself each time we passed a church; now she did so repeatedly, shaking her head. When the gypsies left us at an encampment, which spread like an epidemic outside a village, her hand was a flurry of crossing. 'Oh, Lord,' she muttered, 'Lord, Lord, Lord.'

Today was my birthday.

I was on my way to find George's beloved Father Superior, Gherasim, the man he had gone to visit after we left him in Turnu Severin. I had sought him in Arad, only to discover that he had long since taken up a post in Buzău as Assistant Bishop. I had attempted to reach him by phone but failed to get a line, so I had taken the risk of going there instead. I changed trains in Paşcani, but as there were many hours to wait I stopped for the night.

Paşcani was a concrete town, quite dead. Lining the new high street were purpose-built bars and cafés, bleakly lit, in which no-one sat and drank, no-one exchanged gossip, and purpose-built supermarkets with nothing to sell. In the ghostly lanes the tap tap tap of heels was the only sound, the sound of isolated people going from nowhere to nowhere. I was struck by the ugliness of the women, their crude hair dyes growing out at the roots, their middle-aged hair-dos, their drab and shapeless clothes, their pasty cheeks, their lurid make-up. It was as if an entire nation's aesthetic sense had been bludgeoned into indifference. Poverty and diet were largely to blame, but these women were also restricted by what there was in the shops. If there was only bleach that frazzled the hair, too bad. I wondered why mass production had to reduce everything to its lowest common denominator – surely beauty is as easy to mass-market as ugliness?

Abruptly at the end of the street there rose a cliff, almost sheer, and at the top of several hundred steps, a second town. I spent the night there in a modern hotel full of Soviet Moldavians visiting, optimistically, on a buying spree. I wanted a bath, but there was no hot water; I wanted to speak to Richard, but the telephone did not work; I would console myself with the TV, but it was an empty shell. This was still my birthday.

In his letters George had sometimes seemed egotistical, self-obsessed. *Yes, who am I?* he had asked, rhetorically. *Nobody. Just a guy!* But he did not believe that for a moment. He saw himself as heroic, noble, poetic, his own character in a novel. *Would you like to know who I am: I'm another Julien Sorel. Have you read* Le Rouge et Le Noir *by Stendhal? I guess you have and you can read it again. My life was so similar to Julien Sorel's life! First I tried the military career (the red) and I failed. Then I tried the ecclesiastic career (the black) and I failed again. All that I have to do now is find my death because an ambitious like me is rejected everywhere.* I had not read *Le Rouge et Le Noir*, and was not about to do so at George's command. I had felt slightly irritated: George took himself so seriously. It was that which had appealed to me at first, but once I was back in Cambridge his lack of self-irony became a bore. I said I had read *Le Rouge et Le Noir*, and that yes, yes he was just like Julien Sorel. I had felt a bit guilty about this impatient deceit and had brought a copy of the novel with me to Romania, as if to make amends. And now, more than anything, I did want to know who George was. I retired to bed with the book. By dawn, when I got up to catch the 5 a.m. train to Buzău, I had finished it.

The book was a revelation on level after level. Had George modelled himself on Julien Sorel, or were the similarities between them pure chance, another case of reality imitating art? I would never know. Like George's, Sorel's life was that of an ambitious intellectual struggling to raise himself up from his peasant background, the priesthood being the way out. Like George, Sorel saw himself as a foundling. Like George, Sorel joined a seminary where his intellectual powers far outshone those of his contemporaries. Sorel's success as secretary to the Marquis de la Mole outshone any success of George's, although when he wrote to me he may still have envisaged some such position for himself, and perhaps his time spent working for the local 'sherrif' was the preliminary to that, but like George, Sorel had exceptional powers of memory. Like George, Sorel was occasionally overcome by his own passions until, distracted from his worldly ambitions by his love for women, he ended by refusing to save himself and allowing himself to die.

Look at the physical description of Sorel: short *with irregular but delicately cut features and an aquiline nose. His large black eyes, which in calmer moments revealed a thoughtful, fiery spirit, were at that moment alive with the most savage hate. . . . His trim slender figure gave more promise of agility than strength. The thoughtful expression and the extreme pallor of his face had from early childhood made his father think he had not long to live, or would only be a burden to his family. . . . In Sunday sports in the public square he was always beaten. . . . Who could have guessed that his girlish face, so pale and so gentle, concealed an unshakeable determination to undergo a thousand deaths rather than fail to achieve success?*

I wondered now if George's exhortation that I read the book had been intended not only to reveal himself, but also to be a sort of warning about himself, one I ignored. Sorel was a hypocrite, contemptuous and arrogant. He set out coolly and calculatingly to seduce poor Madame de Rênal, who knew almost nothing about him. *His mind soared free into the upper air, and yet he could not manage to break a silence which he felt intensely humiliating.* (How could I not think of those silences of George's?) *Thus, in long walks which he took with Madame de Rênal and the children, the severe expression on his face was intensified by his most cruel anguish . . . As a final touch to his misery, he was conscious of his own absurdity and took an exaggerated view of it. What he did not see, however, was the expression of his eyes, which were so fine, and bore witness to so ardent a spirit that, as clever actors do, they sometimes imparted a delightful meaning to things that had no meaning at all.* I read this with a beating heart. How much had George fooled me? All that soulful depth – had it been a sham? Had he set out deliberately to seduce me in order to further his own ends? It was quite possible. After all, George had written, *Even now I have the natural mask and nobody knows what is in my soul. Nobody, for nobody is worth knowing. But excuse me, I'm a liar, for God knows what is in my heart. God is my master. And after God, you my friends.*

For her part, poor Madame de Rênal *found a sweet pleasure, bright with all the charm of novelty, in the sympathetic affinities of this proud and noble nature.* Just like me. What a fool I had been. When Julien,

sighing, tells the heartbroken Madame de Rênal, *I really must go away,
for I love you passionately. That's a sin, and what a sin too, for a young
priest!*, I marvelled at George's disingenuousness.

There were hints about George's state of mind. Like George, Sorel
was on occasion subject to fits of melancholy that almost amounted
to madness. *An idea that came into his head drove him almost crazy for
several weeks on end, and finally took possession of him with all the force
of an idea that a highly emotional nature believes it has discovered for itself.*
Later: *This was an effect of the violence and, if I may venture to say so,
the grandeur of those passionate impulses which convulsed this ambitious
youngster's mind. With a being so extraordinary, almost every day was
stormy weather.*

Then there was George's need for freedom. Here is Sorel (who has
now left Madame de Rênal) hidden in a cave on a mountain-side:
*Why shouldn't I spend the night here, he asked himself. I've got some bread
and I'm free! At the sound of this magnificent word his spirit soared aloft;
even with his friend Fouqué his habit of hypocrisy did not allow him to be
free. His head supported on his hands, Julien remained inside this cave,
happier than he had ever been in his life, excited by dreams and by the joy
of being free.*

George's pride too mirrored Julien Sorel's. George had written, *Ali
said I was a wicked man. It was not true. I needed badly a woman. Only
my proudness destroyed me for I could have found thousands of common
girls.*

Even George's literary style was clearly Stendhal-inspired. The
excess, the grandeur of emotions, the romantic self-obsession: *Am I
a coward too, after all? he said to himself. To arms!* Or, *Ah! the brutes! the
brutes!* Expressions that could have come straight from the pages of
George's letters.

Perhaps George's demise – that too – stemmed from *Le Rouge et Le
Noir*. When Sorel was appointed assistant tutor at the seminary,
his mentor Father Pirard (a model perhaps for George's beloved
Gherasim?) acknowledges, *Yes, indeed my son, I have grown fond of
you. . . . Your career will be a painful one; I see in you something that
offends the common run of men. Jealousy and calumny will pursue you. In*

whatever place Providence chooses to put you, your colleagues will never see
you without hating you; and if they pretend to love you it will only be to
betray you all the more effectively.

I left Paşcani early. The hotel receptionist was worried that I had
missed the breakfast for which I had paid, so she made me a packed
one; small kindnesses like these made all the difference. I trotted
back down the precipice free and strong, as if my pack was weightless.
I felt betrayed by the revelations – as I saw them – of George's
character, but at the same time I felt a new distance from him which
was healthy. Like Alice down her hole, he grew and shrank, grew
and shrank. Today he had shrunk.

Bishop Gherasim, I was informed at the monastery in Buzău, had
left for a conference in Bucharest and would remain there for several
days. Undaunted, and having travelled half way to Bucharest already,
I followed him there.

I tracked him down the next day in a huge, gloomy, turn-of-the-
century building with cobweb-strewn walls and a mosaic floor, brown
paint on Corinthian columns, and light made opaque by years of
unwashed windows and the chestnuts beyond that trailed monsoon
rain like tinsel on a Christmas tree. This was the Bucharest Theological College, where Father Iacov had studied. Bishop Gherasim, the
secretary informed me, was already in conference. Would the secretary kindly give him a message? Of course! We entered the conference hall at the back. Men with thick black beards and long black
hair were waving angrily towards the stage, others hissing for silence;
from the balcony overhead others leaned over shaking hands and
white shirt cuffs; the priests and monks wore black habits, the bishops
red and purple-lined pillbox hats. There were no women. On stage,
framed by a purple curtain, sat a row of bespectacled bishops, in the
centre the Metropolitan of Bucharest, magnificent in his square-cut
white beard which was set off by his black veil. His black hat was
high and his crucifix jewelled. The secretary pushed down the aisle
between the raging priests and whispered to a white-bearded bishop
on the far right of the stage. So this was Gherasim. He scanned the

male heads and alighted on me, then whispered to the secretary, who battled back again.

'The bishop thinks it must be a mistake as there are two Bishop Gherasims. You must mean the one from Rîmnicu Vîlcea. He says he doesn't know you.'

'No, I know he doesn't know me. But the Gherasim I want is the Gherasim from Buzău.'

'Yes, that is him.'

'I'll wait then, for a break. I'll catch him as he comes out.'

'As you wish.'

I watched the proceedings. Speaker after speaker rose to berate the Metropolitan for the state of the church in post-revolutionary Romania. Nothing has changed! Priests need higher salaries! The Catholics and Uniates want their land back, but why should they have it when they betrayed us? We want more religious education in schools and universities! All those waving arms and impassioned faces, those straining crowds at the balconies: it was the eighteenth century – David's 'Oath of the Tennis Court' – combined with one of those nineteenth-century group portraits of bearded men in dark suits.

I retired to a table outside and waited. I waited for *five hours*. At last they emerged, chatting and laughing like any delegates during a pause in a conference. I jumped off the table, legs tingling from sitting so long, and followed Gherasim, determined not to miss him. But suddenly all the white-bearded bishops looked alike, and I made several false starts before I found my man. I introduced myself and begged for a few minutes of his time.

'No, you want the other bishop from Vîlcea.' Close up he was disappointing, kindly but short, gap-toothed and stupid-looking.

'No, no,' I insisted. 'It's you.' Brother Gregoriu, the red-haired monk in Putna, had blamed Gherasim for being 'part of the trouble', but he looked so innocent. He grinned and trotted away downstairs to grasp the arm of a colleague who supposedly spoke French. Priests buffeting past us and out of the main doors into the rain, I tried to explain. When I mentioned George Cupar, Gherasim turned to his colleague and said something I didn't catch. He was suddenly in a great hurry.

'Come back after lunch.' He breezed out of the door, still grinning, his arm still through the other's.

'What time?'

'Come back at four.' He hurried down the dripping, cobbled street.

To be sure of seeing him I returned at 3.45. This time I asked the secretary to find me a translator. He obligingly returned with a Ph.D. student called Adrian, who spoke French. Together we sat on the table outside the conference hall and waited. We waited and waited. Although the debate appeared to have begun, there was no sign of Gherasim. Adrian and I chatted. He was serious, training to become a priest, longing to leave Romania to study abroad. He had considered a career in church administration, but found that to get anywhere in the hierarchy he would have to become a monk, which meant remaining celibate. He preferred to be a priest, to be part of the world, not to hold himself aloof from it. I liked him; he was the sort of man George would have been had he had a better education, come from a family of intellectuals rather than peasants.

Adrian told me that he had chosen to study theology not so much because of his love of God but because he knew this would give him access to a truer history of Romania than the student of history, politics or economics. The history of the Romanian church touched on political events which were minimised, ignored or falsified in the ludicrous official history of the country. He had also learnt to debate – the very existence of God was open to discussion – which meant that he learnt there were always at least two sides to every argument, therefore that there were possible truths other than the Communist truth. I wondered if this too lay behind George's dissent. I doubted it. He had been less sophisticated than this Adrian. He had wanted to become a priest because it was a way of using his intellect and making something of himself, and perhaps because he had faith.

I checked the conference hall, and there was Gherasim, back in position on stage, out of reach. He must have returned even earlier than I.

'If you ask me,' Adrian said, 'he's trying to avoid you.'

'Do you think so?'

'Why not? Perhaps he has something to hide.'

We waited until there seemed no point in it. I would return tomorrow.

Gherasim was staying at the Patriarchia beside the Orthodox cathedral. I went there the next morning, without an appointment, to catch him before he left for the conference. Heavy carved doors opened on to a hushed red carpet, marble walls, murmuring voices. Gherasim was in a meeting. I did not mind waiting, I was used to it now, and I stood in the hall to be sure of spotting him before he nipped out of the door and avoided me again. Eventually he trotted down the carpeted marble stairs. At last, this man I had been pursuing from Arad to Buzău to Bucharest. He was racing between meetings, but said he had two minutes to talk. His hands were soft, his manner gentle. Gregoriu had blamed Gherasim for much of what happened to George, and suggested that I challenge him with what I knew, but looking at the small gap-toothed man, I felt sure that Gregoriu was mistaken. Gherasim had clearly loved George, and I could see why George loved him, his Father Confessor. He looked like an honest country uncle.

We spoke in an undertone in the corner. Even when he arrived at Putna, Gherasim recalled, George already spoke four languages, and although this was impressive, and useful for guiding foreigners, it caused him problems. He burnt out. He was too ambitious, too intelligent for his own background. He studied all the time, and also became obsessed by a saint called Doroth who was very humble. George, Gherasim said, made it his purpose to humiliate himself utterly. This sounded unlike George – humble was the last quality I would have attributed to him – but the obsession fitted. When he failed his exams, Gherasim suspected that George had deliberately humiliated himself. George always had to go right to the end. To be cleverer than the others, but not to permit himself to have pride in that; to speak not just one foreign language but four, then seven; to

199

write to me not just often, but daily; to write not just averagely long letters, but letters ninety-two pages long. He was an extremist.

Perhaps his seeming passion for this Saint Doroth was also a career move, a Sorel-style scheme to impress Gherasim. What Gherasim implied was that George did, indeed, become mentally ill.

George had visited Gherasim in Arad a few days after leaving us at Turnu Severin Station. Then George had told him how much he missed him. It was like the sun and the moon, he had said. The moon's light is only reflected light, and when the sun disappears the moon is left in darkness. It has no light of its own. That was how George felt without Gherasim. George grew big again in my mind.

'Did you hear about his attempted escape?' I asked.

'When was that? I didn't hear anything about it.'

'In 1982. Near Arad.'

'Ah ha. I see.' Gherasim nodded. He remembered that in 1982 George had visited him with two other students, saying they had come to buy something. That must have been when he attempted to escape; it made sense.

After moving to Arad he and George communicated less and less. They had no telephone, no money to travel, no safety in writing letters, and above all everyone was preoccupied by their own affairs. I also had problems, he said. I always spoke my mind.

'George's death was a great loss to the church, and to the country,' he added. It was not just a platitude. He had been proud of having such a linguist at Putna. George and Iacov had made it an extraordinary time there. Now there was nobody.

'Why did George die?'

'I do not know.'

Only one other person knew George, he said, a fellow student at Putna, equally brilliant. He had a very different temperament, was more violent, but he was also a linguist, spoke Greek and Slavonic. His name was Melchisedec.

'Can I meet Melchisedec?' I asked.

'No, it's not possible.'

'Why not?'

Gherasim smiled his kindly, toothy smile. 'Unfortunately he is now in Mount Athos.'

So that was that, the one place I could not go. No women are allowed on Mount Athos, not even female goats.

There remained only Costina itself. I was daunted by the prospect. 'A snake pit': Iacov's description. 'Worse than Auschwitz.' Doubtless he exaggerated, but even so I was apprehensive of madness and of human degradation, and ashamed of those fears. However, I could put it off no longer. There was no place else left to try. I returned to Suceava and to the now almost cosily familiar Bucovina Hotel.

I began with the Red Cross; of any organisation, it was the Red Cross who would know what was going on health-wise in the region. At the dark end of a corridor in the Prefectura I knocked on their office door.

Plus number one: somebody there! Two Leather Jackets with long-ish hair, the Marlboro-smoking Eagles-listening type. The room was bright with Scandinavian optimism – pine furniture and Kindergarten diagrams about Red Cross training in Finland.

Plus number two: the Leather Jackets spoke English. They worked as 'yoof' volunteers, taking orphans out for a drive and hoping to meet (and marry) West European (mainly Finnish) volunteers.

Plus number three: they were willing to help. I decided to trust them and told them my story. They offered me coffee and invited me to sit down. The older volunteer, Dan, said, 'What was his name? I was a guide at one time and I used to take tourists to Putna. Maybe I knew him.'

I said, 'Cupar George.'

'Oh yeah, the poet.' Dan nodded.

I clutched at this: not The Madman but The Poet. 'Did you ever read any of his writings?'

'No, but he had a good reputation. I don't know if any was published.'

'Did you come across him?'

201

'Yeah, Cupar George, I knew him. I worked with him in the summer of '86. He had many problems with the Securitate.'

'How did he die?'

'I don't know exactly. Honestly. No secrets. I only heard about it myself in 1989, after the revolution. I was very sorry.'

'I understand he was schizophrenic.'

'Oh no, that's what they say. He wasn't. At least, not when I knew him.'

I heard myself exhale loudly, George made so large and real and tragic again by Dan's lack of indifference.

'Then why was he taken to Costina?'

'Because Costina was a political prison too.'

Theoretically Costina was a home for 'irrecuperables', Dan explained, and for old people who had no family to care for them; it was under the aegis of the newly formed *Inspectoratul Teritorial pentru Handicapați*. Dan doubted I would get any information about George from the *Inspectorat*, nor would I be given permission to visit Costina. The inspectors were of the old guard.

'You'll have to find some other way in,' Dan mused. He had a swoosh of coarse hair and he chain-smoked. 'What about Domnul Popescu?' he asked his colleague.

'Yes, good idea. She could try him.'

Domnul Popescu was an engineer who had several times been incarcerated at Costina although he was not mad, he was alcoholic. It was thought that he might have known George and that, of anyone at Costina, he might be sane enough to talk. They suggested that I ask the *Inspectorat* for a permit to visit Domnul Popescu, but that I should not, under any circumstances, mention George. Dan drew a map on the back of an envelope and marked the *Inspectorat* with an X.

It was housed in a nineteenth-century villa on the other side of town. I was shown straight to the Inspector, but he neither stood nor greeted me, so preoccupied was he at his desk with cubes of salami and cheese. I introduced myself and he, mouth bulging, waved me impatiently to a seat, a shabby man surrounded by dingy lace –

lace curtains, lace tablecloths, lace antimacassars, even a lace mat beneath the spider plant.

I explained that I was a friend of Domnul Popescu, had met him in 1979 (tut tut about the alcohol problems) and that I would like to visit him in Costina. The Inspector was unmoved, so I warmed to my theme and explained that I came from the Red Cross – true enough since I had just come from their office. This did not move him either. Perhaps, I then suggested, something could be done for Costina.

'You mean aid?'

'Yes.'

He wiped his mouth.

'You work for a British aid organisation?'

I hesitated. 'Yes,' I lied.

'I see. Well, Costina is in a terrible state. Aid has been received by so many institutions – there has been so much given to the handicapped children, but there has been nothing for Costina. Old and mad people are not news in your country. But they desperately need aid. There is no running water, no sanitation, terrible overcrowding and no medicines.'

'Perhaps I can help in some way.' Perhaps I could.

He swept the crumbs under a newspaper which mimicked his crumpled, grey look. 'There aren't any doctors there. The only doctor that even visited only stayed for four hours. There are just a few nurses, and none of them are trained.'

'Of course, I'll have to see the place to assess the situation.'

'Very well.'

'You're very kind. When would it be possible? Now?'

'Now? No, no, not now. Tomorrow. And you will take Horia, who works here with us, as your guide. And a car with a driver, which you must provide.'

It sounded expensive, and with Horia as minder it would be difficult to probe into George's imprisonment and death. But there was no alternative.

Another day to kill. I wandered into a café near the hotel which (or so I gathered from the height of the seats) was a special 'kiddies' café. Every town had one, institutionalised 'fun', although the single cartoon tacked to the otherwise bare concrete wall only added to the sense of abandon. Even so, plenty of adults queued up beside me; the cakes tasted of plastic, but the coffee was strong and sweet, the best in town; we squatted at the low tables, knees awkwardly jammed, and stared at each other.

It wasn't such a bad place, Suceava. Streets for strolling in – wide, leafy, clean. With the population explosion that came with Suceava's industrialisation in the 1950s and '60s, virtually every structure in the city – mainly eighteenth- and nineteenth-century neo-classical buildings with wrought-iron balconies – had been levelled. Eight- or ten-storey blocks had been built in their place. But for all the destruction, and the waves of industrial pollution, what Ceauşescu hadn't destroyed were the churches and the white mountain light, the best thing about Suceava.

I passed the police station. A pleasant enough building behind trees, but to me it was redolent with horror since it was also the Securitate headquarters. I envisaged George and his father being bundled out of a van. Ioana had described rooms in Rîmnicu Vîlcea that were not cells so much as offices with basins in. I imagined some barren place, the overhead bulb, the doctor waiting with his syringe, George's fear, and his father, a simple peasant, hunched over cheap cigarettes in the corridor awaiting his release.

I had arranged to meet Dan at the Red Cross office at 10 a.m., but he did not turn up. I waited and waited and while I waited I talked to the secretary, Maria. She had recently visited Costina for the first time, and she expressed shock – horror – at what she had seen. 'I must warn you, it's terrible there,' she kept saying. She described two buildings, one for the normals, one for the not-normals, the violents, which was 'lacking facilities'. No water, few medicaments, little food. Because there was only one 'assistant' in charge of all two hundred inmates, most were kept locked up most of the time. 'The people have nothing, nothing to do,' she said. Amongst the two hundred inmates, she had noted the following ailments:

22 cases of tuberculosis
100 oral infections
15 bronchial infections
6 eye infections
20 dermatological problems including 8 with scabies
2 internal parasites
15 diarrhoea
2 sores

'That makes 182 physically rather than just mentally ill inmates,' I observed.

'Well, of course, some of them have several of these problems at once,' Maria replied. 'TB *and* oral infections *and* skin disease *and* parasites.'

'Of course.'

'The medical equipment at Costina consists of one stethoscope and five syringes.'

'I see. Will they recover, these people?'

'With treatment many would recover. But there is no treatment.' She estimated that of the two hundred inmates, about fifty were not mentally ill but were in Costina for political reasons.

'And George Cupar?' I asked.

'Oh yes, the writer. A tragedy.'

'Was he there for political reasons?'

'He was certainly taken to Costina by force.'

Dan arrived an hour later, having arranged for a Red Cross driver to take us there. We collected Horia from the *Inspectorat*, a fat self-important man. Dan was convinced that George had been killed by the Securitate, and was certain that Horia would have been an informer, if not a Securitate member himself. Now, in the absence of the Securitate, he had probably joined its replacement, the Romanian Intelligence Service: he looked the type, so smug and well-fed. Horia said he had been an activist for Communist Youth. How do you feel about the Communist treatment of the handicapped? I asked him in the car. Oh, he replied, the system was rotten at the top only;

205

everyone else was blameless. And what are you going to do about the situation now? We are waiting, he said in a round-about way, for the laws to be changed. I stared at him. I was staring at Socialist Man, a sort of Homunculus created in a Socialist laboratory, spouting bureaucratic twaddle. I could imagine him a year and a half ago, mindlessly chanting slogans, falling over himself in his worship of the Leader. Overnight, that fount of all goodness had become the fount of all evil, but Horia continued to abnegate all responsibility. He did nothing for himself, only carried out orders.

'I don't trust him,' said Dan in English.

We turned off the main Suceava-Rădăuţi road to Costina, a jolting drive through crooked houses. The village seemed meaner, poorer, than most. I wondered how many of the people we passed – peasants mostly – knew (or cared) what horrors were being perpetrated in their midst. Costina Hospital was right in the centre of the village.

Strict Interzisă Intrarea Persoanelor Străine! None of us had been here before. Metal gates, tangled barbed wire, faces under hats peering suspiciously out of a gatehouse. Horia explained where we were from, and the faces vanished. They reappeared: the director was being summoned. We sat in the car, engine humming. This gatehouse was as far as Doamna Cupar ever penetrated. Her son was brought to see her here by a warder who remained present throughout her visits; George often seemed frightened, particularly during his final visit, the time after his attempted escape. He was badly cut and bruised, but when she asked what had happened he only cried. She never saw him again.

A face between the bars: permission to enter. The gates swung open and clanked shut behind us.

The Director, Domnul Cîmpan, was at once ingratiating and peasanty, with a wheedling voice and a red face framed with black curls, a nose squashed flat as if once broken, and Maxwell eyebrows over bloodshot eyes: a puffy drinker's face.

'*Sărumîna, Doamna.*' My hand disappeared into his ham-like one and was lifted to his fleshy lips. I thought: this man might (directly or indirectly) be responsible for George's death.

Domnul Cîmpan led us through a gone-to-seed garden to the newer of two buildings, or 'pavilions' as he euphemistically called them. It was a 1960s cube, two concrete storeys, not big or frightening, just dilapidated. The front door opened on to the refectory (rows of formica tables, high barred windows), which was being mopped by a loopy-looking, shaven-headed man. He grinned, dropped his mop and waddled over to shake our hands; his were broad and wrinkled and wet. Representatives from an English charity were expected tomorrow, so the saner inmates had been corralled to spruce the place up a bit.

The Director invited us into his office. Though painted battleship grey, it was comfortable enough, with a rubber plant, an important desk, a bed and a drinks cabinet. Cigarettes and pleasantries were exchanged, and Domnul Cîmpan explained – with some pride – that he had been Director of Costina for nineteen years, ever since it opened in 1972. He had done everything he could, he said, holding up his hands in a supplicatory gesture, but he had only six nurses and no running water; all water was hauled from a well in the grounds. Electricity, he added, was spasmodic, and the sanitary installation needed completely rebuilding. There were no showers, no baths, no heating, no laundry facilities, no transport. And he had never, *never* (his voice rose with indignation), received any aid. I think it was this – the indignity of being left out of the aid bonanza – that offended him most.

I sat hunched in my coat beside Dan, looking expectantly from him to the Director and back again, hoping that, with his knowledge of the system and with the authority lent him by the Red Cross, Dan would find a way of challenging Domnul Cîmpan about George. But Dan just sat there listening while Domnul Cîmpan's complaints and self-justifications whined on. I felt sorry for Domnul Cîmpan – his hospital had indeed been deprived, even if he himself was ensconced here in relative comfort – but the politeness was excessive. Yet I was reluctant to interrupt to ask directly about George for fear of revealing the false pretences under which I had come, and getting thrown out without penetrating beyond this office. Eventually I could keep quiet no longer and asked, 'Once you are here, can you ever leave?'

'Yes, oh yes,' replied Domnul Cîmpan blithely. He had a slight lisp.

'But you need permission?'

'Of course. You need permission from me.'

'Not from a doctor?'

'We have no doctor.'

'I thought this was meant to be a hospital.'

'Ah well, that's the problem. No doctor wants to work here. One came, but he stayed only four hours.'

So was this man personally responsible for keeping George here, against his will? I could not ask him that.

'And you need permission from the Handicap Inspectorate, but that would be a formality, confirming my report,' the Director went on. 'Then there is the family. You need permission from your family, and proof that you have somewhere to live and a way of supporting yourself, or of being supported. The family must take responsibility for you.'

So could Doamna Cupar have had George released if she had been so inclined? I wondered again at the scepticism with which Viorica had greeted my praise of her mother's goodness. Surely she could have cared for George at home?

'Is permission to leave ever refused?'

'Oh yes, often. About ten people leave each year. But they are often brought back if it doesn't work out.'

'Was this used as a political prison?'

'People were brought here by the police.'

'People like George Cupar?' I said the name as if in passing.

'Yes,' he answered casually, as if it was quite normal.

'Let's have a look around,' Dan said quickly, frowning at me.

At the top of a flight of steps the Director rattled a gate. A white-coated paunch swinging keys preceded a broken-tooth grin; the gate was unlocked and clanged shut behind us. The paunch belonged to Domnul Suciu, a marvellous man, said the Director by way of introduction, patting him on the back, who had been in charge for

208

nearly twenty years. Domnul Suciu's prickly jowls wobbled as he basked in the Director's praise, and he kissed my hand with unctuous charm, then cadged a cigarette off Dan. He reminded me of someone, I couldn't think who.

There was no sound and few people moved; the air was stagnant too. The first doors opened on to the women's dormitories with rows of narrow, iron-framed beds, eight or ten to a room. The bare concrete floors and the lower halves of the walls were painted a deadly grey; the upper walls had once been white but were now stained with damp and mould. The Director pointed out the stains and complained of the lack of insulation; I pointed out the radiators and he said they did not work. We crowded together in the doorways, nervous of madness and of being voyeurs. Beds are private places, and the horizontal person is at a disadvantage to the vertical one, but privacy and dignity had long since vanished. No-one appeared mad, just old and dirty. Some greeted us weakly and wanted to shake and kiss our hands; others lay huddled under grey blankets, unaware of our visit; but most watched us with a vague blankness, nothing more. One woman sat gazing at the floor, her hands pressed between her knees; a plate of beans and sausages long gone cold lay half-eaten beside her on the rumpled sheets.

Men wore pyjamas and old dressing gowns and woolly hats to keep out the cold. Like the women they lay, apparently resigned to waiting for death. But suddenly a man sat up in bed waving an arm. 'I'm a lawyer,' he shouted, 'and I've been here fifteen years.' His voice bounced around the room. Dan and I turned enquiringly to the Director, who laughed. 'Yes, it's true. We were at school together. Imagine my surprise when the police brought him in and I saw his papers on my desk! Crazy as anything.' He steered us out of the door. Domnul Suciu was watching, and I wondered what punishment would be meted out to this outspoken lawyer once we were out of earshot.

As we left the room my heart turned over. Between the lawyer and the door lay a young man with black hair and a pointed jaw, his moustache and beard black against his white skin. He was in his late twenties, early thirties.

'Why is he here?'

The Director turned back from the door. 'He's a worker.' He dismissed him with a wave. 'Schizophrenic.'

The young man ignored us and continued to stare at the ceiling. I thought his eyes were filled with tears, but perhaps they were just watering. Until then my imagination had been unable to encompass George's suffering. But in that face – sensitive, refined – I saw the hopelessness and the despair that George himself must have felt.

Dan was in the dormitory opposite, whispering to a man who stood as if to attention beside his bed.

'This is Domnul Popescu,' he murmured, one eye on Suciu. Domnul Popescu was middle-aged with large, sad eyes. He wore a grey dressing gown and, like many of the patients, had the vacant look of the sedated. He kissed my hand and whispered in English, 'Good afternoon, Madam.'

'He didn't know George Cupar,' Dan whispered, 'but . . .'

Noting that my attention had been caught, Suciu muscled over. 'This one may be an engineer, but he's a drinker,' he guffawed. He mimed someone swigging and chucked Domnul Popescu on the shoulder. 'His trouble is he likes the bottle too much, ha ha!' Suciu bared a few stained teeth and effectively closed our conversation. His hands were gnarled and broad and I suspected that everyone here, including George and Domnul Popescu, had felt the flat of them. Domnul Popescu stood meekly, sadly, patiently, by the bed, eyes cast down.

Swelter! That was who the corpulent Suciu reminded me of. Swelter, chef of Gormenghast. Costina was not as gothic and fantastic-looking as Gormenghast (if equally mad) but Suciu had Swelter's malevolent bulk, his splenetic brutality. I could imagine him at night creeping from room to room on silent, flat-soled shoes, spreading evil and fear.

He was summoned from the room by a female nurse, and in his absence a spotty youth called to Dan and, seeming to shake his hand, palmed a note into it. He too wore the regulation grey towelling dressing gown and woolly hat, but unlike the others he was alert and angry. He filled his days painting icons on glass, and demanded that I photograph him holding one of his panes. He stared fiercely at the camera.

'I've heard this boy's case already,' Dan said. 'His name's Sandu. He was brought up in the Handicap hospital in Siret – the one you've seen – and now he's kept here because there's nowhere else for him to go. His brother's in another mental institute, but they're both completely sane. They just don't have any place to live. He tried to run away from here so that he could be with his brother, but they caught him and brought him back and now he's stuck here. He wants me to help get him out.'

'Can you help?'

'I can try to plead his case with the authorities, but I don't know that it would do much good.'

'Ask him about George.'

The walls around his bed were lined with his paintings, primitive and brightly coloured – aggressively so. While I admired them, and blocked the view from the door, Dan whispered quickly to him. Yes, he knew George. Yes, he died in Costina. No-one knows why. He died in the other building, the 'old pavilion'.

I was pulled away by an old man with sunken cheeks who produced a Bible from under his pillow.

'God!' he whispered, pointing to himself.

Cîmpan and Suciu swept our procession along the corridor (Horia lumbering along behind) to the 'recreation' room. Suciu fumbled with keys and pushed open the door on to a square cell. Walls dark with filth, a bare concrete floor littered with cigarette butts. No chairs, no tables: a windowless cave. 'This is where they come and smoke,' the Director explained. He seemed almost to like it. I learnt later than Domnul Cîmpan himself lived in one of the smartest blocks in Suceava, a source of envy to other residents, access to which was reserved for those with the very best government contacts and the very best Party credentials. How much was this a bribe to secure his compliance in disposing of certain individuals? The lawyer, for example. George, for example. . . .

Opposite the 'recreation' room were the 'sanitary facilities'. Mildewed walls, three taps without water, and three holes in the ground. It was for both men and women, without even doors to create a semblance of decency. This was what George had been subjected to – and this was the new building.

The Red Cross secretary had said that each night Costina's skeleton staff of three nurses gathered in fear in their private room to smoke and drink and to shut out the mad animals, and in the absence of staff the place seethed with sex. Rape, too, for many of the women were too disturbed to consent to sex, and along with genuine patients with severe mental illnesses, Costina also housed murderers, violent criminals and rapists. The women were taken regularly to Suceava for abortions; they were not as old as they looked. The thought of George abandoned in this underworld, this Bosch-like hell, was too much to bear. Did he, in turn, abandon everything and join the raddled bodies fornicating in their lunacy and filth? Did he sink so low? No, even to consider it for a second was another betrayal.

We were led across a patch of disused ground to the 'old pavilion'.

'Who is sent to this building?' I asked.

'Aggressives and Incontinents,' the Director replied airily. That meant George, no longer a priest or a poet but an Aggressive and Incontinent. A dark passage branched into a sequence of rooms. One had once been the bathroom. Its walls were smeared with excrement. A big, old-fashioned bath remained, but without running water it was unusable. Was this where George was immersed after his attempted escape? I could not ask, at least not yet. We were shown the old hot-water boiler, which had blown up years before and never been replaced.

The atmosphere here made the new building seem lively. The light was dim and the air so foetid it seemed to muffle all sound. One large space, more hallway than room, was filled with rows of grey beds without sheets on which grey men – mostly men – sat or lay. Some shuffled about, zombies adrift in some foggy space, barely aware of our presence. They were surely drugged, though Domnul Cîmpan denied this. He claimed that he did not have the resources, although the Red Cross secretary had said that they used Phenobarbitone indiscriminately. Phenobarbitone is a barbiturate once used in the West as a tranquilliser but now known to have such serious side-effects that it is reserved exclusively for the treatment of epilepsy, and then only as a second line of treatment if other drugs fail. The side-effects are depression, unsteady gait, drowsiness, lethargy, anaemia, all of which these people appeared to be suffering from. It is easy to develop a tolerance to Phenobarbitone, so the dosage has to be constantly increased in order to remain effective, but in overdose it can produce hypothermia, depression, even coma and heart attack. It could certainly hasten death. It is manufactured in Romania so is widely available, and useful for keeping people under control. Even in the TB hospital in Rădăuţi George had been given drugs – presumably tranquillisers – which he said made him feel like a *'half drunk man'*. That, he said, was *'for I seem to be nervous. In fact, I'm not allowed to be angry about anything.'*

When I returned to Costina a year later, once the old pavilion had been renovated by the English charity, the widespread use – and abuse – of both Phenobarbitone and a form of Diazepam, another sedative, continued.

Heads were shaved, bodies wasted. The Red Cross secretary had described the Costina diet as 'empty soup', and the malnourishment was evident. The entire population of Romania was short of food, but as I had seen, those in the outside world, people like Ana in Rîmnicu Vîlcea, had the means of supplementing their meagre rations either by growing food themselves or by wheeling and dealing on the black market; George's little extras brought him by his mother – cakes and clothes – were, she had claimed, immediately stolen by the staff. But she had also said that George, in protest against his incarceration and the conditions at Costina, had organised a hunger strike. Half-starved already, this seemed ludicrously brave. But if he had died of starvation, would not his mother have been informed? After all, it would have been his own fault.

'Was this where George Cupar was kept?' I asked a nurse.

'Oh yes,' she answered. 'In room 2.'

She pointed to an airless tunnel. High on the wall was a barred window. Below, a row of iron bedsteads with barely the space for a man between each. Patients sat on bed after bed, waiting for nothing in their antechamber of death. There was an awful predictability about this room: it was the worst we had seen, the most bleak. God! I couldn't forget George's appeal to me to help him escape. *Listen to me, Helena. My parents are poor, it will be difficult for me to find now a reasonable job, and I can't stay at home out of a job. I could go to study if I had money, but I haven't any. So, please ask your family and friends (Alex included) to call me, to ask your authorities to call me to go in your country.* Only now did I understand his fears. Life without a job and no money meant Costina.

I was beginning to feel that there could have been no degradation too deep, no suffering too terrible, for George, and that death had been inevitable. Had he pushed himself to the limit, and welcomed the abyss? Had he even been conscious of it? Or had he fought it, kicking and screaming? I had no answers, but I felt that he had to go through this, all the way.

'What was wrong with George Cupar?' I asked the nurse.

'Oh, schizophrenic. Very bad.'

What about my illness? Well, a man like me is never ill. I suffer only a social illness. At the time I had interpreted his remarks as being those of the poetic outsider, the 'genius', the 'northern star'. I had failed to see the danger he was in.

'Why did he die?'

Dan whispered, 'Suciu! You can't ask her that. She'll have trouble.'

Suciu loomed over, beaming, jovial, cadging another cigarette, and hustled us out of the building.

We had seen enough. I had intended to visit George's grave but couldn't face it now, and besides I had to maintain the pretence of being a disinterested aid worker in front of Horia, who was anxious for his lunch.

214

Back in Suceava, Dan and I had a drink together in the hotel. We were both shattered. Even he, who had seen many institutions, was shocked by Costina.

'We forgot Sandu's note.'

'Oh yes, Sandu's note.'

Dan produced a scrap of exercise-book paper and read it through before handing it to me. '*Allo!*' it began, but that was all I could decipher.

'It's a warning about the Director. It says that lots of aid has been received by Costina, but all of it has been stolen by him and the staff.'

'I don't believe it!'

'I can believe it,' Dan said quietly. 'Sandu would not invent it. He is very brave. He'd be badly beaten for something like this.'

'So Cîmpan was lying all the time. I knew it!'

'It's normal here. The personnel take the stuff, or the local mafia. You British are so naive.'

This only added to my disillusion. 'How do you think George died?'

'He was murdered by the Securitate. It's sure.'

'You really think that?'

'He was an irritant. Why else would the cause of his death have been covered up? If even his mother doesn't know . . .'

'What do you think was the cause?'

'Who knows? It's possible that the initial injection was some sort of drug used to break him down mentally. Other people have talked about this, and his mother had no reason to invent it. Perhaps he was given another injection at the end. Or perhaps he got pneumonia or hypothermia from being immersed in the water. That was a very common method, you know. I've often heard about it. Some people were wrapped up in wet sheets. It was good because this method left no mark on the body, and in this climate and without heating they usually died in the end. Or perhaps he was beaten by that Suciu.'

'Why should they have wanted to get rid of him?'

'He was a thorn in their side.'

The problem was, I didn't trust Dan. He said he had known George in 1986, but George was already in Costina in 1986. He had also told me that he had escaped from Romania in a boat across the Danube, but that when his mother fell ill he had come back again. Having heard the experience of Veronica Filip, Dan's story sounded too . . . easy. I didn't believe him.

Yes, I had seen much, yet could confirm little. George may or may not have had schizophrenia. If he had, he may or may not have been pushed over the edge by the Securitate, or by Costina itself. He had certainly been taken there by the police, but that did not mean he was not already sick. Schizophrenics are picked up by the police and taken to hospital in any country. It did not necessarily mean that he was a political prisoner. The lawyer who had been there for fifteen years was also taken there by the police, but maybe he was insane too.

In fact, all I knew for sure was that he had been imprisoned in conditions of inhuman squalor. Was this a deliberate policy, or was it simply neglect? The neglect could not be denied. Here was a small institution in a village far from Bucharest – easily shunted aside by the cumbersome bureaucratic machine. But was this neglect caused by lack of funds and indifference, or was there something more sinister behind it? There was nothing fanciful about such an idea. In Nazi Germany it was the successful use of gas to exterminate thousands of mentally ill patients that led to it being used on a bigger scale to eliminate the Jews. When the gassing of mental patients was stopped (public opinion was hostile and, besides, the killer teams were needed elsewhere), the medical profession turned instead to what was called 'discreet euthanasia'. Other than for scientific research, the mentally ill served no purpose for the master race. They were given such demeaning titles as *minderwertig* – 'inferior', or *Ballastexistenzen* – 'human ballast', *leere Menschenhülsen* – 'empty human shells', or *lebensunwertes Leben* – 'lives not worth living'. This expressed society's attitude to the sick, and almost demanded that if their lives were not worth living they be relieved of them. So in selected institutions food rations were reduced to their uttermost and buildings were left unheated in winter, while death was speeded up by patients being given low doses of barbiturates over long periods. Pneumonia usually followed and was terminal, but looked innocent.

In Romania the attitude to the mentally handicapped is one of revulsion and fear. They are known as *Nebun* – 'No Good' – and Communist or post-Communist society has no place for outcasts. I am not suggesting Nazi-style genocide, but elderly and irritating people cost money and were better out of the way. It was well known that Ceauşescu discouraged doctors from treating patients over the age of seventy. In that sense they, and George, were victims of something like 'discreet euthanasia'.

Maybe, on the other hand, George's death was a mistake. It was purely a hunch, but I suspected that the treatment of George – insidious and cruel as it was – was not meant to kill him. That wasn't normally Ceauşescu's way; he was too clever for that. I suspected some form of psychiatric abuse, some form of brutality, that went too far.

One peculiarity was that although it purported to be a hospital, Costina was under the authority not of the Ministry of Health, but of the Ministry of Labour. If George was genuinely sick, surely he would have been sent to a genuine hospital? As I had been told so often, there was no doctor at Costina. But since he was sent to Costina, this suggested that his illness was, as he said, 'a social illness', not a medical one, as in theory Costina was a prison for people with social rather than medical problems. Surely as part of the Ministry of Labour, it was intended to be more like a Victorian workhouse, for people without money or support, people without jobs, people with 'social' illnesses, rather than a hospital. George's social illness was that he had no job, and the reason he had no job was that he refused to conform.

It remained impossible to piece George's story together; so few of the facts were verifiable. I was lost in a mist of hypotheses; facts came at me from every angle, like bits of flying debris, but they dissolved on contact into conjecture, ambiguity, enigma. Nothing fitted into a pattern. I suppose that's the nature of research – a bit from here, a bit from there, large bits missing – but it was particularly true of Romania. For this was looking-glass land, where nightmare and reality had become confused. What little information I received was always subject to my informant's own agenda: some had things to hide, some were discreet, some loyal, some treacherous, some tactful, some evasive. Some exaggerated, some voiced rumours, some were gullible, some were sceptical, some gave me what they thought I wanted, some were simply ignorant of the details. They were all so bewilderingly vague! Was George schizophrenic or not? How did he die? Even now, after so many journeys and conversations and journeys and conversations, even after seeing something of the horror to which George had been subjected in his final days, I had no cast-iron answers.

Five

A year later I returned to Costina. It was April 1992.

From the outside there appeared to be a growing openness in Romania, which encouraged me to hope for more information about George. With time, I thought, people had less to fear from what they had had to hide. In fact, as I was to discover later, few Securitate files had been released, and while in East Germany a commission had been set up to sift through the Stasi's files, the Securitate's were left untouched. In fact it was reported that the Securitate were even now destroying them, and the remains of many had been discovered in a burnt-out pit in Oltenia. However, the mood of Suceava struck me as subtly improved. People still queued for bread, and evening still meant dark and deserted streets, but I sensed less hysteria, more optimism; the mud stirred up by the last two years was settling. Maybe I was influenced by my own mood – the unexpected sunshine, the fact that I was staying not in the Bucovina Hotel but with a friend. Maybe it was also that this time I was not travelling alone; I was five months pregnant and my child, quickening now, tapped new life against my belly.

In the intervening year I had been in touch with the British charity FARA, which had adopted Costina as one of its causes. The charity had installed a doctor and begun the task of cleaning the place up, leaving one volunteer in charge, while Costina's Director, Domnul Cîmpan, had been sacked. Suspected for months of stealing the charity's donations, he was caught leaving Costina with boxes of medicines, food and clothes, and one of the British volunteers had snatched a photograph, which Domnul Cîmpan had been too drunk to notice. This photograph has caused a minor scandal when published in the local press. He had been replaced by a Domnul Bosca.

The gates swung open without hesitation now: no barbed wire, no fierce 'No Entry' signs, no suspicious doorman. From outside the two buildings were unchanged, but this time I noticed the orchard, the nesting rooks and the tiny Orthodox church beyond the fence. It could be a lovely place, I thought with surprise.

The fabric of the newer building remained the same. The same bare grey walls, the same foetid smells. But the locked gate to the wards was wide open. An old woman spent her days at this gate, looking but not yet venturing out, and smiling all the while. People moved about and laughed and kissed my hand. Just a year since my last visit, it was as if lights had been switched on, the Costina illuminations.

Men and women had been segregated, and the state had employed a psychiatrist who, although he was a disreputable character and not a very good psychiatrist, was better than nothing.

He was continuing the assessments begun by a British psychiatrist who had spent several months here. Out of some forty assessments, she had found not one patient who was genuinely insane. One woman I met perched fully clothed on the edge of her bed. While she knitted she discussed her case. A year ago her husband and eldest son, both policemen, had had her incarcerated here as an alcoholic; the real reason was that her husband wanted to marry another woman. In truth she was neither alcoholic nor disturbed in any way, and this nearly two and half years after the so-called revolution.

An older woman, frail but once beautiful, raised a skeletal arm in greeting. Her legs were paralysed from immobility; she had lain in bed in Costina for twenty years. As a professor of politics and economics at Suceava University in the late 1960s, she had said the wrong thing, done the wrong thing, and had promptly been diagnosed as insane. The cause of her madness, it was claimed, was that she had reached the age of thirty and was still unmarried. Costina for life was the prescription. Like other political prisoners, she had had her teeth extracted, which had disfigured her jaw. I wondered about George.

The old pavilion had undergone a more dramatic transformation. This was where the men now lived. Walls were white and clean, hung with posters, and many of the beds were new hospital beds on casters. Gone was George's grey tunnel, gone the drugged gloom. Now the men wandered about at leisure. Two spotty youths ran towards me down the corridor. 'Give us a hundred lei!' I laughed. 'Later, I've left my money in the other building.' They grabbed my hand and jigged about; they had come from Siret but were perfectly sane; they simply had no other place to go. As for Sandu, he had left it for some other institution.

I asked anyone I saw if they had known George Cupar. Some did not understand, others had arrived after his death. There was one old man, someone said. He was fetched. He had hollow cheeks and sunken eyes. Yes, he remembered George Cupar. Yes, he died here. I hoped, *hoped* that this might be the moment.

'How did he die?'

The man shrugged and looked shiftily about him, wanting to escape.

'George Cupar. *Nu mai este.*'

'Yes, I know. I know he is no more.'

'*Nu mai este.*'

'Thank you. I know. But how did he die? Can you remember?'

'I don't know.'

Perhaps he genuinely didn't know. Perhaps he had been too drugged at the time to notice. Or perhaps he was afraid. Perhaps perhaps perhaps. Someone knew, and I suspected it was Suciu, aka Swelter, the male nurse. Unfortunately he was not here; he was working nights and I was not allowed into Costina at night. He still beat people, I was told. One boy had been whipped with steel cables.

221

My only other way forward was through George's medical records.

Domnul Bosca was in his office which was now in an outhouse, a makeshift room. The lower half was painted grey, the upper half mustard. A cabinet housed a jam jar of sugar and a pot of coffee granules; on the wall hung a grey calendar and Mr Bosca's coat. He was a dark nugget of a man in cheap clothes. He greeted me warmly and we realised simultaneously that he had mistaken me for the head of FARA, whom he was expecting from England that morning. Having established my identity he became much less enthusiastic, despite my hard-won letter of introduction from the Ministry of Health, to whose authority Costina had now been transferred. But when I explained that George had been at Putna, Mr Bosca's eyes lit up.

'I used to go there sometimes on business. I think I remember him. Dark and very thin?'

'Yes! But there were two guides. Perhaps you remember the other one, large with a beard?'

'No, I remember them both. I remember being greatly impressed by all the information he told us about the church. Yes, I remember him well. But,' he went on, a cunning look coming over his face, 'about his files. I'm afraid I am very very busy, and the person in charge of the archives is also busy. It simply isn't possible at the moment.' The old game. I had been told by the FARA representative that George's files were in the neighbouring room, along with all the other 'dodgy deaths'.

'Nothing is possible for at least a week.'

'I can't wait a week. I have no other reason for being here in Suceava. I have come all the way from England. I'll be leaving Romania soon.'

'Then perhaps you'll be able to return to Romania some other time.'

'No, no, no. I'll be busy having a baby.' I disliked using this, but it had the right effect.

'Aah. The Doamna is to become a mother!' He was all smiles.

'Then we must do our best to take care of her.' I was required to write out my 'programme' so I listed my questions: how? where? what? when? why? who? Mr Bosca tucked them away in his files. He summoned someone from next door. 'Yes, I think you'll go home satisfied. Or at least, not disappointed. I admit that what you see in the documents may not be the whole truth, but you're a writer, you can use your imagination.'

We waited. He had greased-down hair and monkey features.

The chief nurse entered, red-faced in her white coat, and nervous. She sat down, rubbed her hands together and crossed and uncrossed her legs. Yes, she remembered George Cupar.

Mr Bosca raised his voice. 'I think he was a great patriot. I mean in his soul, not in the usual sense. What happened to him? The Doamna wants to know.'

I wondered how much of his theatricality was for my benefit.

'Paranoid schizophrenia,' the nurse muttered.

'Genuine?'

'Yes, the disease was probably genuine.'

Without a second thought – as if it were quite normal – they were tacitly admitting that there were cases of schizophrenia at Costina which were not genuine. In other words political cases, like the old woman who had had her teeth extracted, like the lawyer I had seen here the year before, possibly like George. I noted her use of the word 'probably'. Agitated by Mr Bosca's questioning, she spoke rapidly. 'He sat in the corner staring into space and refusing to talk, then at other times he talked at random. He got worse.'

'What drugs was he given?' I asked.

'The usual.'

'How did he die?'

'I don't remember.' As chief nurse here, this woman would have been a Securitate informer and would have closely overseen the treatment of any inmate brought in by the police.

'You remember so much about his life, but nothing about his death?' I persisted.

'It was five years ago. We have over two hundred patients, how can I be expected to remember everybody?' She looked from Mr Bosca to me and back again, asking to be believed, twisting in her chair. A records book was produced, and across one line was the familiar story of George's life: date of birth, date of admission to Costina, date of death.

'So.' Mr Bosca cocked his head at me. 'That's all there is. I've done my best.'

There was more, much more. How could I persuade him to help? A bribe was too crude and besides there were too many witnesses. At that moment we were interrupted by FARA's head, a sleek woman who had arrived in Suceava from London the night before. She and I had corresponded about George; Mr Bosca looked on with slight alarm as we greeted each other.

'I know all about your story,' she said to me. 'Please don't let me interrupt.'

'All I want is to see George's file.'

She turned to Bosca. 'I suppose you have the files about this lady's friend?'

Bosca shrugged, admitting defeat. The nurse returned five minutes later with two brown envelopes. I was lucky: a combination of chance and perhaps also of my own ignorance of the subtleties of the situation – of the Russian-doll effect of stories within stories – meant that I was about to learn more about George than his family and friends had ever done. Unlike them, I had been able to try: I had nothing to lose; I could go home. The nurse dropped the envelopes on to the table in front of me.

'There's nothing to hide,' she said.

I leafed through them. 'Where's the death certificate?'

'I don't know. His family probably took it.'

I knew that if someone died at Costina, their death certificate would remain in their files. For the family to obtain the death certificate was no easy matter. George's mother would have had to make an application to the Tribunal, pay a large sum of money and wait. Even if she succeeded, a record of that application would have remained in George's file.

George's mother knew nothing of the death certificate, had never seen it, and would have had neither the sophistication nor the money to make such an application. I could only conclude that the death certificate, if there was one, had been removed by someone else. Who or why remained open to question.

'How did he die?' I asked the nurse again.

'Who knows?'

I had heard this already from none other than the disgraced ex-director of Costina, Domnul Cîmpan. The previous day I had found his name in the telephone directory and invited him for a drink in the Bucovina Hotel. It was that simple. He had dressed for the occasion – grey suit, striped shirt, red tie. Yes, he remembered all about George, but mysteriously nothing about his death.

'We had so many deaths!' he had whined, swallowing vodka. 'You can't blame me if I can't distinguish one from the other!' I had pressed more drinks on him, feeling as if I was supping with the devil.

'Of course it was hard for you, I know.' I had alternately attacked and, as the Romanians put it, 'brushed' him, smoothed him down.

'Yes, it was very hard. If someone was ill we had to call the ambulance from Suceava – we had no vehicle of our own – and often it wasn't available. What to do?'

'But don't you think it's unusual that a man of thirty-two should die, so young?'

'Perhaps he refused his food or something, I don't know.'

The nurse picked up the documents. They were handwritten in ink and difficult to read. 'It says here he tried to escape from Costina but was brought back.' She laughed. 'I remember that. He escaped through a window and went home.' Like a bird trapped in a room, knocking against the glass until it knocks itself out. Putna, Costina, Romania, his own head: prisons within prisons. 'And he took part in a hunger strike,' she added.

'What was his punishment?' I asked.

She looked blank. Both she and Cîmpan claimed to know nothing of 'water therapy': they didn't have enough water for their own use,

225

let alone for punishment. Sometimes they didn't even have a well; all the water had to be brought in by tank, and often it didn't arrive at all. However, FARA's representative had confirmed from conversations with patients and nurses that what water there was had been used to control patients at Costina. One technique was to excite the patient, enrage him, send his blood pressure up, then immerse him in cold water for twelve hours.

Cîmpan had blurted, 'We also never used strait-jackets. Sometimes we did have to tie patients to their beds if they were disturbed and we used sheets for that, nothing else.' Scrunching the tablecloth between his fingers he had appealed to me to take his side.

'Was George Cupar tied down in this way?'

'I can't remember.'

'What was George's punishment?'

'Ooh, nothing serious. I expect he was scolded a little.'

'Scolded!' I tried to imagine Suciu waggling one fat finger at naughty George before sending him supperless to bed. Cîmpan had noticed my disbelief. He had added quickly, voice rising to a whine, 'Of course, it's not surprising if the staff did get a little bit angry when someone escaped, because the police fined them. They lost some of their pay.'

I knew how little they earned; if that was cut because of George I dreaded the consequences.

The nurse left us, and Bosca and the FARA head began their meeting. Why was there still no running water? Why had her pump still not been installed? It is the workmen's fault, they never turn up. Why had a French charity been refused permission to work at Costina despite having plenty of money to offer? Politics, politics, not his fault. I admired the crisp but smiling way she cut through his evasions, but he looked harassed. The nurse reappeared, waving someone's notes, and Bosca made a show of anger: I refuse to have any more of these murderers committed here! This is a hospital now, not a prison, not a dumping ground for murderers!

Meanwhile, I worked through the documents. George had been committed to Costina 'hospital' not by the Bucov de Sus dispensary or any other doctor, but by the Bucov de Sus 'Directorate of Social Assistance'. In other words, George's was a social problem, not a medical one, the problem being that he was unable to work and his mother was unable to keep him. It seemed there was nowhere for him to go but to this – what? – hospital/prison/gulag/concentration camp. A document supposedly in Doamna Cupar's hand and signed by her agreed for George to be brought to Costina and confirmed that all the paperwork was in order.

There followed a slip of paper dated September 1985 acknowledging Doamna Cupar's receipt of a sum of money. Had she been paid in return for his incarceration? Did this lie behind her agreement to his commitment? Did she sell her son's freedom? I couldn't forget Iacov's suspicions, and also Viorica's doubt when I had praised her mother. Perhaps feeling guilty, perhaps telling me what she thought I wanted to hear, perhaps hoping for gifts and money from her son's foreign friend, Doamna Cupar had vigorously denied signing anything.

The early records of George's sojourn at Costina were fairly detailed. On arrival he had been examined by a doctor – so there was a doctor here then – called Sergiu Lupei. Dr Lupei noted George's pallor and apparently irrational judgements and diagnosed *'Schizofrenie paranoidă cu evoluţie deficitară trenantă'*. This translates literally as 'Paranoid schizophrenia with a slow deficient evolution'. In other words, he does not yet exhibit any of the known symptoms of schizophrenia, but he will, he will. This diagnosis was identical to the diagnosis of 'sluggish schizophrenia' which was used for the psychiatric abuse of dissidents in the Soviet Union.

During the Stalinist era in the USSR psychiatry had been used to help political dissidents since the hospitals had better conditions than the labour camps. But after Stalin's death the KGB was no longer so free to use their now infamous methods of terror – the mass arrests, the torture, show trials and executions – since they brought with them worldwide condemnation and political repercussions; instead it became more convenient to brand dissidents as psychiatric cases who required enforced hospitalisation. During the 1950s, '60s and

'70s Professor Snezhnevsky, the chief psychiatric advisor to the Soviet Ministry of Health, so reshaped diagnostic practice that it could now be exploited for those political ends. The most radical element was his broadening of the definition of schizophrenia until it could even include what in the West would be called eccentricity. The most sinister of Snezhnevsky's 'sub-types' of schizophrenia was 'sluggish', which was theoretically slow to evolve but allowed even the most subtle behavioural change to be diagnosed as latent schizophrenia. According to Snezhnevsky, 'Dissent may be due to a diseased condition of the brain where the pathological process develops very slowly and mildly and its other symptoms remain unnoticed for a certain period.' Once the dissident or 'patient' was committed to hospital, the authorities had at their disposal their arsenal of anti-psychotic drugs with which to 'reform' him. Thus psychiatry became a valuable tool.

Dr Lupei confirmed that George's 'Schizophrenia with a slow deficient evolution' was not an urgent case.

While still in London I had had a chance meeting with a visiting Romanian psychiatrist, Dr Cătălina Tudose, the Vice-President of Romania's League of Mental Health. She dismissed with an impatient wave any claims that Soviet-style political psychiatry had ever existed in Romania. It was nonsense; there were schizophrenics all over the world, why not in Romania? People were mistreated in institutions in democratic countries too, and mistakenly locked up. Two years after the revolution and this was still the government line: a blanket refusal to admit that anything untoward had taken place in Romania's psychiatric hospitals. Neglect, yes; lack of funds, yes; but abuse and torture, no. Indeed, after 1989 Amnesty International had followed up several cases of reported psychiatric abuse in Romania but had concluded that all those they interviewed were genuine schizophrenics.

However, many of Romania's psychiatrists trained in the USSR, and what was true of the USSR was mirrored in some way throughout the Communist Bloc. In the West, so much attention had been paid to Soviet psychiatric abuses that the rest of Eastern Europe had been overshadowed, and only now that Romania was emerging from the political penumbra were the psychiatrists speaking out and being listened to. Voicing the opinion opposite to that of Dr Tudose, a group of doctors had founded the Association of Free Psychiatrists, headed by the distinguished Dr Valerian Ţuculescu, whom I met in Bucharest on my way north. He had been the Inspector-General of the Public Health Ministry from 1972–81 but had himself been persecuted in the early 1980s after revealing the mass hospitalisation of dissidents and malcontents. He had discovered that, as in the USSR, before each public festival or presidential visit hundreds of potential trouble-makers were routinely rounded up and confined in psychiatric hospitals where they were treated with neuroleptic drugs, then released once the event was over. After the fall of Ceauşescu, Dr Ţuculescu had made it his mission to expose this and other abuses of psychiatry. He claimed that political psychiatry was first used in Romania after 1965, and the first documented report of the enforced hospitalisation of a Romanian dissident was in 1977 – two years before I met George. By 1990, he claimed, there were three hundred prisoners of conscience in hospitals throughout Romania. This was proportionally equivalent to the number in the Soviet Union. Of those in the USSR, thirty per cent were considered to be dissenters for wishing to emigrate.

George, of course, had tried to emigrate.

Despite the ample proof he had to support his claims, Dr Ţuculescu was greeted with ridicule and attempted vilification by both Dr Tudose and the Romanian press; clearly the government sheltered many who feared retribution. Indeed, since the 'revolution' not one person suspected of torture had been arrested; far from it, they had been promoted and one at least had allegedly become a Member of Parliament. No victims had been rehabilitated.

'The problem,' Dr Ţuculescu had said, 'is that it is hard to define psychiatric abuse. At an international meeting of psychiatrists in 1976 it was agreed that an alienated person is – roughly – he who is not adapted to reality. That's all very well until you wonder: what is reality?'

Ah, there's the rub. The longer I spent in Romania, the more often I asked myself that question.

'Our Communist régime – with the consensus of the people – called reality the Communist structure. Anyone unable – or unwilling – to live within that structure was considered logically insane.'

In the USA during the 1920s and '30s doctors had set about trying to classify what was and was not schizophrenia. Certain criteria of 'reality' were established, and patients who did not meet those criteria were judged to be suffering from mental disorders which were treatable with drugs. Homosexuality, for example, was at that time considered to be the result of a curable mental illness. But in the West, and particularly following revelations of psychiatric abuse by the Nazis, people began to question the ethics of forcing people to conform to certain patterns of behaviour. So Western doctors shifted their attention from society to the disease itself, and laid down certain specific definitions of schizophrenia which attempted to be as precise and as scientific as possible.

While the pre-war branch of psychiatry withered in the West, however, it continued to flourish in the Communist Bloc. It meant that George, who attempted – or was forced – to live outside the Communist structure, was logically insane. Dr Lupei had also recorded that George had 'confused' ideas about religion. To have religious convictions was not normal, much as having special relationships with foreigners was not normal, or wanting to escape was not normal.

'Are you suggesting that some psychiatrists were not necessarily evil, they were simply misguided?' I asked Dr Ţuculescu.

'Yes. You must understand that the Communist régime did not allow for what we call the "private normality space" which we now see as essential for the individual's spiritual life,' Dr Ţuculescu had continued. 'Someone like your friend might have tried to make that space for himself wider, and that is what the régime couldn't tolerate. He was genuinely considered insane.' He added, 'In fact those who believed what they were told, swallowed every word, were the ones who were mad.'

Perhaps, on the other hand, George was insane, driven there by the madhouse in which he lived – both outside and inside Costina. Dr Ţuculescu had gone so far as to coin the term 'the Psychosyndrome of totalitarianism'. He meant the schism of the personality induced by living under a totalitarian regime, in which past and present were grotesquely distorted, in which no-one said what they thought and in which everyone lived a lie, in which people lived day and night with guilt and fear of persecution. The entire population, he claimed, was suffering from this split personality, a personality warped both morally and psychologically. An entire population was slightly mad.

According to Dr Lupei, George's symptoms included laughing without cause, unintelligibility and illogicality. He refused to answer many questions and had a confused understanding of time and space. All of these could have been any man's response to incarceration at Costina. As Dr Ţuculescu said, 'Think of this: whatever happened to him, where the psychiatric hospital is a place of horror instead of a place of cure, simply being incarcerated there is a form of abuse. It is a terror to enter there.' He had not heard of Costina but he knew the sort of place. As in the Soviet Union, there were two grades of mental institution, the first far superior to the second. George was in the second grade, as were the Soviet dissidents. According to Dr Ţuculescu, Costina was part of a Gulag Archipelago that was dotted across the country in remote villages where no-one thought to notice or complain, just as it was dotted across the Soviet Union.

Dr Lupei's initial prescription for George was isolation. Vasile Cîmpan had denied that isolation was used at Costina, but here in the records, in the doctor's hand, was evidence to the contrary. I wondered where they had kept their isolation cell, and what kind of hellish cave it was.

Eight days after Dr Lupei's initial examination, on 25 March 1986, George was described as suffering from agitated dreams, and was staring into space with open eyes. He was prescribed a cocktail of drugs. First on the list was Haloperidol, a major antipsychotic drug. Haloperidol is used for the rapid control of hyperactive psychotic states, but it can induce tremors, restlessness, shuffling gait, blank pallor, nightmares, depression, drowsiness, blurred vision and mood alterations. The most troublesome side-effects are Parkinsonian, including shakiness, which may develop gradually. It is to be avoided if the patient has any history of respiratory disease, or if there are extremes of hot or cold weather. If George had TB or pleurisy, Haloperidol could have been dangerous, and certainly there was extreme cold at Costina. The recommended daily dose of Haloperidol is 2–3 mg, increasing to very high doses of 10 mg in specialist psychiatric units; George was given 30 mg.

Next on the list was Clordelazin, a Romanian form of Chlorpromazine, another neuroleptic used to control anxiety, but with the side-effects of extreme drowsiness, confusion, amnesia and dependence. I hated to imagine under what protest these drugs were administered; Clordelazin is given by injection. What Dr Lupei either did not know, or chose to ignore, is that it can be extremely dangerous to combine different neuroleptic drugs.

The third drug was Bromide, used to control his sexuality. The fourth was Romparkin. As can be guessed from the name, this is not a drug for schizophrenia, but a Romanian-made treatment for Parkinson's disease. George did not have Parkinson's. Romparkin may have been prescribed to counteract the side-effects of the Haloperidol and Clordelazin. However, in the West it is considered bad practice for a doctor to prescribe treatment for side-effects before those side-effects have been given a chance to develop.

Coincidentally – or not – the side-effects of Romparkin are the apparent symptoms of schizophrenia: depression, drowsiness and psychosis, along with nausea, insomnia and palpitations. If given to a patient without schizophrenia it creates the appearance of the disease, and if given to a psychiatric patient it can only make the symptoms worse.

Four months later, George was again examined by Dr Lupei. He was once more reported as suffering from agitated dreams and staring into space, and was prescribed a similar cocktail of five major drugs, administered twice or three times a day. Haloperidol and Clordelazin were again included, along with 'Levo' – Dr Lupei's shorthand for

232

Levomepromazine, a *third* antipsychotic drug, similar to Haloperidol but more sedating. He was also given another sedative, Romparkin again, and another anti-Parkinson's drug called Romergan.

Soon after, and despite being drug-saturated, George managed to run away. Having been recaptured, he was dosed with the same drugs. In November 1986 he was examined again, and more drugs were prescribed, although what they were I could not tell since by now Dr Lupei's handwriting had become illegible.

Was Dr Lupei simply inept? After all, Dr Ţuculescu and his colleagues had admitted to being years out of date. Or were the drugs deliberately given to torture George mentally while making it appear that he was schizophrenic when in fact he was not? If so, no wonder Amnesty International found that all the patients they interviewed did indeed have schizophrenia. No wonder they found no evidence of psychiatric abuse.

Rather than curing him, George's treatment seemed designed to induce paranoid schizophrenia and agitation. As I was to discover later from the testimonials of Romanian political prisoners who had lived to tell the tale, the use of a cocktail of drugs – to punish, to debilitate and control, and even misguidedly to cure – was standard practice. A Romanian-born representative of the Geneva Initiative on Psychiatry, an international foundation for the abolition of political psychiatry, confirmed that George's case was 'absolutely typical'.

But why was he abused in this way? Yes, he had wanted to escape from Romania, was critical of the régime. Yes, he was a thorn in their side. Dr Ţuculescu had pointed out that George was already high-risk, being both a priest *and* a guide – all those contacts with foreigners – but also that he didn't actually have to do anything to be arrested. He simply had to have the intention of doing it. The Securitate was terrified of intentions; their aim was to prevent actions before they took place. They knew they lived on a volcano and that they needed to control it before it erupted, not after. George would have been a potential risk, if not an actual one. And a useful scapegoat too. He would have seemed the ideal victim, not a top-notch opponent of the government but a small man, defenceless, unlikely ever to become famous or to ignite international outrage. He was easy to intimidate and, by being branded 'mad', easy to discredit. And so George was treated not only with cruelty but as a social reject, with contempt.

But was that enough to kill him? Indeed, was he killed or was the death of someone like George simply an incidental hazard, the result of a cocktail too many?

In July 1986 George was taken to Suceava Hospital for a TB test. Cîmpan had told me that he did not recall George having TB and that this test was routine for all patients and was no indication that they were suspected of having TB. At Suceava Hospital I attempted to discover the results of George's test so that I could at least exclude TB from the cause of death. The hospital's deputy director – a friend of a friend – promised me access to George's records. But so often I had come up against a wall of obfuscation, found a chink of light, worked my way through it, only to find another wall rearing up in its place; sure enough, at the last minute access to the Suceava Hospital records was, without explanation, withdrawn.

Abruptly the Costina records ended. George did not die for another eleven months, yet there was not another examination, not a single prescription of drugs, not another mention of his name. Either Dr Lupei had left Costina, or he had given up keeping records, or the records had been removed. For the final eleven months there was not a shred of evidence that George existed at all. Not only was there no death certificate, there was no autopsy report, which Cîmpan had assured me would be here. He claimed that in cases of death, a doctor was *always* called out, and that the autopsy report would remain in the file. I could only assume that if the autopsy report had ever been made it also had been removed. I questioned Domnul Bosca, but what could he say? How should he know? The chief nurse was back in her meeting and could not possibly be disturbed again. Domnul Suciu was away but Domnul Bosca himself would question him and I could telephone him next week. Now, if I didn't mind, he wanted to show FARA's head around the hospital. It had been nice to meet me. He guided me out and kissed my hand.

When I did telephone he said that Domnul Suciu had confirmed that all the files were in order. Goodbye.

I left Costina both horrified and elated by what I had discovered. Horrified by what George had been subjected to, but elated by the evidence that he was, as he would have liked to have been, a hero of a sort – a prisoner of conscience – not for any great acts of heroism but for trying to maintain his self-respect. It was a relief to have come so close to the truth – or at least the likely truth – at last.

I walked out past the gatehouse. Here George had lain before burial. Cîmpan had told me that at first the bodies were kept in a room beneath the old pavilion but that it got too hot in summer so they moved them to the gatehouse, into the visitors' room. Appropriate enough, since the only time most visitors came was to identify the body of some unloved relative. If no-one came then he, Domnul Cîmpan, arranged the funeral himself. He remembered nothing about George's funeral, however, and even expressed surprise that George had trained as a priest. Fancy that!

A caretaker hobbled out from the little green church. Yes, he confirmed, there was a cemetery here. He pointed to rows of carved marble. But the name George Cupar meant nothing.

'He was from the hospital,' I explained, 'from over there.' I nodded towards the trees beside the church, towards the nesting rooks and the high wire fence.

'In that case he would have been buried away down there,' said the old man, pointing to a section against the perimeter, to the paupers' graves hidden away at a discreet distance from the rest. 'They're mostly wooden crosses without names. And many of them were destroyed by hooligans. There's no point looking.'

'I'll look anyway. Thank you.'

The outcasts' graves lined a slope that flowed down towards a ploughed field; a man shouted at his horse, leading his red-tasselled mane up and down the furrows. Ordinary life, so close. Beneath my feet rose mounds of earth, like molehills, covered with buttercup leaves and violets. They were marked with simple wooden crosses tacked together. The first row bore names and dates, the second had nothing but surnames pencilled on in a looping scrawl; the third row of crosses had been torn out and smashed, strewn face-down in the earth. Vandals had had their fun and no-one cared enough to straighten the crosses up, or to remember to whom they belonged.

But beyond them all stood a solitary rusting metal cross, and on this was inscribed 'Here lie the mortal remains of Cupar George.' I stood for a while, looking down, relieved that he had avoided the final sacrilege meted out to his fellow patients, and that someone – his mother, or perhaps Father Iacov and his friends from Putna – had taken the trouble to give him a memorial slightly more permanent than the rest.

I was glad I'd come back. In a sense, George had been rescued. I was too late to rescue him physically, but not too late to rescue his reputation. I had owed him this at least. Yet still I did not know how he had died. Perhaps it was a mistake, perhaps it was deliberate. Drugs, beatings, malnutrition, water therapy – any or all of these. A collective amnesia had gripped the staff and patients of Costina and it seemed that I was not the one to prompt them to recall my friend's hurry-up death. No-one had anything to gain from speaking to me. Besides, what was the interest in this man compared with their own struggles, especially now that he was dead?

George had been shunted into a fog of forgetfulness, along with all the other men and women who had met the same fate. It was easier that way.

I had told Iacov that I needed details, dates, proof, the day-by-day minutiae of George's life – and death; that I wanted my picture of George coloured in from edge to edge. He had laughed at my desire for data, which he had described as 'very English'. Now I knew that I would never be satisfied. I had got as far as I could go. If it was English to want data, then it was Romanian to make do with rumours, myths. There was so little else. Myths filled the void and there they bred, feeding on themselves. Perhaps it is Romanian even to prefer myths to data. Myths add drama to dull old data, and drama feeds the Romanian soul.

The caretaker joined me at the graveside. With the sun shining, spring coming on, it seemed not such a bad place to be. In the end, George had found freedom of a sort.

'I do remember him.' The elderly man nodded. 'He was very young.'

'Why did he die?'

'Who knows? Sometimes bad things happen to good people. It's God's will, not man's.'

With that homily he turned and walked back towards the church.

Acknowledgements

I am indebted to The Authors' Foundation for a grant that helped me write this book.

I would also like to thank Victoria Clark of the *Observer*; Oana Lungescu of the BBC Romanian Service; my agent Derek Johns; Dr Rosalind Ramsay and Dr Ion Vianu for information about psychiatry and its abuse; and Christopher Sinclair-Stevenson for his patience. I was given much-needed advice by Laura Drysdale, Martine Faure-Alderson, Richard Pomeroy, Ivor Porter, Elisabeth Raţiu, George Ross and George Stanica.

I am also grateful to Brenda Walker for permission to reproduce her translation of Ana Blandiana's poem 'Asleep' from *An Anthology of Contemporary Romanian Poetry* published by Forest Books and to quote from her translation of *In Celebration of Mihai Eminescu*, also published by Forest Books.

In Romania unknown people welcomed me into their homes and helped me on my journey. To name them might cause them problems in these politically uneasy times, but they know who they are, and I thank them.

The names of all Romanians mentioned in the book, except those of public figures, have been changed.

While finishing this book, I learnt of the tragic death of Alex Scott. Without him, the journey would not have been so special; in fact, it would not have happened at all.